D0909015

Yale Historical Publications, Miscellany, 109

# THE
# PHILOSOPHES
## AND THE
# PEOPLE

Harry C. Payne

New Haven and London   Yale University Press

1976

Published under the direction of
the Department of History of Yale University
with assistance from the income of the
Frederick John Kingsbury Memorial Fund.

Copyright © 1976 by Yale University.
All rights reserved. This book may not be
reproduced, in whole or in part, in any form
(except by reviewers for the public press),
without written permission from the publishers.
Library of Congress catalog card number: 75-18181
International standard book number: 0-300-01907-6

Designed by John O. C. McCrillis
and set in Baskerville type.
Printed in the United States of America by
The Murray Printing Co., Forge Village, Mass.

Published in Great Britain, Europe, and Africa by
Yale University Press, Ltd., London.
Distributed in Latin America by Kaiman & Polon,
Inc., New York City; in Australasia by Book & Services,
Artarmon, N.S.W., Australia; in Japan by John
Weatherhill, Inc., Tokyo.

B
1925
.E5
P39

For Debby, my wife
In memory of Louis, my father

LIBRARY
ALMA COLLEGE
ALMA, MICHIGAN

# Contents

Preface     ix

Abbreviations     x

Introduction     1

Part I: Perceptions     5

    1   *Le Peuple*—A Class Apart     7

    2   Children of Discord     18

    3   Agents of Ceres     32

    4   A Case of Neglect     42

Part II: Legislation     59

    Introduction: The Legislator's Task     61

    5   The Uses of Belief     65

    6   Instruction     94

    7   The Laborer's Share     117

    8   Equality     148

Conclusion: Dominance and Responsibility     172

Bibliography     192

Index     209

# Preface

Like much historical writing, this essay grew out of a personal interest in a perennial problem—the attitude of the intellectual toward the mass of men. The difficulties seemed especially acute in the case of the philosophes of the Enlightenment who, according to historical legend, believed in the perfectibility and reasonableness of Man but who, again according to legend, scorned and despised the masses. Since surprisingly little has been written on the problem (and much less of a sympathetic nature) the topic seemed worthy of some intensive investigation and rethinking. Though this essay is not intended as an apology for the philosophes, it does attempt to give their attitudes toward and program for the mass of unenlightened men—or "people" as they chose to call them—a sophisticated and open-minded hearing.

My interest in the Enlightenment was first sparked by the writings of Peter Gay on Voltaire and the Enlightenment. As a thesis advisor at Yale University he was a kind and patient critic. He has offered immense help, both in writing the thesis on which this essay is based and in guiding and encouraging my historical studies in general. I owe him the greatest thanks. Professor Robert R. Palmer of Yale University, Ronald Boss, and Harvey Chisick read the original version of this essay in its entirety and offered both encouragement and tough-minded, helpful criticism from which I have profited greatly. I am also indebted to Mr. Chisick for allowing me to read his very valuable thesis on the problem of educating the *peuple* (Johns Hopkins University, 1974) immediately upon its completion. Generous financial support from the Danforth Foundation during my years of graduate study helped pay expenses for research. A grant from the Colgate University Research Council helped in the preparation of the final manuscript and the index. Above all I must thank my wife Debby for her help and support over the past six years.

# Abbreviations

The following shortened forms are used throughout for the sake of brevity and clarity.

In citations of the standard collected correspondences of Voltaire, Diderot, and Rousseau, the collection editor's assigned number appears at the end of the citation.

*VS* indicates Theodore Besterman, ed., *Studies on Voltaire and the Eighteenth Century* (Geneva and London, 1955–).

A bracketed question mark indicates that the place or date of publication appearing on the title page of an eighteenth-century work is of doubtful authenticity.

# Introduction

In 1659 Jacques Bossuet delivered a sermon on "the eminent dignity of the poor in the Church." Asking his listeners to forsake their disdain for the lowly of this world, he distinguished two kinds of vision:

> Those who look at them with corporeal eyes see only baseness and despise them. Those who open upon them the interior eye, that is, intelligence guided by faith, see in them Jesus Christ: they see the images of his poverty, the citizens of his kingdom, the inheritors of his promises, the distributors of his grace, the true children of his Church, the first members of the mystical body.[1]

A century later Voltaire had the opportunity to help one of Bossuet's poor. Using his influence at court, he gained the release of a Protestant shoemaker condemned to the galleys. After he had met the grateful shoemaker, Voltaire wrote to Jacques Necker, who had first requested his help:

> I saw your shoemaker. Truly he is an imbecile. If his friends are just as dimwitted, as I presume, they are as certain of paradise in the other world as they are of the galleys in this.[2]

Bossuet spoke of the poor from the standpoint of a Christian tradition which perceived a special virtue in the wretched of the earth. On one important level of Christian rhetoric, poverty had been portrayed as a type of heroism and special service since the time of the Apostles.[3] Voltaire and his fellow philosophes, however, were irrevocably committed to the "corporeal eye," rejecting much of

1. *Oeuvres oratoires de Bossuet* (Paris, 1928), 3:135.
2. To Jacques Necker, 5 March 1764, Voltaire, *Voltaire's Correspondence*, ed. T. Besterman, 107 vols. (Geneva, 1953–65), (10910). Voltaire volunteered to help others and requested information, but court favor shifted (see nos. 10800, 10863).
3. For other eighteenth-century examples of this style of rhetoric see B. Groethuysen, *The Bourgeois: Catholicism Vs. Capitalism in Eighteenth-century France*, trans. M. Ilford (New York, 1966), pp. 131–39.

Christian belief and style. Concerned with this world alone, they did not distinguish "two visions"; their empiricist frame of mind required a constant effort to match interior idea with exterior experience. The masses appeared base, ignorant, and violent, and the philosophes found no other words to describe them. Even while trying to help the poor, Voltaire could not give up this habit of mind. Instinctively he mocked both the ignorant cobbler and the tradition which promised him a special place in heaven.

The world in which the philosophes lived and thought conspired to separate them—physically and spiritually—from the lower classes, or "people," as they habitually called those below them. As men of letters they cherished an image of themselves as above the common run of men, in a position to observe, criticize, and scorn the failings of others. The writers of classical antiquity had consistently expressed a haughty disdain for the "vile multitude"; the rhetoric of this scorn passed easily and naturally into the vocabulary of the philosophe educated in the classics. To this classical disdain, the philosophes no longer counterpoised a Christian glorification of the poor.

Like their classical models, the philosophes of the eighteenth century enjoyed close ties to the elite. For all their heterodoxy they remained close to, part of, and often reliant upon the wealthy and titled. No major philosophe enjoyed claims to impressive nobility; some like Montesquieu, Condorcet, and Holbach held minor titles, but Diderot was the son of a master-cutler of Langres. Their occupations varied. Many philosophes lived not from their writings but from substantial estates. As large landowners, Montesquieu, Voltaire, Helvétius, Holbach, Gibbon and others derived great revenues from the labor of the people. But even those philosophes not blessed with landed revenues—those like Adam Smith who taught in a university, David Hume who enjoyed several sinecures, Diderot who combined income from land, writings, and patronage—lived among and addressed their writings to the literate few. Wealth and patronage gave the philosophes the leisure and freedom to explore new and sometimes radical ideas. But those same advantages also tended to restrict their perceptions of the "multitude." They viewed the people, in part, simply in the way that landowners and merchants viewed their laborers.

Thus, the partisans of Enlightenment confronted the people across a wide social gulf; their frequent scorn for the lowly betrays the harshness which separation could nurture. Montesquieu observing the Neopolitan people at the "miraculous" liquefaction of the blood of Saint Januarius while he reflected soberly on possible scientific explanations; Diderot staring in amazement from his window at the contortions of the convulsionaries of Saint-Médard; Voltaire angrily recounting the fury of the Parisian populace on Saint Bartholomew's Eve—each could serve as the image of the philosophe confronting the people: scornful, amazed, angry, and, above all, detached.

Despite all these impulses toward detachment, however, the philosophe could not entirely turn his back on the people. The philosophes chose "light" as their image and the spread of "light" as their goal. More propagandists than traditional philosophers, they measured success not by the purity of their syllogisms but by their ability to reach and convince a broad audience. Trying to make enlightenment a social reality, they confronted the mass of illiterate, poor, superstitious men and women who dwelled in the cave beyond the reach of *lumières*. Superstition had long been out of favor with many of the leaders of society, but these leaders still had to deal with the mass of superstitious men. Most philosophes had no doubt that philosophers and *honnêtes hommes* could live virtuously without the threat of divine sanction, but many philosophes feared that their propaganda might undermine the moral power of a belief in God's wrath among a populace already limited in virtue. Sensationalist epistemology had canonized the power of education and environment; it remained to be seen just how radically that environment could be changed to reshape a tradition-bound people. Political reformers resorted to the rhetoric of "natural equality" to justify change but then had to sort out the full implications of that "equality" for a society unequal in every respect. But once philosophers decided to be useful to society, they had to face the people. The poor in Europe of the eighteenth century formed not the "submerged tenth" of a later century but a hulking mass beneath the iceberg's tip of honnêtes hommes. Society, whether they liked it or not, was mostly "people."

The people were not hard to see, but they were hard to see clearly and sympathetically. Social distinctions kept all but the stoutest social explorer, such as Diderot, from haunting the workshops or the cabarets of the people. The philosophes viewed the people, as did most of the elite, from the upper story of a mansion, from the window

of a carriage, from a road passing swiftly through the fields of France
or the working quarters of Glasgow. Neither the means nor the will
to see the life of the people at close hand existed. Hence the Enlightenment's talk about the people tends to employ stereotyped terms. The
people are alternately "stupid," "blind," "useful," "superstitious,"
"gens des bras," "miserable," "insane," "bêtes féroces," and the like.
The formulas will become all too familiar to the reader as he pro-
ceeds. The philosophes took little care to differentiate among groups
within the "people," as did contemporary government officials or as
do modern social historians. From the distance of social and intellectual distinction the masses seemed simply *peuple* and suitable ad-
jectives were ready-to-hand. Still, sorting out these perceptions can
be surprisingly complicated, in that the rhetorical formulas often
express very different and opposing impulses and emotions. Only by
understanding what needs and occasions these perceptions served,
how the philosophes integrated them in their own minds, and how the
weight attached to each changed over the years, can one speak with
some confidence of an "Enlightenment view of the lower classes."
Too often have simple, highly quotable, highly aristocratic phrases
of Voltaire served to represent that view. And only after sorting out
these initial, organizing perceptions can one better understand how
the philosophes proposed to go about reshaping the lower orders so
they might appear different to future philosophes. The story of the
philosophes' confrontation with the people revolves about two poles:
the temptation to remain aloof and the necessity to become involved.
How the "corporeal eye" of the philosophes perceived the people,
how that vision changed over the course of the century, and how these
perceptions dictated a program of change provide the subject of this
essay.

# Part I: Perceptions

# 1 *Le Peuple*—A Class Apart

The French philosophes had many names at hand for society's lower classes. They borrowed most from the aristocratic society in which they moved: *menu peuple, bas peuple, petit peuple, canaille, personnes viles, hommes grossières*. While they frequently used this language of scorn and derision, however, more often than not eighteenth-century French social observers spoke simply of *le peuple*. In France at that time the word *peuple* could be as pejorative as any of the harsher expressions. A man of ancient nobility might mean by *peuple* anyone beneath the first president of the Parisian Parlement. Nonetheless, by the beginning of the eighteenth century the word came to have a certain specific social content, designating that part of the population which depended on the resources of others to find work.[1]

In his *Dissertation sur la nature du peuple*, published in 1755, the satirist Abbé Coyer described the evolution of the idea of le peuple.[2] Harking back to a time when men neatly divided society into clergy, nobility, and third estate (or people), he wrote:

> The people was at one time the most useful, the most virtuous and consequently most respectable part of the nation. It was composed of farmers, artisans, merchants, financiers, men of letters and men of law.[3]

But then, as Coyer recorded, those with higher social pretensions

1. Some of the ground covered in what follows has been intelligently traversed by Roland Mortier in "Diderot et la notion de 'peuple'," *Europe*, nos. 405–06 (Jan.–Feb. 1963):78–88; and by Werner Bahner, "Le mot et la notion de 'peuple' dans l'oeuvre de Rousseau," *VS* 55 (1967):113–27. I have tried to cover the same ground and then go beyond it by pointing to the clarification of a new social category, of which the new meaning of the word *peuple* was one indication. George Boas surveys the vagaries of such words as *populus, peuple*, and *People* in chapter 2 of his *Vox Populi: Essays in the History of an Idea* (Baltimore, 1969), raising many problems but providing no solution.

2. On Coyer, see Leonard Adams, *Coyer and the Enlightenment, VS* 123 (1974), and the entry on Coyer in *Dictionnaire des lettres françaises; XVIIIᵉ siècle*, ed. Cardinal G. Grente (Paris, 1960).

3. Abbé Coyer, *Dissertations pour êtres lues: La première sur le vieux mot de patrie: La seconde, sur la nature du peuple* (The Hague, 1755), pp. 44–45.

gradually seceded from the people. Offices of the robe brought nobility; men of letters, "in the manner of Horace," turned their backs
on the people; financiers and merchants blushed at association with
the rest of the people. Only peasants, servants, and artisans remained.
Even the status of crafters of fine luxury goods had become doubtful,
since their hands "no longer resembled the hands of the people."[4] In
this way Coyer recorded both a linguistic and a social fact: the emer-
gence of a new meaning for the word *peuple* as a result of the increased social pretensions of many commoners. A glance at other
evidence of French usage in the seventeenth century confirms his
analysis.

In 1621 the revised version of Aimar de Ranconet's lexicon,
*Thrésor de la langve francoise*, had listed several uses, but it considered
the word equivalent to the Latin words for lower classes, *plebs* and
*vulgus*, only when qualified in such phrases as *menu peuple* or *commun
peuple*.[5] At that time the lower classes still formed only part of *le peuple*,
meaning either "nation" or third estate. Antoine Furetière's *Dictionnaire universel*, a good indicator of common usage which appeared
some seventy years later, told a different story. In addition to the
standard meanings of a nation, a city population, or just a large
group of persons, the dictionary listed another usage, confirming
Coyer's view:

> *Peuple* is used even more particularly in opposition to those who
> are notable, rich, or educated. The *peuple* is *peuple* everywhere,
> that is, stupid, turbulent, eager for novelties. He is from the
> dregs of the *peuple*. The little *peuple*, the mean *peuple*, the com-
> mon *peuple* is cunning and seditious. There are many of the
> *peuple* in the market place.[6]

4. Ibid., pp. 45–46. The *Encyclopédie*, which paraphrased Coyer closely, no longer left
the superior status of the luxury artisans in doubt; see "Peuple," 12:476. By way of the
*Encyclopédie*, Coyer's analysis became standard; see the articles entitled "Peuple," in *Le
grand vocabulaire françois*, vol. 21 (Paris, 1772) and Robinet, ed., *Dictionnaire universel des
sciences morale, économique, politique, et diplomatique*, vol. 26 (Paris, 1782).

5. The 1621 edition, revised and expanded by Jean Nicot, reproduced by Éditions
Picard (1960), p. 478.

6. *Dictionnaire universel, contenant généralement tous les mots françois tant vieux que modernes*,
2:273 of the second edition [The Hague and Rotterdam, 1694]; first published as *Essai
d'un dictionnaire universel* in 1690. In later editions it became known as the *Dictionnaire de
Trevoux*. On Furetière's dictionary as a good indicator of common usage see entry in
Cardinal Grente, ed., *Dictionnaire des lettres françaises; XVII^e siècle* (Paris, 1954). (Note also
the growing use of *peuple* as an adjective, "a fairly new meaning" according to the *Nouveau
dictionnaire françois*, ed. Pierre Richelet [Paris, 1719], 2:210.)

Later editions of Furetière's dictionary cited the authority of such writers as Vauban, who noted that "the word *peuple* denotes only what the Romans called *plebs*," and La Bruyère, who distinguished two usages:

> There is the *peuple* opposed to the great, which is the populace and multitude. There is the *peuple* opposed to the wise and clever, including the great as well as the small.[7]

The dictionaries indicated that in talking about society, men of letters had seen through the simple legal distinctions of clergy, nobility, and third estate and had defined *peuple* as a social group separate from the rest of society, both nobility and commoners.

French jurists of the seventeenth century kept up with usage. The testimony of legal observers such as Charles Loyseau, Claude Fleury, and Jean Domat carries special weight, since they were the principal social and political thinkers of the seventeenth century.[8] In his *Traité des ordres et simples dignitez* (1623), Loyseau began with the traditional tripartite division of clergy, nobility, and third estate. Noting, however, the vast expanse of the third estate, he drew many distinctions within it. Among these was the point at which professions became *viles*. Holders of "honorable" professions included those as far down as merchant-artisans; holders of "vile" occupations included all peasants and all manual laborers, the *gens des bras*.[9] Loyseau couched his distinction in the judicial language of honor. But his concerns closely followed the lines dictated by economics in a monarchy sensitive to that reality as well.

7. *Dictionnaire de Trevoux*, 5:148. La Bruyère's grouping of the "great" with the stupid populace became a standard irony in the eighteenth century.

8. On the importance of the French jurists and their loss of prestige as social thinkers, see William F. Church, "The Decline of French Jurists as Political Theorists, 1600–1789," *French Historical Studies* 5 (1967):1–40.

9. Fourth ed. (1665), pp. 74–75, 79–80; bound in Claude Joly, ed., *Les Oeuvres de Charles Loyseau, avocat en parlement* (Paris, 1666). Loyseau lamented the usage that classed *laboureurs* and *fermiers*—independent farmers who owned or rented large amounts of land and equipment—among the group of *personnes viles*. He pleaded for raising the social status of these men, a plea which became standard in the eighteenth century. (The importance of the distinction between *vile* and *honorable* in Loyseau has been noted by Bahner, "Le mot et la notion de 'peuple'," pp. 115–16.) Cf. Richelieu, who in his *Testament politique* (1688) divided the third estate into judicial officers, financial officers, and "people." His perspective was fiscal, not judicial or sociological; see part 1, chapter 4, section 5. On the authenticity of the *Testament politique*, subject to long debate and now generally accepted as primarily the work of Richelieu, see the introduction to the critical edition of Louis André (1947), pp. 37–64.

✔ In a similar vein, the abbé Claude Fleury in his *Droit public de France* (written between 1667 and 1669)[10] found the term *third estate* less than adequate. Eschewing terms of legal order or dignity, he divided the lowest estate simply into "rich" and "poor." The "rich" included officers of justice and finance living nobly, the many lesser judicial officers, financiers, and merchants. The much larger group of "poor" encompassed petty shopkeepers, constables, clerks, artisans, and workers of all varieties. Work set these men apart by making them dependent on the rich.[11] Describing this body of "poor," Fleury noted:

> Poor, their numbers incredible; most without assured income. Fortuitous life of trade, work, commission; have no plan; reduced to charity by a change of fashion.[12]

Contingency and dependence, therefore, marked off Fleury's "poor" from the rest of the third estate.

Still another jurist, Jean Domat, writing three decades later in his *Le droit public* (1697), found the threefold legal division of society encumbering and distinguished instead eight ranks, ranging downward from the clergy to the final two, "trades and handicrafts" and "husbandry and the care of cattle." Even within these two he found further divisions necessary. Among practitioners of the trades and handicrafts he found some (no doubt the luxury craftsmen) who had "a kind of Honor that distinguishes them, and places some of them in a Rank above the others."[13] And within the peasantry he divided those who worked for themselves from those dependent upon others.[14] The lower parts of these final two orders comprised what Loyseau had

10. On the date of writing see Church, "French Jurists," p. 11. The work was published in 1769 by J. B. Daragon.

11. Fleury, *Droit public*, pp. 18–19.

12. Ibid., p. 20.

13. Book 1, title 9, section 3, article xxii. Domat composed his work between 1680 and 1696 (see Church, "French Jurists," pp. 14–15). Quotations are from the translation of William Strahan, *The Civil Law in its Natural Order: Together with the Public Law*, second ed. (London, 1737). Domat explained the inadequacy of the old legal divisions as follows: "We could not have avoided the confounding among the Commons, which make the Third Estate, many of the Privy Counsellors, and other Persons who ought to have a distinguished Rank. So that without pretending to do any prejudice to the use of which this Distinction may have, we have thought it proper under other Views to distinguish the Conditions of Men in another manner." (See book 1, title 9, introduction.)

14. Ibid., book 1, title 9, section 3, article xx.

named personnes viles, Fleury had named pauvres, and usage began to name simply peuple.[15]

By the beginning of the high Enlightenment, both common usage and jurists had sorted out a certain group of men, least in dignity but still the majority of the population of France. By a number of terms social observers had seen fit to signify a class united not by any particular legal standing but by a common economic and social position. When Voltaire later spoke of le peuple as "those who have only their hands to live by," or when Turgot divided the classes of farmers and manufacturers between those entrepreneurs who made investments and those who worked only for wages,[16] they employed distinctions which writers had begun to make during the previous century.[17]

The philosophes worked more fully and comfortably with this new division of society than had the jurists and those who shared the legal perspective. To indicate the lowest social grouping, Loyseau resorted to the traditional aristocratic term *personnes viles*, referring more to matters of honor than wealth. Domat saw the need to make distinctions even within the orders of the trades and husbandry, but he did not find a term to make this division clear. Judicial concerns of privilege, esteem, honor, and dignity blocked any full and clear vision of society in economic terms.[18] The philosophes chose to ignore juridical considerations and speak of society in terms of wealth. Typically they divided society not into three estates but rather into

15. Another interesting confirmation of this division of those who work with their hands from the rest of society can be seen in the system of epithets used on some seventeenth-century tax roles. Marcel Couturier, in his *Recherches sur les structures sociales de Chateaudun 1525–1789* (Paris, 1969), cites three epithets commonly used: *noble homme* (largely judicial nobility), *honorable homme* (mostly large merchants), and *honnête personne* (small merchants, master artisans); see pp. 216–22 and 276–78. The division between those having enough dignity to earn an epithet and those who did not closely parallels the other distinctions discussed above.

16. "Réflexions sur la formation et la distribution des richesses" (1766), in Turgot, *Oeuvres de Turgot et documents le concernant*, ed. G. Schelle, 5 vols. (1912–13), 5:569–70, 572.

17. I will not multiply examples from the philosophes at this time, since the body of this essay will contain numerous quotations using "peuple" and dividing society in this manner.

18. Loyseau, in fact, audaciously divided society into those who command—king, officers, magistrates—and peuple—those commanded, including the nobility of the sword, clerics, and peasants. He thereby sought to advance the social pretensions of the judicial nobility of office; see Roland Mousnier, *Etat et société sous François I*[er] *et pendant le gouvernement personnel de Louis XIV*, (n.d.), 1:63–64.

three economic groups: *peuple, état mitoyen,* and *grands.* Within this
framework d'Alembert praised Francis I for favoring the "center of
the nation" and not the extremes, which he defined as "the people,
given over to work necessary for its subsistence" and "the great
*seigneurs,* sufficiently occupied with their idleness and intrigues."[19]
The divisions were very rough, with no pretense to sociological pre-
cision. Yet the philosophes recognized that a merchant who held an
ennobling judicial office might have more in common with another
merchant than with a royal peer, and that both merchants had little
or nothing in common with the peasant who worked the lands they
owned outside the city. While a jurist might debate the relative
nobility of the officeholder and a duke, or feel obliged to class the
second merchant with the peasant as "commoners," the independent
critic could see more clearly the economic and social realities which
bound or separated them.[20]

The evolution of the word *peuple* and the adoption of its new meaning by the French philosophes had no equivalent in other languages.
The French philosophes adopted the new meaning because it squared
with their sense of economic realism[21] and their discontent with the
old hierarchy of birth and honor. Outside France, the tensions

19. *Oeuvres complètes* (1821–22), 4:338. Cf. Diderot, who generally distinguished *riches,
citoyens utiles,* and *peuple*; see Jacques Proust, *Diderot et l'Encyclopédie* (Paris, 1962), pp.
474–80. Holbach habitually divided society into *riches, état mitoyen,* and *pauvres*; during the
eighteenth century *pauvre* often served as a synonym for *peuple.* I do not wish to imply,
however, that the vagaries of language disappeared. The philosophes often still used
*peuple* to mean a nation; they often spoke of *le plus bas populace* or *le menu peuple* to distinguish
a sort of person even lower than mere *peuple.* Nonetheless, the use of *peuple* to distinguish
a social grouping including all those who worked with their hands was most frequent and
is not difficult to distinguish in context from other uses.

20. Roland Mousnier, in a recent article—"D'Aguesseau et le tournant des ordres aux
classes sociales," *Revue d'histoire économique et sociale* 49 (1971):449–64—has indicated this
movement toward a more realistic social analysis in the language of one man. His attempt,
however, to attribute this movement to a "pure movement of ideas" (p. 450) in the
Stoic-Cartesian tradition does not hold, in my opinion. He is correct in seeing nothing
particularly "bourgeois" in this idea, but errs in mistaking the rhetoric d'Aguesseau chose
to use in rethinking social categories with the cause of this rethinking. Coyer probably
has the best explanation for the origins of the limited use of *peuple*; the impulses toward
realistic social and economic analysis, described in chapter 4 below, made the terminol-
ogy convenient.

21. Patterns of marriage and association roughly corresponded to the gross separation
of peuple from the rest of society. See, e.g., F. Furet and A. Daumard, *Structures et relations
sociales à Paris* (Paris, 1965), pp. 7–41, and M. Agulhon, *La sociabilité méridionale* (Aix-en-
Provence, 1966), 1:418–20.

between hierarchies of economic wealth and social honor either no longer existed, as in England and the Netherlands, or had not yet developed to a critical stage, as in most of Europe east of the Rhine.

Still, the equivalent words for *peuple* in other nations carried many of the same connotations as *peuple* in France. A perusal of eighteenth- and early nineteenth-century dictionaries shows that the word *people* almost always carried a first meaning of "nation" and a second meaning equivalent to the Roman *plebs*. Samuel Johnson gives as his second meaning for *people* simply "the vulgar." In England the word *people* more often meant simply the politically active elite—an irony which reflects both England's travails of the seventeenth century and the relative lack of social tension there prior to the late eighteenth century.[22] (With the growth of industrialization, the English word *class* would undergo an evolution similar to that of *peuple* in the face of economic and intellectual change.)[23] German usage, often taking its cue from the French, was quite clear in its disdain for the *Pöbel*.[24] For instance, Herder, with all of his contempt for the superficialities of elite culture when measured against that of the *Volk*, carefully distinguished the more cultured *Volk* from *Pöbel*. The voice of the Volk was as distant from that of mere "people" as from that of intellectuals. *Pöbel* usually meant nothing so much as "rabble."[25]

These varied but similar uses of words for the people reflect the basis for all enlightened talk about the working classes—a sense of the people as a group apart. In terms of social grace the people represented the essence of vulgarity. In terms of mental development the people represented the lowest of accomplishments. In terms of economic standing the people represented a social class defined by its

22. See Jacob Viner, "Man's Economic Status," in J. L. Clifford, ed., *Man Versus Society in Eighteenth-Century Britain* (Cambridge, 1968), p. 29.

23. Asa Briggs, "The Language of Class in Early Nineteenth-Century England," in Briggs, ed., *Essays in Labour History* (London, 1960), pp. 43–73.

24. E.g., Theodore Heinsius, ed. *Wörterbuch der Deutschen Sprach*, 3 (Hannover, 1820): "Pöbel, m., -s, ehemals das Volk ohne allen verächtlichen nebenbegriff, fest aber das grosse Volk von Seiten seiner Niedrigkeit, Rohheit und Ungebildheit, der Hefen des Volks. . . der Pöbel ist sich uberall gleich. . . ." Also, J. and W. Grimm, eds., *Deutsches Wörterbuch* (Leipzig, 1854): "Pöbel . . . (1) volk, volksmenge, einwohnerschaft, leute im allgemeinen, sodann (oft mit einem adjectiv) das gemeine geringe volk, die niedern stände, endlich der grosz haufen, das gemeine, rohe volk, rohe leute überhaupt in bezug auf that, word oder gesinnung."

25. F. M. Barnard, *Herder's Social and Political Thought* (Oxford, 1965), pp. 73–74.

dependence on others to give them work. The grounds for this feeling of separation were hardly new; the philosophes were usually sure that the people had always been "people" in all times and places—vulgar, superstitious, dependent. But sensitivity to this separation seems to have grown markedly during the age of Enlightenment. Nowhere prior to the eighteenth century were intellectuals so concerned about what separated "people" from "nonpeople." The sources of this sensitivity are varied. Christian education and culture had emphasized the unity of believers; the church, at least in principle, offered a set of beliefs and values which all members shared. Secular education and aristocratic ideals growing out of the Renaissance stressed gentility, grace, eloquence, and all of the qualities which set the educated man apart from those beneath him. The philosophes shared these ideals; they were, by definition, honnêtes hommes. The salons and côteries of France, seedbeds of Enlightenment style, reinforced the sense of an aristocracy of intellect mirroring the qualities of the aristocracy of the court.[26] The philosophes lived in a genteel age, on the surface at peace as no age had been before. Withdrawing from the age of great wars and fierce religious battles, much activity of the elite of the eighteenth century focused on status and style—withdrawal from what was base and vulgar. Popular amusements once supported and attended by the English gentry were scorned as vulgar after mid-century.[27] Men of letters, testing the precarious realms of intellectual and financial independence from aristocratic patronage, still shared a sense that letters were an elite vocation, entrusted to the few and closed to the many. They underscored their distance from the multitude as strongly as a nobleman would separate himself from the mere commoner.

Most accepted this separation as a matter of course. Some, however, had reservations. With devastating effect, Rousseau refused to adopt the standards of a genteel society so curiously eager to adopt him. Diderot, at times, had regrets. In the summer of 1759 he visited his hometown of Langres after an absence of sixteen years. "When I walk down the streets," he wrote back to Paris,

26. See Ronald Boss, "The Development of Social Religion: A Contradiction of French Free Thought," *Journal of the History of Ideas* 34 (1973):577–89. I do not, however, share his sense that the idea of separation was either very contradictory or corruptive of the spirit of *lumières*.

27. R. W. Malcolmson, *Popular Recreations in English Society, 1700–1850* (Cambridge, 1973), pp. 68–70, 152.

I hear people who look at me and say, "He's the very image of his father." I know full well that it is not true, and that, whatever I do, it will never be. One of our distinguished priests was perhaps more correct when he said to me, "Monsieur, philosophy has nothing to do with those men."[28]

The master-cutler's son realized that his experiences since going to Paris and becoming a philosophe had permanently separated him from the common men and common wisdom of the provinces. Though he had emerged into high literary society, as few had, from origins close to the people, he recognized that he was no longer an artisan's child from Langres but a Parisian philosophe—a distinct group of men. The philosophe who late in life advised Catherine II of Russia to search for genius in the huts of the people[29] spoke not from any residual warm feeling for his lowly origins but from an awareness of just how far genius and good fortune could separate a common man from his origins.

Historians have often pointed with disapproval to this arrogant sense of separation. The philosophes portrayed the ignorance of the *canaille* too often, too vociferously, and too wittily to pass uncondemned in later, more democratic times. But the philosophes' sense of separation was more than arrogance. The qualities they perceived in the people increasingly seemed less an occasion for self-adulation than a problem to be solved. There is a realism in their haughtiness which should not pass unnoticed, once one cuts through the insensitive rhetoric of scorn of those accustomed to the language of the salon. All societies effect separations and establish hierarchies. Eighteenth-century Europe inherited many such patterns of separation: nobleman versus commoner; elect versus damned;[30] clergy versus laity; first versus second versus third estate; firstborn son versus later sons; honorable versus vile professions; Frenchman versus Englishman versus Spaniard. Almost all of these distinctions had something magical about them. They rested not on empirical qualities of mind

28. To Melchior Grimm, 14 August 1759, Diderot, *Correspondance*, ed. G. Roth and J. Varloot, 16 vols. (Paris, 1955–70), (138).

29. Diderot, *Oeuvres complètes*, ed. Jules Assézat and Maurice Tourneux, 20 vols. (Paris, 1875–77), 3:433; and *Mémoires pour Catherine II*, ed. Paul Vernière (Paris, 1966), pp. 129, 167.

30. Some English preachers intimated that sinfulness coincided with membership in the lower orders; see Roland Stromberg, *Religious Liberalism in Eighteenth-Century England* (Oxford, 1954), pp. 144–46.

or controllable activities of body. Rather they rested on the magic of
birth into a certain family, ordinal position, geographical location;
the magic of salvation and ordination; the magic of having
hands not soiled by labor. They formed the traditional mythopoeic
categories of a social world not yet fully attuned to the
empirical mind of the Enlightenment. The gap the philosophes
perceived between people and nonpeople was not magical;
it had empirical bases, even if the arrogance of the philosophes
appears excessive. The people were, on the whole, illiterate; their
forms of political activity often violent; their amusements vulgar
by eighteenth-century standards; their religiosity often superstitious
in most senses of the word. Nor were the philosophes unaware that
many members of the more fortunate classes shared these qualities;
a common irony of the eighteenth century was to indicate that something of the "people" dwelled even among the greatest. Voltaire
advocated belief in a controlling god for princes and lawyers as well
as peasants. Perhaps even more significantly, the philosophes became
increasingly aware of a "people" not just intellectually but economi-
cally separate. They knew, as indicated in the evolution of the word
*peuple*, that having to labor for subsistence divided the people from
the rest of men—not merely making them vile by the aristocratic
standards of the day but dependent, neglected, and oppressed.

Hence separation from the people, though it gave some philosophes
on some occasions reason for self-satisfaction, more often than not
presented a vexing problem for the men of lumières. Committed
from the early years of the Enlightenment to the destruction of
ignorance and superstition, committed from mid-century to the
exposure of social wrong, the philosophes found in that mass of men
called "people" a problematic and significant variable in the formula
for Enlightenment. In hosts of issues central to the Enlightenment,
the philosophes recognized those who labored for their subsistence as
a separate entity with interests and difficulties different from the
merchant, the duke, the king, and the man of letters. Adam Smith
systematically took into account the role of "labor" in the creation
and sharing of the wealth of nations as earlier political economists
had not. Holbach's atheism might appear ideal for the philosopher,
but its impact on the mind of the people remained vexing in a world
attuned to the use of religion for social control. Quesnay's "single
tax" made sense, many believed, from the perspective of the state,

but the perspective of the people was different and had to be explored. The questions and complications multiplied once social critics fully recognized the existence of the people—as both ignorant "multitude" and dependent "laborers"—and took its existence into account. The moralist Coyer regretted the gradual secession of men of economic and social standing from the old order of peuple. He saw only the growth in pretentiousness and snobbery, not the growth in realism. The philosophes accepted this separation with few qualms and, as philosophers bound to change the world, began to work out its implications.

# 2 Children of Discord

No one portrayed the brutality of the people more insistently than Voltaire. In his writings the people often appeared as a tyrannical and ferocious beast, the embodiment of unreason. His epic poem *La Henriade*, written early in his career, described the terrifying Parisian mob, possessing no mind of its own and turned at will at the whim of its leaders. On the Day of the Barricades, May 9, 1588, the leader of the Roman Catholic League gained control of Paris with the aid of the populace. Voltaire painted the scene:

> Guise, tranquil and proud in the midst of the storm,
> Let loose the people or held back its rage,
> Governed the springs of sedition,
> And moved this vast body at will.
> All of the people ran furiously to the palace:
> One word from Guise and Valois was dead.[1]

When popular favor later turned against the League, the goddess Discord appeared to its leader Mayenne, assuring him:

> Fear nothing from this foolish and fickle people,
> Whose minds are mine, their hearts are in my hands:
> Soaked with my gall, prey to my furies,
> Soon you will see them further my designs,
> Fight with audacity, and die with joy.[2]

Here and elsewhere the people seemed to Voltaire the unreasoning and barbarous children of Discord; the specter of the mob on Saint Bartholomew's Eve haunted his work.[3] More than a half-century later he still could not rid himself of the image of a cruel and

1. *La Henriade*, Third Song, lines 251–56. I have used the critical edition of O. R. Taylor.
2. Ibid., Fourth Song, lines 151–56.
3. E.g. ibid., Second Song; Voltaire, *Dictionnaire philosophique*, ed. Julien Benda and Raymond Naves (Paris, 1967), "Fanatisme," p. 197; Voltaire, *Essai sur les moeurs et l'esprit des nations et sur les principaux faits de l'histoire depuis Charlemagne jusqu'à Louis XIII*, ed. René Pomeau, 2 vols. (Paris, 1963), 2:494–97.

irrational people. To support his argument for a religion to contain the people, he sternly warned his readers in 1771 that "everyone is not a philosopher. We have to deal with many scoundrels who have seldom reflected, with a multitude of brutal, drunk, thieving little men."[4]

One could multiply many times such observations by the flock of philosophes.[5] They often spoke of the man of the people as an animal totally separate from the philosophe, magistrate, or priest. But the philosophes' view of the people's mind and character reached beyond simple class snobbery, though it fell far short of serious sociology. The people dwelled in a world far different from the genteel and cosmopolitan society of the philosophes. The nature of that world as it appeared to the philosophes significantly shaped their view of the future prospects and direction of enlightenment. Their perception of the people's mind deserves a closer look.

Holbach defined reason in *Essai sur les Préjugés* (1769)[6] as "truth discovered by experience, meditated upon by reflection, and applied to the conduct of life."[7] His definition could serve for the entire Enlightenment. Despite their emphasis on the priority of sense experience, the philosophes recognized that true knowledge lay only in the disciplined comparison and combination of those original

4. Voltaire, *Dictionnaire philosophique*, "Enfer" (addition of 1771), p. 526.

5. See Peter Gay, *The Enlightenment: An Interpretation*, 2 vols. (New York, 1966, 1969), 2:517–22, for a judicious survey of their views. Voltaire has proved most quotable on the stupidity and cruelty of the people; see the same author's *Voltaire's Politics: The Poet as Realist* (Princeton, 1959), pp. 220–23, and R. Mortier, "Voltaire et le peuple," in W. H. Barber et al., eds., *The Age of Enlightenment: Studies Presented to Theodore Besterman* (London, 1967), pp. 137–51.

6. Werner Krauss, in "Über eine Kampfschrift der Aufklärung: der *Essai sur les préjugés*," in Krauss, ed., *Studien zur deutschen und französischen Aufklärung* (Berlin, 1963), pp. 273–99, has argued that the *Essai* is more likely the work of Dumarsais. His arguments, based on two discrepancies between the *Essai* and Holbach's known work, seem frail. In a more recent study, Rudolph Besthorn has proved that the work is largely that of Holbach, although perhaps with the aid of a collaborator; see "Zur Verfasserfrage des *Essai sur les préjugés*," in *Beitraege zur romanischen Philologie* 8 (1969): 10–46. On the authenticity, dating, and publication of Holbach's various works, I have relied on the thorough studies of the Krauss circle. In addition to those cited above, see M. Naumann's "Zur Publikationsgeschichte des *Christianisme dévoilé*," and R. Besthorn's "Zeitgenössische Zeugnisse für das Werk Holbachs," both in Krauss, ed., *Neue Beiträge zur Literatur der Aufklärung* (Berlin, 1964), and especially the textual analyses of Besthorn in his *Textkritische Studien zum Werk Holbachs* (Berlin, 1969).

7. Holbach, *Essai sur les Préjugés, ou, de l'Influence des opinions sur les moeurs & sur le bonheur des hommes* (London, 1770) (more probably published Amsterdam, 1769), p. 6.

sense data. All men share a virtually identical quantity of sense experiences; the relative ability or inability of men to use that experience provides the standard by which to judge the quality of their minds. The model philosophe (as those who adopted that title portrayed him) does not try to transcend the world of senses and passions; rather, he guides himself through that world by reflecting on his experience and foreseeing the results of possible actions.[8] The author of "Philosophe" in the *Encyclopédie*, borrowing from an earlier tract, compares this ideal to the people. "Other men," he writes,

> are driven by their passions, without reflection preceding their actions. These are men who walk in shadows. On the other hand, even in passionate moments, the *philosophe* acts only after reflection; he walks at night, but a torch precedes him.
>
> The *philosophe* forms his principles on the basis of an infinite number of individual observations. The people adopts the principle without thinking about the observations which produced it: it believes that the maxim exists, as it were, by itself; but the *philosophe* takes the maxim right to its source; he examines its origin, he recognizes its value, and uses it only as it suits him.[9]

The number of philosophes in the world is of necessity quite small. A philosophe needs a certain leisure to reflect, and few men have that leisure. But ease alone could not guarantee a philosophic mentality, the author concludes, since most wealthy men indulge their passions too much to take time for meditation.[10]

In contrast to the wealthy, the people did not have leisure to abuse. Holbach used this fact to defend his *Christianisme dévoilé* (1761) against those who feared he might undermine the people's belief. "The people reads no more than it reasons," he responded; "it has neither the leisure nor the ability to do so."[11] It was the fate of the common man, Holbach thought, that the sheer weight of his labor

8. On the definition of the philosophe and the history of the tract entitled "Le philosophe," see Herbert Dieckmann, *Le Philosophe: Texts and Interpretation* (St. Louis, 1948).

9. *Encyclopédie*, 12:509.

10. Ibid., pp. 510–11.

11. Holbach, *Le Christianisme dévoilé, ou, Examen des principes et des effets de la religion chrétienne* (London, 1756) (probably published Amsterdam, 1761), introduction, p. v.

for the necessities of life allowed no time for reason. Others must think for him.[12]

Trapped in the world of the senses and the passions, the common man—as the philosophes perceived him—believes everything he thinks he sees. Enlightenment accounts of the origin of superstitious beliefs often emphasized this critical failing in the popular mind. Idolatry began, they argued, not with the deliberate deception of priests but with the inability of the people to distinguish symbol from reality. In the entry "Ecriture" in the *Encyclopédie*, De Jaucourt described the workings of the people's mind in ancient Egypt: Wise men of Egypt placed hieroglyphs on public objects. When the people saw these symbols on monuments, religious assembly places, and ceremonial objects, they "stopped stupidly at the figures they had before their eyes," not comprehending the symbolic truths represented. The people quickly adopted the hieroglyphs as cult objects.[13] Voltaire, in another entry to the *Encyclopédie*, described the similar workings of the mind of the Roman populace. In defense of the upper classes of ancient Rome, he argued that they never worshiped statues as gods, considering them only representations of higher divinities. But "the superstitious Roman populace, without the use of reason and struck with religious horror when it viewed statues of Diana or thunder-bearing Jupiter, easily slipped into worshiping the statue itself." In his own day, he added, priests still had to instruct their charges to ask intercession from beings in heaven and not from images of wood and stone.[14]

This theory of the degeneration of symbol into cult in the mind of the people enjoyed wide acceptance; even Holbach, inclined as he was to blame treacherous priests for many of the world's evils, accounted for the birth of idolatry as had De Jaucourt and Voltaire. Ancient sages, he thought, admired the universe as a great Whole which they deified and then represented symbolically. The "vulgar," in turn,

> stopped at the emblem, the symbol under which Nature was

12. Ibid., p. 4.

13. *Encyclopédie*, 5:360; cf. the similar explanation offered by Diderot in "Divination," *Encyclopédie*, 4:1071, citing Abbé Pluche as his source.

14. "Idole, idolâtre, idolâtrie," *Encyclopédie*, 8:501; repeated almost verbatim, *Dictionnaire philosophique*, pp. 239–40. His arguments were not entirely unfounded; see the complaints of clerics on the idolatry of the populace in Groethuysen, *The Bourgeois*, p. 16.

shown to them, with its parts and its functions personified: its
limited mind never allowed it to rise higher: only those deemed
worthy to be initiated into the mysteries knew the reality behind
these emblems.[15]

Legislators resorted to speaking to the people in the language of
myth and allegory and then soon gave way to the temptations of
outright imposture.[16]

According to the philosophes, the people could not distinguish
symbol from abstract truth, appearance from reality. This susceptibility moved Saint-Lambert to insist in the *Encyclopédie* that "the
people is led neither by reasonings nor by definitions; one must
impress its senses, and by distinctive marks announce its sovereign,
nobles, magistrates, and ministers of religion; their exterior must
announce force, goodness, gravity, holiness."[17] Leading the people
becomes, for Saint-Lambert, a matter of the proper manipulation of
appearances. Although the empirical "reason" of the philosophes
did not resemble the higher "Reason" of Plato, their "people" were
still his: hapless dwellers in the cave of appearance.

Limited to sensation, the people seemed to crave the wondrous and
spectacular. In a letter to Sophie Volland written in the summer of
1762, Diderot described the furor in Geneva over the creed of the
Savoyard priest in Rousseau's *Emile*. "Precisely because this profession of faith is a kind of galimatias," he explained, "the heads of
the people will be turned by it. Reason, which presents nothing
wondrous, does not astound them enough, and the populace wants
to be astounded."[18] Years earlier Diderot had witnessed the credulity
of the Parisian people: a supposed "miracle" in which a man threw
off his crutches and walked—in reality, Diderot saw, supported by
three or four friends. "Where is the miracle, stupid people?" he
wondered on reflecting upon the incident. "Don't you see that this
impostor only exchanged crutches?" The source of such miracles, he
concluded, lay in the predisposition to see them: "I would surely
swear that all those who have seen spirits feared them beforehand,

15. Holbach, *Système de la Nature, ou des Loix du monde physique et du monde moral*, 2 vols.
(London, 1770) probably published (Amsterdam), 2:35.

16. Ibid., p. 36. For other contemporary versions of the same story, see F. Manuel,
*The Eighteenth Century Confronts the Gods* (New York, 1967 [1954]), pp. 121–25.

17. "Luxe," *Encyclopédie*, 9:767.

18. 25 July 1762, Diderot, *Correspondance* (263).

and all those who saw miracles there were bent on seeing some."[19]
The desire for novelty thus seemed to drive the people to accept
whatever appeared most ridiculous to the philosophe. "If the people
were allowed its way," Voltaire once wrote, "there would be a
hundred Jesus Christs per week everywhere."[20] To the philosophe
who valued the stability of calm reasonableness, the volatile imagina-
tion of the people appeared both ridiculous and dangerous.

This penchant for novelty often took the form of unreasoning
caprice, as the people's mind shifted with each appearance. In
Voltaire's plays the populace ends up on the side of right or wrong
not through any exercise of judgment but through clever manipulation by leaders. The champions of the just cause confront, and
frequently founder on, the irrational whims of a mercurial people.
If justice is served after a fashion amidst popular tumult in *Oedipe*
(1718) and *Rome sauvée* (1758), the populace chooses much less wisely
in *La mort de César* (1731) and *Mahomet* (1741). The action of *La
mort de César* is typical. After the assassination of Caesar, Cassius
harangues an enthusiastic and responsive populace (act 3, scene 7).
Caesar, however, had instructed Antony at length in the art of
beguiling the the mindless "tiger," the Roman people (act 1, scene
4). Antony takes the podium, displays the body of Caesar, and soon
controls the public mind. The fickle crowd now screams its support
for Antony, who then leads them toward vengeance and his own
succession (act 3, scene 8). *Mahomet* concludes with a similar struggle
for the support of the people. Justly enraged at the supposed "pro-
phet" who duped him into committing parricide, Seide leads the
crowd to Mohammed. Seide falls dead, however, from a poisonous
wound received in an earlier struggle; Mohammed seizes the occasion to claim magical power over life and death; the crowd, always
prey to appearance, obeys his will (act 5, scenes 3 and 4).[21]

19. "Pensées philosophiques" (1746), in Diderot, *Oeuvres philosophiques*, ed. Paul Vernière (Paris, 1964), p. 43.

20. To Joseph Vasselier, 24 June 1769, Voltaire, *Correspondence*, (14725). Similarly,
Montesquieu argued that, given the chance, the people would continuously expand the
cults of saints and the Virgin; see "Pensées," no. 431, in Montesquieu, *Oeuvres complètes*,
ed. André Masson, 3 vols. (Paris, 1950–55), 2:163.

21. On the general image of the people in eighteenth-century French theater, see John
van Eerde, "The People in Eighteenth-Century Tragedy from *Oedipe* to *Guillaume Tell*,"
in *VS* 27 (1963):1703–13. He finds Voltaire's portraits typical, but he does find in a few
writers a more sympathetic and sustained role for men of the people.

So much power did the philosophes attribute to the people's need
/ for novelty and excitement that they chose to explain the crowds of
the people at executions in terms of this need rather than in terms of
any inherent cruelty. In an aside in *Jacques le Fataliste* (c. 1774)
Diderot denied that these crowds gave evidence of inhumanity
among the populace. "Give an amusing fête in the boulevard," he
wrote,

> and the execution square will be empty. The people craves
> spectacles and runs to them, because it is amused when it enjoys
> them and even more amused by the story it tells when it returns
> home. The people is terrible in its fury, but the fury does not
> last. Personal misery has made it compassionate; the people
> turns its eyes from the spectacle of horror it had sought; it breaks
> down and returns weeping.[22]

Similarly, Holbach attributed these crowds to a childlike need to be
strongly moved.[23] Helvétius and Rousseau concurred, finding the
people's behavior analogous to the love of the great for the artificial
spectacle and cruelty of the stage. The people found its sensation on
the more accessible stage of the execution square.[24]

More often than not, however, the philosophes judged the people's
moral character even less favorably. As we have seen, Voltaire
spoke insistently and eloquently on the people's cruelty and
violence. The same Diderot who defended the people's reputation
on the matter of executions betrayed fears of popular violence in the
article "Boucher" in his *Encyclopédie*. Some had proposed placing all
butchers together in the suburbs to improve the health of the city of
Paris. Despite the logic of this argument, Diderot opposed the plan.
Such action, he feared, might endanger public tranquility by bringing together "violent, undisciplined" men "whose hands and eyes

22. Diderot, *Oeuvres romanesques*, ed. Henri Bénac (Paris, 1951), pp. 669–70.

23. Holbach, *La Morale universelle, ou les Devoirs de l'homme fondés sur la nature*, 3 vols.
(Amsterdam, 1776), 1:148–49.

24. See Helvétius, *De l'esprit*, in *Oeuvres complètes*, 5 vols. (Paris, 1795), 2:52, and Rousseau's "Lettre de J.-J. Rousseau à M. Philopolis," in *Oeuvres complètes*, ed. Bernard Gagnebin et al., 4 vols. to date (Paris, 1959–), 3:236. Helvétius ascribed the crowd's action to a
pure desire for new sensation. Rousseau insisted that the people sought merely to arouse
the primal instinct of pity as well as the more mundane goal of becoming *orateur du quartier*.
Rousseau was responding to criticism of Charles Bonnet (alias "Philopolis"), who had
used the crowds at executions to refute Rousseau's contention that pity is a natural instinct. See Rousseau, *Oeuvres complètes*, 3:230, note 1 (found on p. 1385).

are accustomed to blood." Diderot preferred to scatter their "natural fury" about the city.[25]

Turgot extended Diderot's fears to include the entire people. As an alternative to the French system of courts, the English jury system seemed plausible to some reformers. Turgot, however, found the people unfit to judge. In a letter on criminal justice he analyzed the people's moral condition:

> The people is hardened by its misery. It is almost indifferent to life, exposes itself to death over the smallest matters, and sees death approach without emotion. No matter what is said, the sentiments of nature are much less alive among it than among men of a higher station. Love itself is weak among our peasants, and often they will miss their cow more than their wife or son, because they can better calculate the price of the cow than of the privations of the heart.[26]

Turgot did not blame the people for its cruelty but found that cruelty inevitable.[27]

Even in his egalitarian years during the Revolution, Condorcet—who followed Turgot on most matters—considered the people morally deficient in its existing condition. In his second "Mémoire sur l'instruction publique" (1791), he advocated using animal fables to arouse *sensibilité* among the children of the people. "Above all, let us not forget," he argued,

> that in the man occupied with base work which dulls his compassion and wraps him in personal concerns, the habit of callousness produces that penchant for violence which is the great enemy of the virtue and liberty of the people, and is the only excuse for tyrants, the only specious pretext for all unequal laws.[28]

25. *Encyclopédie*, 2:352.

26. *Oeuvres de Turgot*, 3:528. Turgot was speculating in the light of the reforms of Chancellor Maupeou, who had disbanded the traditional sovereign courts of France in January 1771.

27. Turgot's sense that the peasant was conditioned to favor his cow over his family was shared by other observers. See André Bourde, *Agronomie et agronomes en France au XVIII^e siècle* (Paris, 1967), 2:1025, and Diderot, *Oeuvres philosophiques*, p. 499.

28. Condorcet, *Oeuvres complètes*, ed. M. F. Arago and A. C. O'Connor, 12 vols. (1847), 3:235–36. He also echoed Turgot's opinions on juries, urging society to choose judges "who do not share popular prejudices, so that neither the nature of the crime nor the im-

Condorcet thus appealed to the political and social fears of his readers to gain support for his scheme of moral education and legal equality.

The philosophes' "natural history" of the people's moral insensibility followed two paths. In the first instance, they reasoned, as did Turgot and Condorcet, that the people's hard lot dulled its sensitivity to the sufferings of others. (Rousseau, among others, would eventually argue that the opposite was true.) In other cases, they argued that the people's lot condemned it to ignorance and that ignorance bred immorality. That the people had little time to think because of the demands of labor almost all philosophes agreed. "The laborer's share," John Locke wrote, "being seldom more than a bare subsistence, never allows that body of *men, time or opportunity to raise their thoughts above that*, or struggle with the richer for theirs."[29] Three-quarters of a century later the perspective had not changed a bit. Comparing the mind of the upper classes to that of the laborer, Adam Smith found a great gap. The activities and the leisure of the rich demanded and nurtured complex and sophisticated thought. It is otherwise with the common people, he observed.

> They have little time to spare for education. Their parents can scarce afford to maintain them even in infancy. As soon as they are able to work, they must apply to some trade by which they can earn their subsistence. That trade too is generally so simple and uniform as to give little exercise to the understanding; while, at the same time, their labor is both so constant and so severe, that it leaves them little leisure and less inclination to apply to, or even to think of anything else.[30]

Some like Shaftesbury and Smith considered the moral sentiment innate and strong. But most philosophes assumed that ignorance narrowed the moral ability of the person, locking his mind into false prejudices, preventing him from seeing the long-run effects which made actions right and wrong. A mind constrained by continuous labor was also a mind crippled in moral judgment.

pression it makes on their minds leads them to condemn an innocent man." (*Vie de Turgot*, in *Oeuvres complètes*, 5:192).

29. E. J. Hundert, "The Making of *Homo Faber*: John Locke Between Ideology and History," *Journal of the History of Ideas* 33, no. 1 (Jan.–Mar. 1972):6.

30. *Wealth of Nations*, ed. E. Cannan (New York, 1904), 2:269.

This assumption of the necessary relationship between knowledge and virtue is as old as philosophy itself. No doubt it betrayed a good measure of social bias and fear. But it also lay at the heart of the philosophes' ideal—the reasoned and calm investigation of the consequences of actions. Holbach compared the ignorant man to the blind deaf-mute

> who walks randomly on the road of this world at the risk of running into others or falling down at any moment. In a word, without experience or learning it is impossible to be good.[31]

With characteristic aggressiveness Helvétius stated the assumption even more positively: "Destroy ignorance and all the germs of moral evil will be destroyed."[32] Implicitly, then, those condemned by their estate to ignorance, the people, would necessarily lack the preconditions for virtue. The Physiocrat Mercier de la Rivière made explicit the social content of this assumption to support his plan for public instruction. He described the fate of the masses, who lacked both human reason and the shrewder animal instincts: "Their blindness places them lower than brutes, making them more miserable than animals, more difficult to lead, and more tempestuous." Like children in their gullibility, he continued, the people dwell in "a state of habitual delirium . . . ignorance differs in no way from madness, when you consider each according to its disastrous effects."[33] La Rivière chose extreme rhetoric to support his cause, but even in calmer moments the spirit of his analysis remained implicit in much of what the philosophes had to say about the people.

For the philosophes, therefore, no virtue rested in the socially primitive. Their ideal man belonged to the leisured, sophisticated class of honnêtes gens and pursued virtue through useful action. The fabled "noble primitive" that the philosophes occasionally evoked—Montesquieu's Troglodytes, Voltaire's Scythians, Diderot's Tahitians —served only to point to excesses and unnecessary artifices in the life of leisured society. A real return to nature seemed, however, a return to barbarism. Although Diderot cast the supposedly "primitive"

31. *La Morale universelle*, 1:276. Holbach did, however, think that the knowledge necessary for virtue might become accessible to all; see chapter 6 below.

32. *De l'homme* (1772), in *Oeuvres complètes*, 4:11. Helvétius saw a direct relation between ignorance in nations and their moral baseness; see ibid., pp. 4–5.

33. *De l'instruction publique; ou considérations morales et politiques sur la nécessité, la nature et la source de cette instruction* (Paris, 1775), pp. 23–24.

Tahitians in a glorious light in his *Supplément au Voyage de Bougainville* (1772), he criticized any attempt to find superior virtue in the ignorant peasant.[34] On the contrary, he linked moral improvement to economic improvement; to Catherine the Great he contended that "the purity of morals has followed the progress of clothing from animal skin to silk."[35] Whatever virtue the philosophes chose to attribute to primitive peoples distant in space and time, they found the primitive peasant who worked their lands exceptional only in ignorance and, too often, cruelty.[36]

Though the philosophes assumed that leisure nurtured both knowledge and virtue, they never automatically associated increased virtue with increased wealth. Like most moralists of their time, they often delighted in lumping the very rich with the poor in the same moral class. Helvétius, in an entry to his notebook, defined virtue as "wisdom which reconciles passion with reason and pleasure with duty." Immediately afterward he made two succinct social observations—"virtue does not speak like the people" and "the people often dwells in the great."[37] Helvétius thus automatically associated lack of virtue with the people, as a product of ignorance. But he could not resist seeing that this baseness was often as true of the rich and powerful as it was of the people.

Holbach similarly warned against the moral dangers of great wealth and its consequent languor; many of the higher orders of society were, he thought, as estranged as the people from the habit of thorough thinking.[38] Even Turgot, who so doubted the people's capacity for moral judgment on juries, also distrusted the ability of the very rich and powerful to judge fairly. "One must select," he warned, "neither the dregs nor the froth of nations" to sit on tribu-

34. Michèle Duchet ably dispels any extreme interpretations of Diderot's "primitivism" in "Le primitivisme de Diderot," *Europe,* nos. 405–06 (Jan.–Feb.1963) : 126–32.

35. "Plan d'une Université" (1775), *Oeuvres complètes,* 3:429–30. Though the philosophes found the best hope for civilized *moeurs* in developed societies, they did not view progress in moeurs as either inevitable or permanent. For themes of decadence in the Enlightenment, see H. Vyverberg, *Historical Pessimism in the French Enlightenment* (Cambridge, Mass., 1958), chapters 17–20, the last on Diderot.

36. There are, of course, a few exceptions, but only a few. Diderot wrote to his Sophie, "I love to talk with the peasant; I always learn something from him." 20 October 1759, *Correspondance* (153). In a *pensée* Montesquieu observed, "I like peasants; they are not wise enough to reason craftily." (*Oeuvres complètes,* 3:302, no. 1109.)

37. *Notes de la main d'Helvétius,* ed. A. Keim (Paris, 1907), p. 78.

38. *Système de la Nature,* 2:289.

nals.[39] The philosophes thus joined those moralists who perceived the corrupting influence of wealth and power. Yet in the end they had to address their plans and reforms to that class. The rich at least had some of the preconditions for enlightenment; the people seemed locked into permanent ignorance and sporadic fury.

The words which came to the philosophes' minds to describe the people often conjured up images of animality and even madness: *bêtes féroces, furieux, imbéciles, fous, aveugles.* "The people will always be composed of brutes," Voltaire jotted in a notebook; some time later he added, "The people is between man and beast."[40] Such rhetoric flowed freely from the pens of Voltaire and other philosophes, and readers have often taken these sentiments for the substance of the Enlightenment's view of the people. We can doubt that Voltaire really considered the people only half-human—he emphasized the common humanity of all men on equally numerous occasions. The philosophe knew full well that the men of the people largely worked peaceably and anonymously in the fields and shops of Europe. But the people impressed him first as the children of Discord.

Social reasons for this rhetoric of scorn are not hard to find. By training and association the philosophes belonged to the elite; they had no monopoly on contempt or despair at the intellectual and moral capabilities of the masses. Samuel Johnson, no philosophe, was as disdainful as any concerning the manners and mind of the populace.[41] The humanitarian poet William Cowper wrote movingly of the poor who, "inured to drudgery and distress / Act without aim, think little and feel less."[42] But behind the scorn of the philosophes one can discern a measure of fear for the future of Enlightenment in the face of both the abysmal ignorance seen lurking in the lower orders and the violent passions which those masses came to represent in the social realm. The philosophes adopted the role of apologists for passion informed by reason, defending the legitimate role of passion against the fears of Christian and even Stoic moralizing. But in turn they feared the role of the violent passions inaccessible to reason.[43]

39. *Oeuvres de Turgot*, 3:529.

40. *Notebooks*, ed. T. Besterman, 2:534–60 (vols. 81 and 82 of *The Complete Works of Voltaire*, ed. Besterman [Geneva, 1968]).

41. Robert Voitle, *Samuel Johnson the Moralist* (Cambridge, Mass., 1961), pp. 112–13.

42. Cited in Stromberg, *Religious Liberalism*, p. 131.

43. That the philosophes misunderstood violent passion or unreason is suggested by Michel Foucault, *Madness and Civilization: A History of Insanity in the Age of Reason*, trans.

The people, not educated in the ways of calm gentility, was the rhetorical victim of that fear. The church understood irrationality as the effect of a universal sinfulness; the people stood a more than equal chance for redemption in another world. The secular mind of the philosophes rejected that explanation and consolation. The philosophes could understand irrationality only in social terms, in the inability of reason to penetrate beyond the leisured, educated few. Redemption could come only through education into the ways of enlightened self-interest, and that education seemed, at least until the later years of the Enlightenment, totally inaccessible to those who had to live by their labor.

The association of certain social orders with certain psychological and moral faculties dates back to the beginnings of political thinking. Plato's *Republic* mirrors the structure of the soul. The aristocratic society of the eighteenth century likewise made an easy transition from the "aristocratic" qualities of the soul to the aristocratic elite in society; virtue, honor, nobility, courage, and similar attributes were often considered the prerogative of the upper orders. (The philosophes, as we shall see, showed healthy disrespect for this particular assumption.) Not surprisingly, those who dissented from the Enlightenment in the later years of the century used the same kind of framework but reversed the assumption: they projected superior wisdom and virtue onto the life of the peasant. Apologists for the peasantry, largely in Germany, found in the unreflective, passionate life of the peasant the cure for society, not a threat to its stability. They agreed with the philosophes that the peasant was by his social nature cut off from the reflective, complex habits of the civilized honnête homme—that was the peasant's glory. Early in the century, the Alpine poetry of Albrecht Haller juxtaposed the corrupt teaching of urban society to the unrefined empirical experience of peasant wisdom.[44] Praise of the peasant mind grew proportionately to the reaction against Enlightenment in the late eighteenth century. The German social observer Justus Möser described passion as "the noble gift of God surer than the most enlightened reason." The simple peasant, he wrote, "follows a long experience, or a venerable prej-

---

R. Howard (New York, 1967) from the French *Histoire de la folie* (Paris, 1961). His view of "the Age of Reason" is, however, badly stereotyped; the name itself is a misnomer.

44. John Gagliardo, *From Pariah to Patriot: The Changing Image of the German Peasant, 1770–1840* (Lexington, Ky., 1969), pp. 67–68.

udice, and it is dangerous to disturb him."[45] The German Sturm und Drang and a growing body of sentimentalists throughout Europe after 1770 found in the natural immediacy of peasant life the source of a truer wisdom.[46] In so doing they rejected both Enlightenment epistemology and social biases—a predictable process in view of the links that the philosophes had forged between knowledge, reflection, and leisure. The sentimentalists' criticisms were fair, but their alternative hardly more realistic, indeed much less so.

The philosophes' fear of the people should not be exaggerated. Though urban and rural violence existed, it was usually sporadic, narrow in its aims, easily controlled. The philosophes did not stand in fear and awe of a growing urban, organized, politically powerful working class such as nineteenth-century intellectuals had to face. No one predicted, as many in the nineteenth century would, that society and culture stood in complete jeopardy in face of the rising masses. The people was no more nor less imposing than it had been for centuries. Furthermore, the ignorance, violence, and superstition of philosophes' "people" became, as it did not for most elitists of the eighteenth century, a problem begging for a program. The philosophes scorned and feared the people not in order to dismiss them from consideration—whatever the fatalism of occasional observations—but to confront, explain, and, perhaps, change the situation. However rudimentary their sociology, it represented the beginnings of a scientific appraisal and pointed the way toward a cure. Above all, one should not forget that we are dealing here with one form of rhetoric, and that all rhetoric is occasional, drawn from a reserve of expressions and formulas to meet the perceptions of the moment. This rhetoric suited the needs of inbred scorn and fears, but only those needs. Other perceptions could and did evoke other rhetorics and other ways of dealing with people. Fear and scorn represented only one way in which philosophes reacted toward the people and only the beginning, however basic and important, of their involvement with Discord's progeny.

45. As quoted in ibid., p. 68.
46. Ibid., chapter 3, and Roy Pascal, *The German Sturm und Drang* (New York, 1953), chapter 3.

# 3 Agents of Ceres

Someone attuned to the philosophes' colorful rhetoric of scorn for the people would turn to the article "Peuple" in the *Encyclopédie* fully expecting a diatribe on the people's unreason. Instead, he would find that the author, De Jaucourt, entered a plea for respect toward the masses. The worker, he wrote,

> rises with the sun and, without looking at the fortune which smiles above him, puts on his clothes for all seasons; he digs our mines and our quarries, he drains our swamps, he cleans our streets, he builds our houses, he constructs our furniture; even when hunger comes, all goes well with him; when the day is done, he goes to bed painfully in the arms of fatigue.

Beset by the cruelty of the elements and powerful men, the peasant, as De Jaucourt describes him, goes about his business: "He is sober, just, faithful, and religious, without considering what he will get in return." He marries for love, toils diligently, and shares his fortune— unlike the wealthy—among *all* his children. "Such is the portrait," the article concludes, "of the men who compose what we call 'peuple,' and who always form the most numerous and most necessary part of the nation."[1]

De Jaucourt's somewhat maudlin, pastoral portrait of the average peasant seems disingenuous, hardly the image of the ignorant, ferocious beast so often painted by the philosophes. Elsewhere in the *Encyclopédie* De Jaucourt himself had not been above speaking of the people in such terms; he had hardly considered the people's religiosity a point of merit.[2] But when he made an official pronouncement on the people, he suppressed his scorn and presented an account of the arduous life of the worker and, perhaps less sincerely, an optimistic view of his moral character.[3] By the standard of reason the

1. "Peuple," *Encyclopédie*, 12:476, drawing heavily from Abbé Coyer.
2. See above, chapter 2, note 13, and "Fé, Fo, Foé," *Encyclopédie*, 6:460.
3. Cf. Holbach, *La Morale universelle*, 2:250: "Poverty when it works should never be scorned. Laborious poverty is usually honest and virtuous; it deserves scorn only when it gives way to idleness and vices for which, too often, opulence gives the example."

people stood condemned, but by another measure, equally dear to the philosophes, the people earned praise and support. That measure was utility.

The editors of the *Encyclopédie* often polemicized on the dignity of the useful mechanical arts. In a noteworthy passage in his "Preliminary Discourse," d'Alembert narrated a history of society's scorn for its workers. The philosophe can do little to correct this attitude, he noted, but he can at least trace its origins. In d'Alembert's version of man's early history, the collective action of the weak broke the initial rule of the strong few. Men still felt compelled, however, to feel superior to others. Those who adopted reason as their standard attacked the strong by exalting the mind over physical strength. But both the intellectually and physically strong then relegated base and routine work to those considered lowly. Nonetheless, the mechanical arts have their revenge on the liberal arts, since these skills are always more useful. For this reason, d'Alembert argued, we should not scorn these servants of society, despite the superior dignity traditionally associated with the activity of the mind.[4]

Diderot similarly castigated the prejudice against useful work which had tended to fill the cities with "vainglorious reasoners and useless contemplatives" and the countryside with "ignorant, lazy, and scornful petty tyrants." Society's values, he argued, had no relation to society's needs. Men praise those "occupied in making us believe we are happy" rather than those "occupied in making sure we really are." "How strange are our standards," he mused. "We demand that people occupy themselves usefully, and yet we scorn useful men."[5]

The praise of useful—and attack on useless—men became a familiar refrain during the Enlightenment. In the years before the propaganda of the Physiocratic party turned attention to the countryside, most of this praise fell to the artisan. The attempt by certain men of letters and science to rescue the reputation of the mechanical arts from the disdain of aristocratic culture had long been underway. During the High Renaissance artists such as Leonardo and Dürer, humanists such as More and Bruno, as well as numerous literate artisans had pleaded the cause of the useful arts. Francis Bacon gave the apology philosophical dignity, and other scientists and philos-

4. *Encyclopédie*, 1:xiii.
5. "Art," *Encyclopédie*, 1:714.

ophers continued his polemic throughout the seventeenth century.[6] Mercantile economics in France, placing a premium on the luxury arts, gave official sanction to the praise of manual crafts. At Colbert's insistence the *Académie royale des sciences* began in 1675 the ambitious project of describing all of the mechanical arts in detail for the use of both laymen and craftsmen. Although the Academy's *Description des arts et métiers* did not begin to appear until after the publication of the first volume of the *Encyclopédie*, it became a source and model for the latter's subsequent sections on the arts.[7]

The philosophes' apology for the mechanical arts had, therefore, a long prehistory. In 1716 Claude Joubert wrote of the manual arts:

> Their products are evident and real, while so much from other arts are purely imaginary, valued only from the perspective where imposture and seduction have placed them. Arts and trades deserve public esteem and recognition with as much justice.[8]

A half-century later the perspective had changed little; Diderot echoed Joubert's sentiments, asserting, "The poet, the philosopher, the orator, the minister, the warrior, and the hero would all be naked and have no bread without the artisan, the object of his cruel scorn."[9] Feared as rioter and scorned as believer, the artisan drew praise from Diderot in his role as producer.

Such appreciation of the worker was not limited to the *Encyclopédie*, with its somewhat parochial concern for the mechanical arts. Voltaire consistently expressed in *Essai sur les moeurs* (1756) his admiration for those persons, largely unknown, who had provided society with the tools of civilized life and whose inventions remained the heritage of

6. Paolo Rossi has ably recounted the history of this current of ideas in *Philosophy, Technology, and the Arts in the Early Modern Era*, trans. S. Antonasio (New York, 1970) from *I Filosofi e le Machine* (Milan, 1962); see especially chapters 1 and 3, and appendix 3. F.G. Healey concentrates on the *Encyclopédie* and the *Description des arts et métiers* in his article, "The Enlightenment View of *Homo Faber*," *VS* 25 (1963):837–59. For a necessary corrective to Healey's view that there was little concern for these matters during the seventeenth century, see Rossi, chapter 3. Healey's attempt to see something radically new in these efforts (pp. 845, 848, 850) is misleading.

7. Healey, "Enlightenment View of *Homo Faber*," pp. 843–48. On this and other predecessors of the *Encyclopédie*, see Jacques Proust, *Diderot et l'Encyclopédie*, chapter 6.

8. In *Secrets concernans les arts et métiers*, quoted in French in Healey, "Enlightenment View of *Homo Faber*," p. 845.

9. "Métier," *Encyclopédie*, 10:463. Though officially anonymous, the entry reflects Diderot's style and sentiments.

the artisan class. In the dark night of the Middle Ages, he acknowledged, men still managed to preserve and even extend the realm of
the useful arts. Merchants and artisans survived despite the storm of
feudal war, and, like mice, "dug their habitations in silence while the
eagles and vultures tore each other apart. Even in these base centuries
one found some useful inventions, fruits of that mechanical genius
which nature gives to certain men most independently of philosophy."[10] In his introduction of 1761 to a new printing of the *Essai*,
he credited the artisan class with being the precondition of any
higher culture: "There had to be blacksmiths, carpenters, masons,
and laborers before there could appear a man with enough leisure to
meditate. Without doubt all the manual arts preceded metaphysics
by several centuries."[11] A product of an age which admired Colbert,
Voltaire recognized the value of the arts.

Holbach did not limit his praise so exclusively to the mechanical
arts. His frequent arguments for the possibility of a society based on
recognition of mutual need and respect included appreciation of the
worker's role. "Nothing is more unjust or base," he wrote in *La
Morale universelle*,

> than the insulting manner with which haughty opulence regards
> those artisans who every day contribute to furnish him those
> needs and pleasures which his weakness could not obtain for him.

And a little later he added:

> By the strangest of follies, the rich man scorns and disdains the
> laborer, the farmer, the nourisher of nations, without whose work
> there would be no harvests, no livestock, no manufacture, no
> commerce, none of the arts indispensable to society.[12]

The specter of the fearful progeny of Discord disappeared behind

---

10. *Essai sur les moeurs*, 1:757–58; similarly, see the undated "Chapitre sur les arts," in
ibid., 2:819–20, 835–36. On the appreciation of the mechanical arts, Abbé Pluche was no
less enthusiastic. Inviting physicists and philosophers to descend from the celestial spheres,
he wrote: "They will find in these arts, though common and base, practices so exact that
you would be tempted to consider them the work of some extraordinarily enlightened
genius who had taken it upon himself to teach them to the human race." (*Le Spectacle de
la Nature, ou entretiens sur les particularités de l'histoire naturelle* [Paris, 1770; first ed., 1746]
6:418–19.)

11. *Essai sur les moeurs*, 1:12.

12. *La Morale universelle*, 2:250–51.

the image of the peaceful agents of Vulcan and Ceres. Holbach's
style of perceiving the people became part of the common rhetoric of
the Enlightenment. Reformers, unable and unwilling to appeal
directly to the masses, appealed instead on their behalf to the holders
of power. The Badenese reformer Johann Reinhard prefaced his
proposal for economic reforms for the working orders by simply
pointing to the people's central place in the creation of wealth.
"Unpropertied and hardworking people are," he wrote to his
margrave,

> an indispensable necessity in a large nation, which cannot exist
> for even a short time without them, without going entirely to
> pieces. Yes, it is certain that just this class of people constitutes
> the foundation of the wealth of a nation.[13]

The economic societies of Spain propagandized in a similar manner
and at length on the dignity of labor to a nation accustomed to
aristocratic disdain of dirty hands.[14] Adam Smith, in analyzing the
sources of the wealth of nations, emphasized that the laboring class
was the principal generator of wealth and well-being. Policies which
worked to its benefit, he insisted, worked to the benefit of the nation
as a whole. The same could not be said for those who lived from profits, whose interests rarely coincided with the nation's.[15]

There is, to be sure, often something superficial in this praise, especially when posed against the philosophes' expressed contempt for
the people as moral agents. In criticizing the scornful they criticized
themselves. They spoke from the perspective of the economic needs
of society, recognizing that the people's work provided the basis
of all social life, and pleaded for recognition of the status of the
people on the ladder of utility. But the people's function, not the
individual worker, received their attention and praise; the plates of
the *Encyclopédie* display techniques and machines, not real workers.[16]

---

13. As quoted in Helen Liebel, *Enlightened Bureaucracy Versus Enlightened Despotism in
Baden, 1750–1792, Transactions of the American Philosophical Society.* 55, part 5 (Philadelphia,
1965), p. 66.

14. R. J. Shafer, *The Economic Societies in the Spanish World (1763–1821)* (Syracuse,
1958), pp. 81–82.

15. *Wealth of Nations*, 1:248–50.

16. See Jacques Proust, "L'image du peuple au travail dans les planches de l'Encyclopédie," in *Images du peuple au dix-huitième siècle* (Paris, 1973), pp. 65–86.

Recognition of a special dignity in agriculture did not mean recognition of such dignity in the individual day laborer.

Helvétius attempted to explain and justify this distinction in *De l'esprit* (1758). Why, he asked, do nations that supposedly consult their own interest in all judgments always honor the poet and the geometer more than the laborer and winegrower, though the latter two are demonstrably more useful? Helvétius responded to this puzzle with little difficulty—excessive praise would lower the value of public esteem. Were the public to extol activities which everyone can do, the power of its praise to cultivate the seeds of genius would dissipate. "The public realizes," he concluded,

> that in the case of agriculture, the art and not the artist should be honored; and that if long ago, under the names of Ceres and Bacchus, people deified the first farmer and the first winegrower, this honor, so justly awarded to the inventors of agriculture, must not be squandered on manual laborers.[17]

Within this framework the philosophe could praise the labor and function of the common man without attributing any particular moral stature to him. In defending the dignity and value of the useful arts, the philosophes occasionally pleaded for the dignity of the worker himself, but only occasionally. They never escaped the conviction that most physical labor, whatever its necessity and value for society, undermined the laborer's moral and intellectual potential. They often praised the active life in the tradition of Aristotle and Cicero, but they did not equate the activity of the honnête homme with the labor of the peasant. The philosophes in no way adopted a "work ethic"—Calvinist, bourgeois, or otherwise—which could see equal virtue in all forms of time-consuming, productive activity. The brief, anonymous entry "Travail" in the *Encyclopédie* captures some of the ambiguity of the philosophes' position. Work is, it says,

> a daily occupation to which man is condemned by his needs, and to which he owes at once his health, his subsistence, his serenity, his common sense, and perhaps his virtue. Mythology,

17. *Oeuvres complètes* (Paris, 1820), 1:270–71. Helvétius attributed this idea to Charles Duclos, a close associate of the philosophes; see chapter 15 of Duclos's *Considérations sur les moeurs de ce siècle*, in *Oeuvres complètes*, for similar sentiments.

which considered it an evil, made it the child of Erebus [son of Chaos] and Night.[18]

The entry here is cautious and traditional, seeking to establsh something of the dignity of labor in a hostile society. In less guarded moments, the philosophes' views approached much more closely those of mythology. The offhand division made by Charles Duclos is much more typical:

> With the exception of the low people, which has ideas relating only to its needs and is usually deprived of every other concern, the rest of society is everywhere the same. Good company is independent of rank, and can be found only among those who think and feel, who have just ideas and upright feelings.[19]

The pursuits of the magistrate, the man of letters, or (perhaps) the merchant, Duclos and the philosophes thought, developed and fulfilled his humanity. The work of the peasant or the simple artisan limited and distorted that quality; labor was his burden, not his glory.

The philosophes thus spoke of the people in two voices based on the separate standards of reason and utility. While despairing at the people's unreason and cruelty, their "corporeal eye" could not deny economic reality: the people was in fact "the most numerous and most necessary part of the nation." We are faced with the paradox that they both scorned the people and criticized those who did precisely the same. But the paradox is much more apparent than real. There is no absolute contradiction in considering men both brutish and useful. The twin standards of reasonableness and utility were vital to the philosophes' critique of society. The philosophes never spoke of the people as both unreasonable and useful in the same breath; different occasions brought different judgments. As a group of intellectuals who thought they had hit upon a style of worldly, critical reasonableness by which to judge the rest of society, they perceived with dismay and alarm the barbarity of the lower classes in the annals of history, the gullibility of the people with regard to the "miracles" in the streets, and the volatility of the people at times

18. *Encyclopédie*, 16:567.
19. *Considérations sur les moeurs de ce siècle*, pp. 109–10.

of scarcity and fear. Speaking in the voice of intellectual moralists, therefore, the philosophes freely and fiercely condemned the irrational canaille.

But the philosophes spoke from many perspectives and in many voices. The pose of the moralist might suit certain occasions and perceptions; the pose of the legislator suited others. Analyzing critically what each part of society owed to the others and to the whole, they easily recognized—and reminded those with authority—that the largest and most productive part of the nation was that same, much-maligned people. They insisted that those entrusted with leadership suppress their scorn and disdain for the people and see what was relevant to the exercise of leadership—the people's utility.

A famous exchange between Voltaire and the social critic Simon Nicolas Linguet provides a telling instance of the division between these two voices. Linguet wrote to Voltaire in 1767 to bring his first major work, *Théorie des lois civiles*, to the attention of the literary patriarch. With characteristic lack of tact, Linguet took the occasion to question the goal of general enlightenment. It would be fine, he argued, if you could limit lumières for the amusement only of the idle and the rich. But since the rays of light inevitably spread to the lower orders, discontent will grow among the people once it learns that it too has a mind. All social order might then he lost.[20] Although his doubts were indiscreet, Linguet had every reason to expect that his desire to keep the people in line would meet with the approval of Voltaire, whose repeated advocacy of a social religion for the people was well known in Paris. But Voltaire responded indignantly. First he distinguished those who work only with their hands from skilled craftsmen. The former, he argued, would always have the Mass and the tavern as their culture, but the latter were beginning to read and were capable of learning. Then he expanded his criticism, throwing Linguet's words back at him. "No, sir," he wrote,

> *all is not lost when the people is put in a position to see that it has a mind.*
> On the contrary, all is lost when you treat it like a herd of bulls.
> Because sooner or later it will gore you with its horns.

Had the people been educated, Voltaire continued, fanatics could

20. Linguet to Voltaire, 19 February 1767, Voltaire, *Correspondence* (13075).

never have led the masses into the religious and civil excesses of the past two hundred and fifty years. He concluded, "It's not your business to prevent men from reading."[21]

The haughtiest of the philosophes thus drew a line between calling the people animals and treating them as such.[22] Voltaire had learned respect for the skilled craftsmen in his involvement with the Genevan lower orders during the struggles of the 1760s. But his stern reaction defending *all* of the people reflected a distinction made implicitly by many philosophes between ridiculing the people's ignorance and creating or perpetuating it. In his *Testament politique* Cardinal Richelieu had compared the people to mules, spoiled more by long rest than hard work; burdensome labor should neither crush the people, he argued, nor give it time to reflect.[23] The philosophe admitted that the people was often mulish, but thought it deserved better than to be kept that way.

The voice of the moralist expressed aristocratic scorn and philosophic frustration. The voice of the legislator expressed the loftier concerns of the philosophe trying to measure the just contribution of all men to a society. Both rhetorics were traditional, the first dating back to the dawn of philosophy, the second to the High Renaissance. Neither perspective entailed any specific program of action toward the people; each rather set limits to actions and expectations. Try as you might to enlighten men, the moralist said, but remember that the people is composed of ignorant and cruel men who can never understand you. Scorn the people if you must, the legislator replied, but remember that the people provides the economic substance of the nation and must receive a measure of care and respect.

Both voices existed side by side throughout the Enlightenment, serving the needs of varying moods. The occasion for anger at the people's unreason never disappeared from the writings of the philosophes, especially those of Montesquieu, Voltaire, Gibbon, and Diderot. But among many of the later generation of leading philosophes—Turgot, Condorcet, Helvétius, Holbach, Smith—such observations are more rare. Not that they had more faith in the *vox populi* than their mentors; they trusted the judgment of the peasant

21. Voltaire to Linguet, 15 March 1767, Voltaire, *Correspondence* (13143).

22. Also noted by M. Roustan, *Les philosophes et la société moderne au xviii^e siècle* (Paris, 1906), p. 370.

23. *Testament politique*, ed. Louis André (Paris, 1947), pp. 253–54.

or the behavior of the crowd no more than Voltaire did. Conditions did not seem, however, to call for the scornful rhetoric of earlier years, especially in formal writings on society and its problems. A new perception, developing and maturing from mid-century on, altered the rhetorical balance in favor of the voice of the legislator. As they pressed their investigation of society during the decades after 1750, the philosophes discovered that in many ways the people was not merely the principal support of society but also its principal victim.

# 4  A Case of Neglect

Humanitarianism was in vogue in the eighteenth century.[1] A concern for *humanität* and its most unfortunate children, though hardly confined to the circle of the philosophes, provided an essential horizon against which they explored and talked about society. The "deserving poor," the crippled, the sick, the insane, the enslaved, and all special cases of misery benefited from the humanitarian "spirit of the age." To refined aristocrats trying to redefine "nobility" in an age when martial virtues were in eclipse, humanitarian concern provided a new definition for overlordship and stewardship. For the clergy, especially Protestant, humanitarianism provided a plausible substitute for religious "enthusiasm," a cast of mind discredited by the excesses of the previous two centuries. For men of letters it provided a high-minded cause with which to associate their new stature and nerve. For all humanitarianism represented a just perception of ills inadequately met in previous ages but now, in an age of relative ease, apparently open to cure. Without this humanitarian climate any appreciation of the more general oppression and misery of the laboring people would have been impossible. Such appreciation, however, was neither widespread nor automatic. Humanitarianism focused its energies on the obvious distress of certain groups; most of these groups belonged to the people. But to see the people as a class as the victim of society required a much deeper, more radical insight into the economic and legal underpinnings of the Old Regime. Such insight eventually was achieved, but only in the later decades of the Enlightenment and primarily in France, where the philosophes' perspective on power nurtured a more radical vision.

Certainly perception of the people's misery was not lacking elsewhere. But nowhere else in the European Enlightenment did the will and incentive exist to pursue the implications of this insight with the clarity of the French. The English elite was, as a rule, too much at

1. On the humanitarian background to Enlightenment see Gay, *The Enlightenment*, 2:24–55. On humanitarianism in France, see Shelby McCloy, *The Humanitarian Movement in Eighteenth-Century France* (Lexington, 1957).

ease with the political and social solutions of the Augustan age to express anger for the people. English discussion of the people remained remarkably confined to the problem of poor laws, the most vexing social problem of the age.[2] Scottish philosophes, largely academics by training, remained more comfortable within the speculative sociology of Montesquieu than in the critical, programmatic social thought of the Encyclopedists.[3] The most perceptive of their number, Hume and Smith, were also those most closely in touch with thought in French circles. The principal centers of the Spanish Enlightenment, the economic societies, did not court danger as did the French philosophes, but rather remained respectful of traditional authorities while suggesting ways to increase production.[4] The most significant social observers and commentators in the Germanies were administrators, trained in cameralist science, often accurate in their assessment of fiscal and economic ills, but understandably not given to questioning the social bases of their society.[5] Hence for much the same reason that the European Enlightenment looked to France for leadership, the French philosophes led the way in the perception of radical abuse in society.

Perception always involves perspective, a certain angle from which even the most critical, discerning eye views the world. For the social critic, one important perspective is his own experience of power and authority. The French philosophes viewed the structure of authority in eighteenth-century France much as we see it today with the perspective of history—as an ambiguous, multifaceted affair. The myth of unity and permanence which Louis XIV had encouraged was simply not congruous with the obvious realities of France after his death. Church quarrels, court factions, conflicts between sovereign law courts and royal administrators, and repeated demands for reforms broke any semblance of monolithic power. The philosophe occupied a particularly good position from which to

2. On English debate about the poor and the widening humanitarian concern within that debate, see Dorothy Marshall, *The English Poor in the Eighteenth Century* (London, 1926), chapter 1; Brian Inglis, *Poverty and the Industrial Revolution* (London, 1971), pp. 26–44; A. W. Coats, "Economic Thought and Poor-Law Policy in the Eighteenth Century," *Economic History Review*, 2d series 13, no. 1 (Aug. 1960): 39–51.

3. See Gladys Bryson, *Man and Society* (Princeton, 1945).

4. See Shafer, *Economic Societies*, and Jean Sarrailh, *L'Espagne éclairée de la seconde moitié du xviii<sup>e</sup> siècle* (Paris, 1964).

5. See Liebel, *Enlightened Bureaucracy*, and Albion Small, *The Cameralists* (Chicago, 1909).

observe these divisions and ambiguities, living as he did on the fringes of power: close enough to the center to benefit from authority and appreciate its uses, far enough away to feel its wrath and see its inequities.

The philosophes certainly did not have to rely upon pure projection to feel frustrated with authority; at crucial moments each had felt its anger. Voltaire's journeys to England, Berlin, and finally to the Swiss border marked stages in a long love-hate affair with the world of vested power. An early visit to the prison at Vincennes taught Diderot the capriciousness of French censorship, and his career as editor of the *Encyclopédie* involved a continuous search for harbors of official goodwill amidst an angry sea of clerical opposition and royal censorship. Helvétius, a wealthy farmer-general turned philosophe, saw great trouble in the wind after being audacious (or foolish) enough to sign his name to *De l'esprit*. Turgot found his efforts at reform first mildly encouraged in his years as intendant at Limoges but then ultimately frustrated after he became first minister of France. Holbach, to be sure, never experienced a serious brush with the law, but Holbach also never signed his name to any work.

The record is, however, far from unambiguous. Voltaire occasionally felt the anger of royal power, but he continued to court that power as much as criticize it. The role of philosophe gave Diderot access to the highest social circles; prison was a shock and mental torture but it was not the galleys or the scaffold. His career flourished long afterward. Helvétius despaired at his ill-fortune after the storm over *De l'esprit*, but the actual dangers proved unequal to his fears. Friends at court saved him from personal harm, and the simple precaution of anonymity would have prevented any genuine danger in the world of censorship and tacit acceptance of eighteenth-century Paris.[6] Holbach's hand in the clandestine press of the 1760s and 1770s did not go unrecognized, and yet he lived safely at Grandval. Only the poor peddler who sold his works ran the risk of the galleys.[7]

Persecution was, therefore, a real threat to the philosophe, but usually only a threat. The protection and encouragement of the

6. D. W. Smith, *Helvétius: A Study in Persecution* (Oxford, 1965), chapter 4.

7. See Diderot's account of "l'affaire Lecuyer" in a letter to Sophie Volland, 8 October 1768, *Correspondance* (503), and the account in Pierre Naville, *D'Holbach et la pensée scientifique au xviii^e siècle* (Paris, 1967), p. 108.

Choiseuls, Malesherbes, and Pompadours within the powerful elite kept him relatively safe. Anonymity and foreign presses provided additional sanctuary. But merely indicating the limits to the persecution of the philosophes would understate their involvement in the structure of power. Royal and aristocratic patronage provided a fair, if sometimes unpredictable, amount of revenue and security. Official gazettes, literary salons, administrative offices, and royal academies drew the philosophes into official circles. The rewards of the monarchical system of patronage encouraged hope for success within it. The philosophes thought that if the rules were made more fair and if the holders of power correctly saw their enlightened self-interest, the existing system of power could handsomely serve the needs of society and enlightenment.

Despite these sources of hope and satisfaction, the philosophes' impulses toward criticism remained strong. Committed to a critical, secular analysis of the world, they could not help but see and express the realities of power more clearly than a Bossuet or a Loyseau, who had seen society in terms of legal or juridical hierarchies. The best of the philosophes, like the best philosophers of all times, were able to explore fully the logic of their ideas. The logic of Enlightenment pointed toward a tough-minded appreciation of the uses and abuses of power. Sporadic persecution and continuous clerical opposition kept the philosophes effectively outside of the sanctum of complete respectability. The experience of victimization clearly helped open their eyes to the plight of other victims in other circumstances.

Perhaps most important, the ruling power they viewed at close range was not of one mind. Louis XIV and his inner côterie had set royal policy for the fifty-four years of his personal reign. Only in the very last years had men with power—Vauban, Boisguillebert, Fénelon voiced major policy dissents, and their opinions had more impact after Louis's death than before.[8] Fénelon evoked humani-

8. On the general climate of criticism see Lionel Rothkrug, *Opposition to Louis XIV: The Political and Social Origins of the French Enlightenment* (Princeton, 1965). His analysis (chapter 3) of the relationship between royal investigation and social criticism is, I think, just, and helped my views on the later period. His subtitle is, however, misleading at best. In the area of social criticism, the economic calm of 1720–50 largely quelled the criticism of the years Rothkrug discusses, only to revive for similar but less dramatic reasons in the 1750s. The philosophes read and knew the writings of this earlier period, but their criticisms developed out of evidence, impulses, and crises much closer to their own day. And this economic criticism was only one part of "the French Enlightenment." Werner

tarian sympathy for the plight of the peasant; the works of Vauban and Boisguillebert, proposing fiscal and economic reforms on the basis of detailed intendants' reports, set the pattern followed by scores of intendants and lower administrative officials during the eighteenth century. As one of its first acts the Regency invited suggestions for measures to restore the fiscal health of France after the devastation of Louis XIV's wars.[9] Throughout most of the century, intendants and subdelegates, freed from the hand-to-hand exigencies of those wars, examined and reported the problems of their areas. Such investigations became a regular part of the process of assessment and taxation. Far from discouraging these efforts, the ministers who had to manage the fiscal structure of France encouraged and ordered them.

The complaints, discoveries, and proposals of administrators became part of the talk of literary circles, as the ties between the literary and administrative elites were strong both in the salons and in the Encyclopedic enterprise. Several men belonged to both elites.[10] If during the first half of the eighteenth century the man of letters proved his modernity by being conversant in physical science, after mid-century proof rested more in concern for fiscal and economic issues. Any proposals to change tax policies inevitably involved the entire economic and social structure of France—privileges, commercial policy, economic priorities, distribution of burdens. The relative economic calm from 1720 to 1750 kept the level of criticism at a minimum. The clandestine literature of the age mirrored this calm, concentrating its energies on priests and shying away from any more acute investigation of the plight of the laboring classes.[11] But beginning with the controversial tax proposals of Controller General Machault in 1749, ministers, *parlementaires*, clergy, and philosophes became embroiled in a continuous series of controversies over pro-

---

Gembruch neatly summarizes the views of the major opponents to Louis XIV in the long article "Reformförderungen in Frankreich um die Wende vom 17. zum 18. Jahrhundert," *Historische Zeitschrift* 209 (1969): 265–317. For an able summary and analysis of Vauban's *Projet d'une dîme royale*, see R. Mousnier, *La Dîme de Vauban* (Paris, 1968). A. Cherel is exhaustive on the influence of Fénelon in *Fénelon au xviiie siècle* (Paris, 1917). On Boisguillebert, see Hazel Van Dyke Roberts, *Boisguilbert: Economist of the Reign of Louis XIV* (New York, 1935), chapters 8 and 9.

9. Montesquieu, *Oeuvres complètes*, 3:24; for his response see pp. 24–31.

10. E.g., among others, Turgot (intendant, controller general) Damilaville (*premier commis* in the bureau of the *vingtième*), Boulanger (royal engineer).

11. J. S. Spink, *French Free Thought from Gassendi to Voltaire* (London, 1960), chapter 15.

posals to ameliorate the weak financial condition of France. Scores of books, periodicals, and prize competitions contributed toward widening the debate. "More works on political economy have appeared during the last ten years in France," Marmontel observed in 1759, "than had appeared until then since the revival of letters."[12] Inbred curiosity and social ties to the court impelled the philosophes to enter the economic debate and offer their critical observations. Their peculiar position—outside the highest echelons of the administrative elite but privy to its thoughts and sometimes victims of its power—allowed them to adopt a perspective and rhetoric more critical than those inside. As an intendant and minister, Turgot could speak of the inadvisability, inconvenience, and even unfairness of feudal privileges, but had to guard his words constantly; his friend Condorcet could speak of feudal *banalités* as simply "the robbery of the poor by the rich."[13]

Within the context of the widening economic debate grew the assumption that the men of power and influence must take responsibility for the health and stability of the nation. The actual effectiveness of royal administration varied widely; performance certainly never matched the dictates of royal edicts. Nonetheless, during the eighteenth century this administration took most aspects of public life under its view. The administration of justice had always been the central function of monarchy. Since the time of Henry IV the monarchy had sporadically intervened into the economic workings of the countryside, trying to restore common lands, introduce new crops, spread new techniques, and alleviate suffering from disasters.[14] But many royal projects had begun only in the seventy years after 1680: the royal *corvée* for road building; extensive public works in the cities; the attempt to enforce public instruction for all children; the organization of a militia with mandatory liability, first for the peasant, later for the urban worker; proportional taxation of most income to bring fiscal stability; concerted efforts to halt mendicity and organize charity. Prior to the eighteenth century the role of the monarchy in the life of the average Frenchman had varied with the personal resourcefulness and strength of the king. With the growth of the intendancy and its functions, the administrative institutions gave

12. *Mercure*, June 1759, quoted by Roustan, *Les philosophes et la société moderne*, p. 382.
13. In "Réflexions," *Oeuvres complètes*, 11:287.
14. Bourde, *Agronomie et agronomes*, 1:133–76.

the monarchy a strong public presence, regardless of the king's personal stature.

The philosophes largely accepted the implications of administrative growth of the monarchy. They sought an institution more respectful of individual liberties, more responsive to the opinion of a wider elite, and more resourceful in its legislation for the nation. But the philosophes (with the notable exception of Turgot) were men of letters, not intendants. They accepted the supposition that a few men must always be responsible for the welfare of the many. As outsiders, however, they could see the necessary corollary—the few must take responsibility for the people's misery as well as its health. If the well-being of the people required the exercise of resourceful leadership, the philosophe recognized that the people's wretchedness pointed to the failure of that leadership. The philosophes thus occupied a natural perspective from which to perceive the victimization of the people. As their social vision matured in the decades after mid-century, they gave voice to that perception.[15]

After 1750 social criticism in France focused primarily on conditions in the countryside. "I cannot help but feel sad," Condorcet wrote to Turgot in 1770, "when I compare the luxury of Paris with the misery of Limousin, and when I think that this luxury is in part drawn from the subsistence of these unfortunate men."[16] Condorcet voiced an opinion then common among administrative and literary circles—that the monarchy had seriously neglected and exploited the countryside for the benefit of the court at Paris. The critical inquiry into the state of the French countryside had begun several decades earlier during the crisis years after 1690. The tracts of Vauban, Boisguillebert, Fénelon, and Saint-Simon helped break the myth of unity fostered by Louis XIV and pointed to the deepening misery of the countryside.[17] Vauban pleaded for fiscal reform partly in the

15. For an analysis of a closely related phenomenon—the increasingly activist definitions of "philosophe"—see Charles Stricklen, "The Philosophe's Political Mission: The Creation of an Idea, 1750–1789," *VS* 86 (1971):137–228. Franco Venturi writes intelligently—though with different emphases from those above—on the unique role of France in Enlightened social criticism in *Utopia and Reform* (Cambridge, 1971), chapter 5. Cf. the similar position and role of philosophes in the antique Roman order in Ramsay MacMullen, *Enemies of the Roman Order* (Cambridge, Mass., 1966), chapter 2.

16. *Correspondance inédite de Condorcet et de Turgot, 1770–1778*, ed. Charles Henry (Paris, 1883), p. 2.

17. See note 8 of this chapter, above.

name of the menu peuple, "the most ruined and miserable part of the kingdom . . . [but also] the most considerable in numbers and in the real and effective services it renders."[18] The other reformers spoke similarly of the people's lot, but they had formed no unified "party" of opposition.[19]

The issue of the *vingtiéme*, Controller General Machault's proposed five percent tax on all income, broke the fiscal calm in 1749 and unleashed a flood of writings on economic problems which continued until the eve of the Revolution. The fiscal speculations of economists such as Mirabeau, Graslin, Goudar, Gournay, Quesnay, Baudeau, and scores of others were not written specifically from the perspective of the people. The emphasis in economic writings shifted from mercantile concentration on bullion and power to the problems of national wealth and production;[20] the overall perspective remained, however, oriented to the needs of the state—increased revenues, growing population, a favorable balance of trade. The problems of distribution, wages, and standard of living—the people's share—generally entered only circumstantially.[21] The philosophes, however, were more detached than most economic writers from immediate involvement with the needs of the state. They could adopt the stance of the "enlightened amateur" and see economic issues from all sides, including the perspective of the people. From that perspective they could express moral outrage as well as intellectual doubts.

Voltaire's two most significant ventures into the issue of tax reform provide a good illustration of the changing perspective. He published in 1751 a "Dialogue entre un philosophe et un contrôleur général des finances" to propagandize Machault's proposals to tax privileged income.[22] Although he mentioned the plight of the overtaxed poor, the tone of the piece is one of administrative consultation, "an obscure citizen" advising the controller general how best to raise revenues. Seventeen years later Voltaire chose a very different tactic in his popular story "L'homme aux quarante écus."[23] The

18. Quoted by Mousnier, *Dime de Vauban*, p. 36.
19. See Gembruch, "Reformförderungen."
20. On this important change in attitude, see Gay, *The Enlightenment*, 2:344–68.
21. For good surveys of the scores of economic schemes in eighteenth-century France see Joseph Spengler, *The French Predecessors of Malthus* (Durham, N. C., 1942) and J. F. Bosher, *The Single-Duty Project* (London, 1964).
22. Voltaire, *Oeuvres complètes*, ed. Louis Moland, 52 vols. (Paris, 1877–85), 23:501–06.
23. Voltaire, *Oeuvres complètes*, 21:305–68.

obscure citizen is no longer a consultant but a victim, a peasant bat-
tered on all sides by tax farmers, Physiocratic schemers, and monks.

A decade's experience as a seigneur in the poor border region of
eastern France had made the difference in the two approaches. While
Voltaire's contacts with literate Genevan artisans raised his opinion
of some of the people, his role as master of Ferney deepened his
awareness of life at the bottom of society. The peasant's burdens—
tax farmers, salt taxes, tithes, uncertain harvests, brigands—became
immediate realities to him. His letters from the early months of his
tenure bristle with anger at the authorities who harassed the peasants
on his lands. Describing the rapacity of the tax farmer, he wrote:

> Unfortunate men with hardly enough money to eat a little black
> bread are stopped every day, plundered, and imprisoned for
> having put on their black bread a little salt procured near their
> huts. One half of the inhabitants dies in misery and the other
> rots in prison. . . . I am buying the estate of Ferney only to do
> some good there.[24]

Voltaire took his role as the benevolent seigneur of Ferney most
seriously. During the two decades after his purchase of this estate he
spoke for the peasantry on many issues, among them removing the
region from internal customs barriers, commutation of the oppressive
salt tax, and freeing several thousand peasants still subject to servile
duties.[25]

As spokesman for his region Voltaire acted in his own interest as
well as the interests of his peasants. But his new perspective even
impelled him to rewrite some of his history to voice measured sympathy for the "ferocious beast." In the original version of *Essai sur
les moeurs* (1756) Voltaire had described Thomas Müntzer and his
disciples: "They developed that dangerous truth which is in every
heart: that all men are born equal, and that while the popes had
treated princes as subjects, the seigneurs had treated the peasants like
beasts." Passing judgment on the Anabaptist leaders, he continued:

> One must agree that the demands made by the Anabaptists and

24. To Antoine J. G. le Bault, 18 November 1758, Voltaire, *Correspondence* (7234).
25. Voltaire is best served by his copious correspondence on the economic problems of
his region after his move to Ferney. On Voltaire as benevolent seigneur see Fernand
Caussy, *Voltaire, seigneur de village* (Paris, 1911).

written down in the name of the cultivators of the earth were all quite just; but this action unleashed bears while making a reasonable demand in their name.

Five years later he found cause to revise this passage in light of his experience:

> In truth, the manifesto of these savages in the name of the cultivators of the earth might have been signed by Lycurgus: they demanded that only tithes in kind be levied on them; that a part be used for the care of the poor; that they be permitted to hunt and fish for food; that the air and water be free; that forced labor be moderated; that wood be left for warming fires; they claimed the rights of the human race, but they supported them like ferocious beasts.[26]

The emphasis thus changed from the "dangerous truth" and unwise leadership to the just demands of an oppressed peasantry.[27]

Voltaire never developed any full-scale vision of class oppression as a way to explain or question the shape of society. His tolerance for great inequalities surpassed that of most major philosophes. Late in life he briefly summed up his estimate of the people's lot. Writing to the veterinarian Claude Bourgelat he observed:

> The great misfortune of the peasants is stupidity and another is neglect: no one thinks of them except when the plague devastates them and their herds. As long as there are pretty opera girls in Paris, all is well.[28]

Voltaire knew the stupidity of the people from his earliest years as a philosophe. He came to recognize society's neglect of the people only with the lessons of experience and involvement.

None of the other major philosophes except Turgot worked so directly in the countryside as did Voltaire, but all, as landowners, had sufficient experience with the workings of fiscal policies of the

26. *Essai sur les moeurs*, 2:236–37, and note on p. 963.

27. Cf. his similar remarks of 1763 on the more recent uprising of the Camisards: "One must also admit that the war made by the savage populace of the Cévennes under Louis XIV was the fruit of persecution. The Camisards acted like ferocious beasts, but their wives and children had been seized; they tore apart the hunters who pursued them." ("Remarques sur l'Essai," in ibid., p. 933.)

28. 18 March 1775, Voltaire, *Correspondence* (18264).

Old Regime in France. The pattern of Voltaire—a maturing social awareness and growing sensitivity to the people's problems—recurred in the careers of many members of the enlightened community as men of letters entered the economic debates. Even within the collective work of the *Encyclopédie* the changing perspective is manifest. Many articles in the early volumes adopted a cautious stance on social and economic issues. The author of "Corvée (ponts and chaussées)," Nicolas Boulanger, merely outlined means to make forced labor at royal command more efficient.[29] François Quesnay dismissed the problem of high grain prices in "Grains," callously warning against the low price of bread lest the peasants become lazy and arrogant.[30] (In later years the corvée became a target of attack for most philosophes, and Physiocrats revised their thinking to assert that their plans would bring improvements for the peasant as well as the state.) Articles written in the late 1750s and early 1760s and included in the final ten volumes (1765) reflected new concerns and new awareness.[31]

The articles by De Jaucourt show this changing sensibility. A doctor by profession and an admirer of Montesquieu's aristocratic policies,[32] De Jaucourt would seem an unlikely spokesman for the people. Nonetheless, he chose several occasions in later volumes to plead the people's cause. In "Impôt" he called for a tax system based on distributive justice; in "Milice" he proposed reform of the hated militia; in "Peuple" he condemned overtaxation of the poor; in "Sel" he pointed to the gross inequities in both the salt tax and the arbitrary *taille*; and in "Taxe" he outlined a plan to raise funds at the expense of the rich whereby the state might liquidate the remaining feudal burdens of the peasant.[33] De Jaucourt might be seen as the typical philosophe: by vocation not involved in economic matters,

29. *Encyclopédie*, 4:283–88.

30. *Encyclopédie*, 7:831.

31. The division between the early and final volumes is not absolute. For appreciation of the hard lot of the peasant expressed in the volumes before the suspension of 1759, see "Chaumière" (anon., 3:257), "Disette" (anon., 4:1036), and "Economie (morale & politique)" (Rousseau, 5:337–49). These early articles, though sympathetic, proposed few specific cures.

32. E.g., see his *Encyclopédie* articles "Démocratie" (4:816–18), "Naissance" (11:8–9), and "Noblesse" (11:166), all sympathetic to a highly aristocratic view of society, though ambiguous on the problem of privilege.

33. *Encyclopédie*, 3:604; 10:505; 12:476; 14:927–28; and 15:947, respectively.

yet drawn into economic issues and emerging with better insight into the inequities of his society.

One can suspect that De Jaucourt also spoke for the editor Diderot in his articles for the *Encyclopédie*. Diderot rarely addressed himself to economic issues but gave reformers a platform in his project. He did, however, speak out for proportional taxation in the late article "Vingtième,"[34] and in "Indigent" he spoke pointedly of society's scorn for the poor it creates. "One of the most harmful consequences of bad administration," he wrote, "is the division of society into two classes, one living in opulence, the other in misery." In such a society indigence appears worse than vice. The vicious man is welcomed while the indigent man is shunned. "There are no indigent men among the savages," Diderot concluded without further comment.[35] Indigence was thus, in his view, a product of "bad administration," not of any inherent laziness or arbitrary fate.

During the 1760s Diderot had seen hope for economic stability and order in the social doctrines of Physiocracy, but by 1770 circumstances had moved him toward opposition. His admiration for the anti-Physiocrat Abbé Galiani and his alliance with a court faction opposed to the Physiocrats involved him in the controversy over freedom of the grain trade. A voyage to the countryside had recently reminded him of the fears and dangers which even the mere threat of famine engendered[36] when he hastily composed an angry *Apologie de l'Abbé Galiani*. Rather than deal with the Physiocrats at the level of theory, Diderot chose instead to accuse them of having failed to see the realities of the peasant's life. "Trying to represent the countryside by four wealthy farmers," he wrote, "is to forget the misery of the multitude."[37] Diderot accused the Physiocrats, with all of their theories, of having offered only "theoretical bread."[38] Even their "sacred right of property" he considered illusory when placed against the need for bread.[39] Though the rhetoric of his apology was ex-

34. On Diderot's role in the composition of "Vingtième," see Proust, *Diderot et l'Encyclopédie*, pp. 487–88, and on Diderot's involvement in economic questions, ibid., pp. 453–74.

35. *Encyclopédie*, 8:676.

36. Diderot, *Oeuvres complètes*, 17:345; letter to Sophie Volland, 23 August 1770, Diderot, *Correspondance* (627).

37. Diderot, *Oeuvres politiques*, p. 90; cf. similar remarks on pp. 97, 122.

38. Ibid., p. 115. His phrase is *pain possible.*

39. Ibid., pp. 90, 118.

ceptional, conveying obvious anger and frustration, he continued afterward to show an understanding and concern for the needs of the people and to perceive how frequently the leaders of society failed to meet those needs.

The examples might be multiplied. Turgot, Condorcet, and Holbach similarly adopted more radical, critical visions of the relation of rich and poor, powerful and weak. By the 1770s it had become almost commonplace for philosophes to point to society's laws and see in them symptoms of a more general social abuse. Helvétius formulated this view of society as early as 1758. In a note to *De l'esprit* he compared the lot of the peasant to the life of the savage. He found the latter superior, though not from any particular "nobility" in savage existence. The fear of prison, excessive taxes, seigneurs, arbitrary officials, and humiliation by the rich brought misery to the peasant; the savage had at least his feeling of liberty and equality. "In civilized nations," Helvétius noted,

> the art of the legislator has often consisted only of directing an infinite number of men toward the happiness of a small number; to hold, for this purpose, the multitude in oppression, and to violate all the rights of humanity in their case.
>
> Might not one suspect that the extreme felicity of a few individuals is always tied to the misfortune of the majority?[40]

Others shared and expanded Helvétius's perception as the investigation of the ills of the nation repeatedly placed responsibility on the shoulders of the rich and the privileged.

Accusations of abuse, neglect, and treachery by the rich became a persistent theme in the writings of Holbach and Condorcet. Holbach extended this judgment to all nations in all times. "By a vice common to all governments," he wrote in *La Politique naturelle*,

> the most numerous part of nations is usually the most neglected; it would seem that societies were formed only for the Princes, the Rich, and the Powerful; you would swear that the people enter into the association only to spare those who are already most fortunate the trouble of working.[41]

40. *Oeuvres complètes*, 1:146–47, note 1.
41. *La politique naturelle, ou Discours sur les vrais principes du gouvernement*, 2 vols. (London [?], 1773), 2:186.

In Holbach's view of history the rich and powerful continually used society's laws for their own gain, perverting in this way the very purpose of law—to give equal protection to all.[42] Condorcet singled out the *gabelle*, the salt tax, as the symbol of a more general perversion of all law by the rich. "All schools agree," he wrote,

> that in the moral sciences, the consent of the human race is a proof of truth. But the codes of criminal law, England alone excepted, are all, like those on the gabelle, founded on the same principle; all seem to be drawn up according to this maxim: That the weak and the poor should be sacrificed for the tranquility of the powerful and the rich. And this verse, "What does it matter that lowborn blood be spilt?" might serve as an epigraph for all collections of penal laws.[43]

From this perspective even the people's supposedly inherent viciousness and stupidity appeared less a part of its natural condition than the product of centuries of abuse.[44] The people seemed to these more radical philosophes not Bossuet's children of God or Voltaire's children of Discord, but the neglected children of unjust and unworthy leaders.

The rhetoric of Condorcet and Holbach surpassed that of most philosophes in its strength and directness, but all of the enlightened circle shared to some degree in their perception of fundamental abuse. The language of French radicalism found echoes and admirers throughout the spectrum of Enlightenment thought. In discussing the inconveniences of excessive inequality of wealth, Hume noted with characteristic dispassion that "where the riches are in a few hands, these must enjoy all the power, and will readily conspire to

42. *Système de la Nature*, 1:150.

43. *Oeuvres complètes*, 7:23–24. Condorcet's view of English criminal law was wishfully myopic. Condorcet repeated this idea on a number of occasions. See "Réflexions sur la loi criminelle," *Oeuvres complètes*, 7:3–24, from which this passage is drawn, and scattered remarks throughout his economic writings—e.g., *Oeuvres complètes*, 4:381, 467; 11:189, 190.

44. E.g., Holbach, *Système de la Nature*, 1:289–90: "Man is wicked not because he is born wicked but because he is made so; the great and powerful crush the indigent, the unfortunate, with impunity; and the latter risks his life to avenge the harm received from them; openly or in secret he attacks an unkind fatherland which gives everything to some of its children and seizes everything from others." See similarly ibid., pp. 231–33, and *La Morale universelle*, 2:180. Condorcet dwells at length on social creation of crime and ignorance in his essay opposing the utility of deceit; see *Oeuvres complètes*, 5:361–62.

lay the whole burthen on the poor, and oppress them still farther, to the discouragement of all industry." He later added quite simply that under absolute monarchy, the government of much of Europe, poverty of the common people "is a natural, if not infallible effect."[45] Though no radical social critic, the naturalist Buffon found occasion in the article "Boeuf" in his *Histoire naturelle* (begun in 1749) to object to the lot of the raisers of cattle, unable to eat any of the meat they raise, "reduced by the necessity of their condition, that is by the cruelty of other men, to live like horses on barley and oats or coarse vegetables and spoiled milk."[46] The Italian philosophe Beccaria, in his analysis of crimes and punishments, did not hesitate to point to inequities caused by the tyranny of rich over poor. In a strikingly clear portrayal of the perversion of laws, Beccaria reconstructed the reasoning of a would-be criminal weighing the advantages of crime against the threat of capital punishment:

> What are these laws that I am bound to respect, which make so great a difference between me and the rich man? He refuses me the farthing I ask of him, and excuses himself by bidding me have recourse to labor, with which he is unacquainted.
>
> Who made these laws? The rich and the great, who never deigned to visit the miserable hut of the poor, who have never seen him dividing a piece of moldy bread, amidst the cries of his famished children and the tears of his wife. Let us break those ties, fatal to the greatest part of mankind, and only useful to a few indolent tyrants. Let us attack injustice at its source. I will return to my natural state of independence. I shall live free and happy on the fruits of my courage and industry. A day of pain and repentance may come, but it will be short; and for an hour of grief I shall enjoy years of pleasure and liberty. King of a small number as determined as myself, I will correct the mistakes of fortune, and I shall see those tyrants grow pale and tremble at the sight of him, whom, with insulting pride, they would not suffer to rank with their dogs and horses.[47]

45. "Of Commerce," *Essays Moral, Political and Literary* (Oxford, 1963), pp. 271–72.
46. As quoted in Bourde, *Agronomie et agronomes*, 1:1008.
47. *An Essay on Crimes and Punishments*, trans. E. D. Ingraham (Philadelphia, 1819), pp. 102–03.

Beccaria did not choose to refute his hypothetical assassin. Rather he pointed to the superior deterrent power of lifelong imprisonment and, more important, looked forward to a time when those with the power might legislate with a view to the welfare of the people. Beccaria's radical insights into law found translators and admirers throughout the continent.[48] Across the continent, his most famous successor as utilitarian law reformer, Jeremy Bentham, reached even more radical legal and political conclusions, seeing class oppression in extant legal and political institutions and looking to democratic political reforms that would wipe away aristocracy, a vice which "stained and corrupted and deformed" all laws.[49] The Parisian grub-street social critic Linguet found the laws of Europe so rooted in class oppression that he was unable to see any way to undo oppression without undoing the fabric of society in its entirety.[50] Despite Rousseau's idiosyncracies his radical insight that laws had from their inception served the rich and oppressed the poor passed into the mainstream of Enlightenment thought.[51]

From Rousseau's *Discours sur l'inégalité* to the legal reformism of Beccaria to the proposals of agricultural reformers throughout Europe[52] to poems on the life of the countryside (such as Saint-Lambert's *Saisons* and Goldsmith's *Deserted Village*), the perception of oppression and the willingness to talk of it in tough-minded terms became an integral part of Enlightenment social vision. Many men still spoke of society in terms of an idealized hierarchy, with rich and poor performing mutual service. The philosophes often looked to that ideal in formulating their legislation. But to Diderot in 1774 monarchical society seemed best depicted as a pyramid of balls:

> The ball at the summit presses down on the three or four which form the level below; that level presses down on another level;

48. Venturi, *Utopia and Reform*, chapter 4.

49. Mary Mack, *Jeremy Bentham: An Odyssey of Ideas* (New York, 1963), chapter 9; quotation on p. 421.

50. See Darlene Levy, "Simon Linguet's Sociological System," *VS* 70 (1970): 219–93.

51. I have purposefully left Rousseau's special approach to the people to the concluding chapter. Needless to say, however, his radical language helped encourage others; Beccaria, for instance, admired Rousseau and paraphrased him frequently.

52. Sarrailh, *Espagne éclairée*, pp. 505–32; Gagliardo, *Pariah to Patriot*, pp. 41–48; F. Venturi, *Italy and the Enlightenment* (New York, 1972), chapters 9 and 10.

below this one is a third; and so on down to the base, or last level, which touches the earth, and which is crushed by the weight of all the others.[53]

Diderot spoke for a mature Enlightenment whose eyes had been opened by three decades of experience on the fringes of power.

53. "Observations," *Oeuvres politiques*, p. 378; he used the same image in "Entretiens," ibid., pp. 305–06.

# Part II: Legislation

# Introduction: The Legislator's Task

While the philosophes often cast the problems of society in terms of the victimization of the poor by the rich, they could not consider this condition irreparable. They perceived the people not as one pole in a permanent struggle of rich versus poor, but rather as a helpless mass unable to do much more than labor and pray. Only in revolt against the most dire oppression or, more often, under the leadership of dynamic men did the people appear as an active agent in the philosophes' histories. The people's condition and behavior provided a barometer of the quality of its leaders. For the philosophes, eighteenth century society suffered not from inevitable class conflict but from a failure of leadership.

The philosophes' experience within the power structure of Europe encouraged them to hope that independent criticism might bring the holders of power back to a more humane and beneficent judgment of their self-interest. The philosophes' ambiguous position in that society—appreciative of power and high culture yet aware of the crushing burdens on the people—led them toward the classic assumption of the moderate reformer: that there exist policies by which virtually everyone can gain. Social redemption could come, they thought, through the reconciliation of all orders, not the victory of one over the other.

The reformers often projected this sense of need for enlightened leadership onto the figure of "the legislator." As a cultural hero, the legislator provided the Enlightenment's answer to the Christian saint or the Renaissance prince. Half-mythical, half-historical, the figure of the legislator who shapes and unifies his society dominates the political and historical writings of the philosophes. They learned of the power and role of legislators mostly from ancient history—especially Plutarch—and chose their heroes from among the forceful men who rose above social and religious conflict to reestablish lasting peace. Montesquieu's *De l'esprit des lois* is at one level a guidebook to the work of the legislator; Voltaire's *Essai sur les moeurs* provides a catalogue of the failures and successes of legislators; Helvétius designed his psychological studies *De l'esprit* and *De l'homme* in part to serve the legislator in his quest for public happiness; Beccaria and Bentham pursued the logic of Helvétius's determinism toward a total overhaul of law according to the standard of utility. The philosophes themselves often seized opportunities to act the role of modern Solons or at least to advise those with the authority to become such. Locke had pointed the way with his constitution for Carolina. Voltaire played such a role for the region around Ferney, pleading its causes, developing its economy, instructing its inhabitants. Diderot eagerly followed La Rivière as legislator for Russia, adopting the style of "King Denis" as he composed memoranda for the use of Catherine the Great. Holbach offered his *Ethocratie* as a comprehensive plan of legislation for France, then under the promising leadership of Louis XVI and Turgot. And Rousseau, who analyzed the task of the legislator in *Du Contrat social*,[1] undertook the role on request for the distant lands of Corsica and Poland. The philosophes' sense of power was not entirely mistaken, for as the Enlightenment reached full bloom, administrators with enlightened sympathies infiltrated the governments even of such "backward" regions as Spain and central Italy.

The philosophes' ideal legislators were not so much utopian philosopher-kings as pragmatic philosophe-kings, working within the constraints of existing laws, customs, religion, climate, and class divisions. The results consequently varied over a wide spectrum: Solon's Athens was not Lycurgus's Sparta or Romulus's Rome; Diderot's projected Russia was not Holbach's vision of France or Montesquieu's England; Rousseau's ideal Geneva was neither his own ideal Corsica nor his ideal Poland. But despite the differences dictated by objective conditions of nations and subjective temperaments of leaders, one task unified the efforts of the philosophes' legislators: the search for social balance and harmony. Plutarch supplied many of the tales of legislators that shaped the philosophes' view of antique leadership; his final judgment on Numa Pompilius[2] gave early expression to this continuing legislative ideal:

> Thus much, meantime, was peculiarly signal and almost divine in the circumstances of Numa, that he was an alien, and yet

1. *Du Contrat social* (Amsterdam, 1762), book 2, chapter 7, found in *Oeuvres complètes*, 3:347–70.
2. Second king of Rome, supposed to have ruled 715–673 B.C.

courted to come and accept a kingdom, the frame of which
though he entirely altered, yet he performed it by mere persuasion, and ruled a city that as yet had scarce become one city,
without recurring to arms or any violence. . . . but, by mere
force of wisdom and justice, established union and harmony
amongst all.[3]

The task of the eighteenth-century legislator remained, for the
philosophes, the task of Numa: to find laws which might bring harmony to the interests of the poor, the middle orders, the rich, and the
state. They believed that the task, though difficult, could be performed, and that the resources of enlightenment were crucial to its
success.

Among the realities which shaped the philosophes' projected legislation was their perception of the people's role, capabilities, and
condition. Bringing enlightenment and change to the lower orders
would, they knew, be a most difficult project, and they often
expressed doubts about any significant progress. Numa and many
other successful legislators had directed and manipulated the people's religious sensibility toward ends both worthy and unworthy.
The power of religion as legislative instrument was part of the received wisdom of history to a century which studied history with
profit but without bowing to tradition. Beccaria, an exponent of
clear rationality in the mature modern world, appreciated the uses
of religion in man's infancy and adolescence. No exponent of error,
he still maintained that "religious error" had been "of the utmost
service to mankind." Those who dared to deceive were "the greatest
benefactors of humanity," harnessing and uniting the passions of the
vulgar, in the transition from savagery to civilization.[4] Herder admired the legislative instincts of Moses. If the Israelite chief deceived
his people by pretending divine guidance for his legislation, Herder
reasoned, he showed only the highest instincts and wisest political
savvy.[5] The Austrian cameralist Josef Sonnenfels was prosaic and
clear in his appreciation of the uses of belief. His twenty-fourth thesis
of cameral science reads simply:

Religion is the most effective instrument to further moral con-

3. *Plutarch's Lives; The Translation Called Dryden's*, rev. A. H. Clough, 5 vols (Boston, 1878), 1:167.
4. *On Crimes and Punishments*, pp. 152–53.
5. Barnard, *Herder's Social and Political Thought*, pp. 63–65.

ditions. Secular legislation will be insufficient on several points
if not supported by the bond of religion and its "punishments."

Irreligion, he concluded in the next thesis, is thus a state crime,
undermining its "most powerful restraining powers."[6] Gibbon was
much less prosaic but no less firm in his admiration for the uses the
Roman senatorial class made of religion to lead the masses. "The
various modes of worship which prevailed in the Roman world," he
observed, "were all considered by the people as equally true, by the
philosopher as equally false, and by the magistrate as equally
useful."[7] The situation clearly struck him as just.

These were not the words of vicious exploiters but of humanitarian
reformers, not of fanatics but of advocates of toleration. The philosophes earned a reputation as the most secular of men in a secular age.
But just how far their disenchanted vision could reach without undermining social order remained problematic. The people of the eighteenth century seemed, for the most part, little different from the
vulgar people of the time of the first legislators. The philosophes'
discussion of legislation for the people began, therefore, not with a
program so much as with a debate on tactics: could religion still serve
the needs of the legislator in an enlightened age?

6. As quoted in Robert Kann, *A Study in Austrian Intellectual History: From Late Baroque
to Romanticism* (New York, 1960), p. 173.
7. *Decline and Fall of the Roman Empire* (New York, 1932), 1:25–26.

# 5  The Uses of Belief

## THE SHAPE OF THE PROBLEM

The philosophes used many conceptual tools to analyze society, such as the fabrication of "natural" or "hypothetical" histories of institutions, the elimination of ideas and words with no corresponding objects in the world of experience, the exploitation of disagreements among authorities to subvert those authorities. Historians have, however, generally overlooked one of their most fruitful tactics—the continual division of social functions into "private" and "public" spheres. The liberal ideology of the eighteenth century coalesced with the decision of certain philosophers, most notably John Locke, to give priority to the individual's private rights in matters of religious belief, political persuasion, economic activity, and legislative power. The intellectual transfer of these areas of human experience from the public to the private domain has been justly celebrated as the hallmark of eighteenth-century liberalism and a central contribution of Enlightenment thought.[1]

But the path ran both ways. Reformers often found the opposite technique equally vital to justify incursions by the public power on the many remnants of feudal liberties. Privileged nobles and office-holders had long considered the administration of justice, the enforcement of feudal dues, and performance of royal commands as forms of private property. To buttress proposed reforms, philosophes often insisted that these functions were by nature "public." In times of social chaos private individuals had usurped them, they argued, and the public power could now reclaim its rightful domain. Rousseau, it might be said, pursued this logic to its fullest conclusion in *Du Contrat social* (1762) by insisting that everything must be made in principle public through the logic of the social contract in order to

1. E.g., the recent article by Betty Behrens, "Cultural History as Infrastructure, Part 2," *VS* 86 (1971):14–24. I would argue that the movement was twofold—both a clarification and heightening of respect for the rights of the individual and a growth of understanding of and appreciation for the power of legislation. If the philosophes wished to tie the hands of the prince, they still saw much for the legislator to do.

65

insure legitimate social order. Not surprisingly, Rousseau's concluding chapter, designing a public religion sponsored by the state
and intolerant of dissent,[2] has raised the ire of liberal thinkers since
Voltaire. But Rousseau's vision of religion as a preeminently public
function was not as idiosyncratic as some might believe. Voltaire
rejected Rousseau's intolerance, not the substance of his social religion nor the animus behind it. Even for the liberal thinkers of the
eighteenth century, religion was not the exceedingly private matter
that we usually consider it. The religious sphere rested, rather, at
the cutting edge of the division of public from private.

Quite early in the Enlightenment most reformers resolved the
problem of personal belief on the side of a wide tolerance of individual preferences.[3] But the reach of religious institutions in Europe
extended far deeper into society than the level of personal belief.
The established churches performed many functions and services
which apparently belonged to the public sphere. The powers enjoyed by the clergy as a privileged order—taxation, censorship,
judicial functions, fiscal immunities—appeared unwarranted to all
philosophes. But the action of the clergy among the lower orders of
society seemed, at least in principle, much less odious. To be sure,
the parish priest and vicar taught "superstition" to the people, but
the people seemed destined for superstition in any case. The parish
priest also taught the duties of social obedience and the basic principles of morality. He provided what rudiments of education existed
in the countryside. He relayed information between the villagers
and the city-dwelling royal officials. The philosophes appreciated
the necessity of these tasks, especially in view of the people's legend-
ary volatility. The people needed leadership at its own level, and the
church appeared to be the inevitable holder of that responsibility.

By mid-century the Encyclopedic circle had reached a certain
modus vivendi with the established public powers of the church,
mediating the claims of a liberal tolerance, Erastian reality, and
social order. But as Holbach, Boulanger, Diderot, and others broad-
ened the attack on religion to the point of professed atheism, they
necessarily reopened the issue of the social value of religion. Their
discussion normally took place within two established traditions,

2. Book 4, chapter 8.
3. Even John Locke, however, excepted supposedly disruptive and antisocial beliefs,
notably atheism and Roman Catholicism. See *A Letter Concerning Toleration* (1689).

"Bayle's paradox" and the doctrine of "double truth." Pierre Bayle had upset traditional wisdom in the late seventeenth century by contending that a society of atheists was possible and, indeed, preferable to a superstitious society.[4] His reasoning disturbed even the most tolerant writers who still assumed that public morality rested on religious belief and, hence, that any religion was better than none. Bayle argued from the lessons of history; superstitious societies had been violent and vicious, while the famous atheists of classical antiquity seemed the most peaceable of men. To his less daring contemporaries, religion and morality seemed inseparable, and they judged his pairing of atheism with morality a fundamental and perverse paradox.[5]

Bayle's insights opened the eighteenth-century discussion of the links of religion to society but did not give the issue a specific social content. The many opponents of Bayle's position made no open class distinctions. Society as a whole needs religion, they argued, since all men require a motive to avoid secret crimes and vices. In contrast, a much older literary tradition, the so-called double truth, began explicitly from social premises. Since classical antiquity philosophers had contended that in each society there are two religions: a purely philosophical faith for the political, social, and intellectual leadership, and a superstitious faith for the masses. At the end of the seventeenth century English deists revived the doctrine, in part to give their purified religion a historical pedigree.[6]

The doctrine found its way into French circles. Montesquieu enthusiastically endorsed its wisdom in an address to the Academy of Bordeaux in 1716. Within the religious policy of the ancient Romans, he discovered, as did Gibbon a half-century later, much merit in their overt use of religion for leading the masses. "It was neither fear nor piety," he began,

4. *Pensées diverses écrites à un docteur de Sorbonne à l'occasion de la comète* (Paris, 1682), chapters 160, 161, 177.

5. Ronald I. Boss, "Rousseau's Civil Religion and the Meaning of Belief: An Answer to Bayle's Paradox," *VS* 84 (1971):123–29. Boss's essay is the best treatment to date on the problem of "social religion" in eighteenth-century France, discussing the views of Voltaire and d'Alembert as well as that of Rousseau. While Boss discusses the problem in the framework of Bayle's paradox—the most important problem in the period he considers—I will show how Bayle's problem receded in the eyes of Voltaire and others during the 1760s and 1770s as purely legislative, utilitarian considerations moved to the fore.

6. For the antique and deist background, see Manuel, *The Eighteenth Century Confronts the Gods*, pp. 64–69.

which established religion among the Romans, but the necessity for all societies to have one. The first kings were no less attentive to the regulation of the cult and ceremonies than to giving laws and building walls.

I find this difference between the Roman legislators and those of other nations: the former made the religion for the State, and the others the State for the religion.[7]

The detachment of Roman leaders from popular religion placed them in a strong position to rule, Montesquieu argued. Not overly concerned with moral scruples, they had but one motive, "to inspire in a people which feared nothing the fear of the gods, and to use this fear to lead them at will."[8] Montesquieu's perspective was purely Machiavellian;[9] the demands of the state took priority over the ideal of truth. The Roman populace cooperated with insatiable gullibility; the more incredible the doctrine, the more readily the people accepted it. The extreme irrationality of Roman cults made them perfect political instruments, since men of wisdom could not possibly succumb, leaving them dispassionately above the mob and in command of every situation.[10] Even the virtuous Cicero, Montesquieu noted, privately expressed disbelief while he publicly condemned all unbelievers.[11] The magistrates led the people to useful extravagances while in private they practiced a simple religion honoring a supreme deity. The technique was no secret among men of letters; even Saint Augustine knew of its existence.[12] By actively taking command of the religious aspect of society the Roman leaders avoided

7. "Dissertation sur la politique des romains en matière de religion," in *Oeuvres complètes*, 3:38.

8. Ibid.

9. Literally as well as figuratively. Montesquieu was no doubt well aware of Machiavelli's admiration of those policies and shared that admiration. See Machiavelli's *Discourses*, book 1, chapters 11–15. On Montesquieu's ambivalent but often favorable opinions of Machiavelli, see A. Bertière, "Montesquieu, lecteur de Machiavel," in *Actes du congrès Montesquieu* (Bordeaux, 1956), pp. 143–58, and Paul H. Meyer, "Politics and Morals in the Thought of Montesquieu," in *VS* 56 (1967): 845–91.

10. *Oeuvres complètes*, 3:40.

11. Ibid., p. 44. Montesquieu, as he matured, evidently grew more open to the possibility of useful lies. In a youthful "Discours sur Cicéron" (c. 1709), he praised Cicero for trying to lead the people away from religious excesses provoked by unscrupulous magistrates, a wishful distortion of Cicero's opinions; see *Oeuvres complètes*, 3:17. Cicero's thoughts on social religion were widely known and appreciated by the philosophes, especially Hume and Gibbon; see Gay, *The Enlightenment*, 1:152–57.

12. Montesquieu, *Oeuvres complètes*, 3:44; see *The City of God*, book 4, chapter 31.

the fate of ancient Egypt (a transparent analogy to contemporary France), where an independent clergy became parasitical, lazy, and factious.[13] Implicitly Montesquieu offered the Roman example as a model for his times.

Montesquieu's crudely manipulative version of the double truth differed somewhat from the version that became the mainstream of philosophic opinion. Samuel Formey rendered a less arrogant account in his *Encyclopédie* article "Exotérique & esotérique," in which he praised the policy of the ancient Greeks who maintained pure truths within the company of philosophers and magistrates while allowing the public its crude polytheism. "It was not points of doctrine taught differently in public and in private," he explained; "it was the same subjects, but treated differently according to whether one was speaking before the multitude or before the chosen disciples."[14] The difference lay, therefore, at the level of symbolism, not of central truths. Following the English bishop William Warburton,[15] Formey asserted that the Greeks had learned the policy of a double truth from the Egyptians who, for the public good, pretended to communicate with the gods and preached the dogma of divine punishments and rewards, all the while maintaining mystery cults to preserve the truth of God's unity. The testimony of ancient authorities revealed that all men holding public trusts—rulers, priests, warriors—were indoctrinated into the mysteries. These men in turn maintained the public cult, turning the superstition of the masses to the public good.[16]

The belief in the necessity of a double truth had a curiously wide appeal among supposedly high-minded philosophes. Diderot even reflected favorably on the possibility of Latin remaining a language

13. Montesquieu, *Oeuvres complètes*, 3:47.

14. *Encyclopédie*, 6:273.

15. Bishop Warburton's *The Alliance of Church and State* (1736) and *The Divine Legation of Moses* (1738–41) provided a compendium of arguments for supporters of state-supported and controlled religion. The French philosophes and other writers on religious matters frequently plundered his works, though not always to his purposes. On Warburton's French influence, see the articles of Clifton Cherpack, "Warburton and the Encyclopédie," *Comparative Literature* 17 (1955):226–39, and "Warburton and Some Aspects of the Search for the Primitive in Eighteenth-Century France," *Philological Quarterly* 36 (1957):221–32. For summaries of the arguments of Warburton's tomes, see A. W. Evans, *Warburton and the Warburtonians: A Study in Some Eighteenth-Century Controversies* (Oxford, 1932), chapters 2 and 3.

16. *Encyclopédie*, 6:274.

in which philosophers could pursue their most daring speculations without unduly disturbing popular belief.[17] The doctrine of a double truth attracted philosophes in several ways. As a deist a philosophe could, as did Formey, consider all cults as a variation on one natural religion and thus see the people's cult as a harmless gloss on pure belief, satisfying the popular need for images and miracles. On a social level, the tradition of a double truth presented an image of societies in which public officials and men of learning shared a common perspective, separated from baser men. Considered in this manner, an age of double truth could seem a worthy model for Enlightenment emulation, since, as Voltaire and others often lamented, the holders of public power too often shared the opinion of the mob. An age in which leaders were sufficiently self-conscious to direct the people toward the common good while secretly enjoying the dictates of natural reason appealed as much to Voltaire in 1760 as it had to Montesquieu in 1716. And on the purely pragmatic level, the philosophes usually doubted that the people could live without superstition; in that case the existence of a double truth made the best of a regrettable but inevitable situation. Enlightenment discussion of religion's social value generally took its frame of reference from these two literary traditions. Bayle's paradox raised the question of the relative merits of any religion against the possibility of a moral atheism. The tradition of a double truth gave the question of social religion an overt class content. As the perspective of the Enlightenment shifted after mid-century from more purely philosophical to more practical legislative matters, the central concern of discussion understandably also shifted from the more general issue of Bayle's paradox to questions of separation, deception, and manipulation raised by the heritage of a double truth.

### THE CERTAINTIES AT MID-CENTURY

In a rare display of virtual unanimity, the writers of the *Encyc-*

17. "Aius Locutius," *Encyclopédie*, 1:241. For other descriptions generally favorable to the workings of the double truth, see the articles "Augures" (Abbé Mallet), 1:876; "Cabale" (Abbé Pestré) 2:476; "Casuiste" (Diderot), 2:757; "Divination" (Diderot), 4:1071–73; "Hébraique" (anon.), 8:85; "Idole, idolâtre, idolâtrie" (Voltaire), 8:503; and "Lettrés" (anon.), 9:433. Diderot's defense of the idea of a double truth must have offended some of his readers. Under the *errata* at the beginning of volume 3, he noted an addition to "Aius Locutius" which directed his reader to the article "Casuiste" for a further explanation of his position. See 3:xv.

*lopédie* agreed that all societies need a god, and specifically one who rewards good and punishes evil. Almost every article dealing with the relation of religion to society lauded the social utility of a religion, Christian or natural. Abbé Yvon first raised the problem in his article "Athée." He began his long-winded, tortuous sermon by explicating the widely known view held by Plutarch and Bayle that atheism harmed society much less than did superstitious religion. Although Yvon conceded that superstition affronted the godhead more than atheism by attributing vicious qualities to the deity rather than none at all, he repeatedly denied the viability of atheism in a moral society. Most nations commonly called "atheistic," he contended, in reality adhered to some form of natural religion.[18] In any case, he denied the notion that a "moral sentiment" or human laws had sufficent strength to contain men fully. Obligation entails a master who obliges, he reasoned; only a god who rewards all good deeds and punishes all evil can oblige the members of society in the universal fashion society needs. Despite a passing specific reference to the desire to "force the multitude to practice virtue,"[19] Yvon and the other exponents of religious utility in the *Encyclopédie* argued from the more general grounds that virtually all men need the constraint of an omniscient master.[20] To give weight to his views, Yvon offered the testimony of poets, legislators, political commentators, and even atheists who had shared his concerns. Plutarch, Seneca, Sextus Empiricus, Polybius, Strabo, Pomponazzi, and Warburton had all borne witness to the impossibility of an atheistic society. Yvon thought he walked in good company.[21]

Yvon rejected atheism but proposed no legal punishment for professed atheists; others were not so cautious. Samuel Formey argued in "Athéisme" that unbelief degrades human nature and denies all principles of morality, politics, equity, and humanity. Philosophic virtue always collapses before fear, interest, and passion. Only "a God who sees and conducts all" can give virtue its proper rigor. On this basis, Formey pronounced professed atheism contrary to natural law and hence punishable under the civil law.[22] Even the

18. *Encyclopédie*, 1:799.
19. *Encyclopédie*, 1:805.
20. E.g., the anonymous articles "Christianisme," 3:382; "Société," 15:256; and "Théisme," 16:243.
21. *Encyclopédie*, 1:811–14.
22. Ibid., pp. 816–17.

author of the article "Tolérance" proposed punishment for the professed atheist and admiringly cited the intolerance of Rousseau's *Du Contrat social*.[23] Among some of the apostles of tolerance, therefore, the realm of freedom could extend only so far; public order still appeared to require a religion.[24]

These Encyclopedists largely ignored any difference between the people and the rest of society. The temptations of riches as well as the exigencies of poverty could drive men to vice; both rich and poor therefore needed a god. The difference, in the *Encyclopédie*, between the religion of the people and the religion of honnêtes gens resided not in central beliefs but in the form of cult. If religion were made only for the philosopher, Diderot observed in "Cérémonies," then sensible signs and acts might not be necessary to recall the dictates of faith and duty. Sensible impressions alone, however, move the common man. "Never could the eloquence of Antony," he concluded, "have worked like the robe of Caesar."[25] De Jaucourt, in the article "Culte," recognized the danger that sensible objects might be mistaken for the substance of religion by the simple people. Nonetheless, he argued that without these objects the people might forget the divinity entirely.[26] The author of "Christianisme" even insisted that the people would accept no religion except one with the trappings of revelation. Though the substances of revealed and natural religions differed not at all, he wrote, the people could only learn truth from impressive revelation, not from the reason which it never obeys.[27]

The boundaries of the Encyclopedic discussion of social religion remained quite narrow. The authors all assumed, at least for public consumption, that atheism presented a genuine danger to the moral fabric of society and that all men needed a religion which included a rewarding and punishing god. The dogma necessary for society was simple enough. "A God, a providence, a future life, rewards and punishments for the good and bad" formed the entire substance of

---

23. Romili *fils*, *Encyclopédie*, 16:394.

24. In "Législateur," however, Saint-Lambert warned strongly against using religion as the principal support of the laws, and considered religion only an auxiliary tool for the legislator; see *Encyclopédie*, 9:359.

25. *Encyclopédie*, 2:839.

26. *Encyclopédie*, 4:550–51; see also "Enfer," 5:667 and "Religion naturelle," 14:81–83, both by De Jaucourt, for similar judgments.

27. *Encyclopédie*, 3:385.

religion given by the "natural light," according to Abbé Mallet,[28] and most others accepted that minimum doctrine. Natural religion was therefore both useful and true; deception presented no problem. The author of "Divinité," though obviously defensive about the manipulative use made by legislators of the doctrine of a future life, still insisted that the belief remained of obscure origin and that it dwelled in the hearts of all men.[29]

The author of "Christianisme" explored the matter further. He criticized those legislators who purposefully mixed true religion with dupery, but he found in the evident social utility of the doctrine of a future life only another proof of its theological certainty:

> In sacrificing the true to the useful, [legislators] did not see that the blow which struck the first struck the second at the same time, because there is nothing which is universally useful which is not exactly true. These two march as it were abreast; and we see them act on minds simultaneously. Following this idea, we should sometimes be able to measure the degrees of truth in a religion by the degrees of utility that states derive from it.[30]

The machinations of leaders did not, in the end, invalidate the truth of the doctrine of future rewards and punishments. At mid-century a rewarding and punishing god remained a belief worthy of the philosophe as well as useful for all men. Within this providential vision, the doctrine's evident utility merely confirmed its basic truth. If the Encyclopedists' insistence on the need for this kind of religion betrayed implicit fear of the people (which comprised, after all, most of "society") they did not rely on this fear to argue for imposture or artificial constraints. The true and the useful neatly coincided.

## A PROBLEM FOR THE LEGISLATOR

The easy coincidence of metaphysical truth with human utility

28. "Déistes," 4:773; see also De Jaucourt's "Religion naturelle," 14:79, where he stated that natural and revealed religion have the same core beliefs, differing only in that revealed religion also supposes "an immediate mission by God himself, attested by miracles and prophecies."

29. *Encyclopédie*, 4:1073.

30. *Encyclopédie*, 3:382; see also Abbé Yvon's "Athée," 1:812, for almost identical phrases, probably the source for the former. The convergence of the true and the useful was a major theme of Bishop Warburton's writings, from which Yvon and others drew. See Evans, *Warburton*, chapter 3.

could and did easily collapse as the concerns of the Enlightenment became more pragmatic and legislative. For the would-be legislator utility was enough, and truth became an unnecessary hypothesis.

Montesquieu initiated the movement away from truth as a serious concern in discussing the social utility of religion. As we have seen, he had openly admired the religious policies of Roman leaders; his perspective matured but never fundamentally changed. In one of the *Lettres persanes* (1721) Ibben candidly observes that if the belief that one being is actually composed of two provides a "better guarantee of the actions of men" than another belief, then the legislator should include that belief in the civil law.[31] Some time later Montesquieu noted with regret the supposed ill effects on the manners of the people of William Whiston's tirades against prophecies, even though he privately sympathized with Whiston's religious liberalism.[32]

In these early observations, Montesquieu still reasoned within the tradition of the ancient Roman double truth. The more mature Montesquieu of *De l'esprit des lois* (1748) avoided overt admiration for deceptive practices but still disregarded entirely the problem of truth in discussing religion's relation to society. Adopting the perspective not of "a theologian but of a political writer,"[33] he considered religion only in its sociological role. In this light he rejected the contentions of Bayle. As proof against Bayle he offered not the violent populace but the prince "who fears and hates religion. . . . like the wild beasts that bite the chains which keep them from pouncing on those who pass by."[34] He admired Christianity as the religion best suited for moderate governments, giving the standard of utility clear precedence. "From the nature of the Christian and Mohammedan religions," he argued,

> we should without further investigation embrace the former and reject the latter, because it is much easier to see that a religion should humanize the manners of men than that one religion alone is true.[35]

31. *Oeuvres complètes*, vol. 1, part 3, pp. 158–59.
32. *Oeuvres complètes*, 3:286. On Montesquieu's religious belief see Robert Shackleton, *Montesquieu: A Critical Biography* (Oxford, 1961), pp. 349–53, and Pauline Kra, *Religion in Montesquieu's Lettres Persanes, VS* 72 (1970).
33. Book 24, chapter 1. (*De l'esprit des lois* may be found in *Oeuvres complètes*, vol. 1.)
34. Book 24, chapter 2.
35. Book 24, chapter 4.

Even without the proofs of revelation, Montesquieu argued, religions could still inculcate respectable ethics.[36] More flexible than the Encyclopedists, he recognized that a religion with no divine punishments and rewards might suit the needs of society, provided that a civil law compensate with immediate and severe sanctions.[37] And, as he pointed out in his eclectic manner, belief in an afterlife could produce such horrible practices as the suicide of loved ones expecting to rejoin persons recently deceased.[38] The tragedy of such acts, he implied, lay not in any possible divine wrath but in giving priority to distant, dubious rewards over the enjoyment of this life. His worldly, sociological perspective allowed him to see religion as a flexible legislative instrument with both good and harmful results. The legislator must choose wisely.

A pair of letters written by Turgot in 1753 confirm that within this climate of ideas even a religious moderate could easily give utility marked precedence over truth.[39] Accepting the ideal of pure tolerance, Turgot then posited a duty on the part of the state to prevent the confusion and indifference which neutrality toward religion might create. He feared the fierce conflicts and barbarous superstitions which a people, left entirely to its own devices, might nurture. To counter this threat, he advocated public instruction, "an education for the people which would teach it probity; which would place before its eyes a summary of its duties in a form that is clear and easy to practice."[40] Most men, he thought, are incapable of choosing their own religion in any rational manner; the state therefore should present them with a clear, established example. Thus, despite his ideal of pure tolerance, Turgot considered religion too important to leave entirely to individual initiative.

Turgot's state church would have had its subsistence guaranteed by public lands supporting a number of curés sufficient to spread public instruction to villages and towns. He presumed that the majority religion would probably become the state-sponsored cult. But since the basis of choice should be utility, he acknowledged that a

---

36. Book 24, chapters 8, 9, and 10, on the Pégu tribe, the Essene sect, and the Stoics, respectively.
37. Book 24, chapter 14.
38. Book 24, chapter 19.
39. For the substance of what follows, see Turgot, *Oeuvres de Turgot*, 1:387–91, 423–25.
40. Ibid., p. 389.

majority religion might be unsuitable. The state, he argued, should tolerate but not protect or sponsor a religion which encouraged celibacy, defied political authority, or maintained inflexible dogmas. Hence he found the Roman Catholic church inappropriate. Moderate Protestantism or Arminianism appeared more acceptable, but he considered them weak buttresses against irreligion. "Would not natural religion," he concluded, "systematized and accompanied by a cult, prove more solid by defending less terrain?"[41] When called upon to defend this position, he later asserted that the historic role and greatest benefit of Christianity had been to propagate this natural religion.[42]

Turgot considered his state religion in no way an imposition of falsehood upon an unwary populace. His religion made no distinction in dogmas between people and nonpeople, though he did direct his program of instruction toward the lower orders. He advocated nothing which he did not himself consider true. Nonetheless, he insisted in the spirit of Montesquieu, as others had not, that the issue should rest on purely utilitarian grounds.

Turgot's views could be controversial for the Christian believer but not for the philosophe. Voltaire, on the other hand, singlehandedly turned the question of social religion back to the idea of imposture for the masses, thus provoking a mild, continuing storm in the philosophic camp.[43] As we have seen, writers in the *Encyclopédie* generally divided "popular" from "true" religion at the level of cult and not basic belief. At mid-century, those philosophes had assumed that all religions possessed a common core, a *religion naturelle*, which included the doctrine of future rewards and punishments. The beginnings of the open propaganda of the Parisian atheists—Holbach, Boulanger, Damilaville, and (at least in private circles) Diderot— changed the perspective for discussion. Voltaire accepted for himself

41. Ibid., p. 391.

42. Ibid., p. 425. One can find this idea already broadly implicit in his *sorbonnique* of 1750, "Discours sur les avantages que l'éstablissement du christianisme a procurés au genre humain," in ibid., pp. 194–214.

43. On the matter of Voltaire's social religion, Gay's account in *Voltaire's Politics*, pp. 259–69, is thorough and balanced. I have tried, however, to place Voltaire's ideas in a wider context in which his "crude deism" for the masses (p. 267) can be seen as identical to the "natural religion" accepted by most philosophes at mid-century. I have also tried to show that Voltaire's particular choices of rhetoric and tactics were not as typical of the Enlightenment as a whole as Gay's and other accounts might suggest. Cf. ibid., pp. 259–61; *The Enlightenment*, 2:522; and Manuel, *The Eighteenth Century Confronts the Gods*, p. 68.

the belief in a beneficent God but not the reality of an afterlife; he assumed, probably in error, that most enlightened honnêtes gens believed as he did. At the same time his radical distrust of the people drove him to fear the extension of atheistic propaganda to unprepared, violent popular minds. Unwilling to believe naively in the truth of an afterlife with rewards and punishments, he fell back on an obvious standard, social utility. In opposing the radicalism of the atheists, Voltaire argued from the late 1750s to the end of his career that the people needs a punishing god to contain its violence and that the legislator must, therefore, provide one.

Voltaire repeated his formula—*un Dieu rémunérateur et vengeur*— scores of times over the course of the conflict. Belief in such a god, he thought, constituted the very minimum that society as a whole must accept. He did not always limit this requirement to the people, although it was never very far from his view. All men face the temptation to act irrationally, rich as well as poor; all men, therefore, need some psychological barrier to harmful action. "It is absolutely necessary for princes and for peoples," Voltaire concluded his entry "Athéisme" to his *Dictionnaire philosophique*, "that the idea of a supreme Being, creator, governor, remunerator, and avenger, be inscribed in men's minds."[44]

The substance of Voltaire's social religion was simple. It differed little from that of the Encyclopedists, Turgot, and Montesquieu. But Voltaire simply did not believe in the god of his social religion, and in addressing his recommendations to the public he made no pretense of doing so. Voltaire assumed that those who would read his work sympathetically were enlightened initiates who would see the need for a "vengeful god" without believing in its existence. Voltaire once described a fictional priest addressing "a good and honest Huguenot minister" who had disavowed the idea of eternal damnation. "My friend," he insisted, "I do not believe in eternal hell any more than you do; but it is good that your servant, your tailor, and even your lawyer believe it."[45]

When confronting the hosts of "brutal, drunk, thieving little men"[46] Voltaire preached the need for one lie: the possibility of eternal damnation. For the Ciceros and Senecas of the world he

44. *Dictionnaire philosophique*, p. 43.
45. Ibid., "Enfer," p. 180.
46. Ibid., (addition of 1771), p. 526.

considered proper a "pure adoration of the supreme Being." Such a
religion might descend as far down as the "healthy" part of the people—literate artisans, shopkeepers, and the like. For the violent and
superstitious low people, the best one could hope for would be the
reasonable worship of a god offering indefinite punishments and
rewards.[47]

Although he made a bow to the tradition which stressed the need
for a religion throughout society, Voltaire repeatedly stressed social
distinctions to make his point. He perceived the problem of a social
religion (as the Encyclopedists had not) squarely in the tradition of
the double truth. The phenomenon fascinated him from its first
appearance in his notebooks—"Double doctrine among almost all
the ancients"—and throughout his later writings.[48] For Voltaire
more than any other philosophe, the idea that society could be
divided into the educable genteel few and the ignorant many appealed
both as an explanation and a consolation in the face of adversity. The
image of philosophers in ancient Egypt, Greece, and Rome sharing a
common spiritual bond with the leadership of society reaffirmed his
chosen tactic for the success of enlightenment—conversion of the
holders of power.

But despite the cold cynicism of his rhetoric, Voltaire often displayed a measured optimism in his personal version of a double truth.
At somber times his thoughts coincided with that of the ancients,
allowing a purified religion for some and all manner of superstition
for the canaille, as long as it remained controllable. In 1762 he wrote
to a friend:

> I do not believe that our philosophes want to stop our wine-
> growers and laborers from going to Mass, but I do think that they
> want to stop honnêtes gens from being the victims of a supersti-
> tion, as absurd as it is abominable, which serves only to enrich
> lazy scoundrels and pervert feeble spirits. Those who want their

47. The words are those of "Fréret" in the dialogue "Le dîner du comte de Boulainvilliers" (1767), in *Oeuvres complètes*, 26:555–56. For similar statements, see also "Traité
sur la tolérance" (1763), *Oeuvres complètes*, 25:101–102; and *Dictionnaire philosophique*,
"Fraude," pp. 210–11, and "Superstition," p. 398.

48. *Notebooks*, 2:488. For various accounts, mostly favorable, of societies with "double
truths" see *Essai sur les moeurs*, 1:77, 93–96, 103, 130–31, 181, 223–24, 238–39; and 2:683,
906, 908. The double truth is also a recurrent theme in the *Dictionnaire philosophique*; see
articles "Apis," p. 30; "Christianisme," pp. 118–19; "Idole . . . ," pp. 236–50.

friends to think like Cicero, Plato, Lucretius, Marcus Antoni-
nus, etc., are not so wrong. As for the canaille, one should not
consider it.[49]

But in preparing more detailed visions of a future popular religion,
he clearly desired not to allow superstition free rein, even among
the people. In a noteworthy addition to the article "Guerre" in the
*Dictionnaire philosophique*, Voltaire distinguished between religion
naturelle, which included a "just and vengeful God" from *religion
artificielle*, with all the vicious trappings of superstition.[50] He advocated for the people not the idolatry of oracles, soothsayers, and
priests, but this same natural religion, much as it had been defined in
the *Encyclopédie* and practiced by the guardians of pure religion in
ancient times. Had Voltaire been the legislator, the religion of the
canaille would have been the natural religion of the Stoics, the early
Egyptian priests, and the Chinese literati. While Voltaire passed
beyond these wise men in the refinement of his personal religon, he
found no legislative value in imposing his theology on society. All
metaphysics being subject to debate, he argued, the legislator could
choose on the basis of social utility. Voltaire found the natural religion of history suitably utilitarian in that it kept a bridle on the mob
while avoiding the dangers of superstition.[51]

Voltaire did not doubt that the people, left to itself, would create
and nurture the most bizarre superstitions, but he did not want the
people left to itself. Instead he sought to turn its religious instinct to
the public good. At the most cynical level this meant yoking the violent passions of the masses with the "noble lie" of an eternal hell. At
a more benign level, it meant converting religion into an educative
and administrative tool, once the literate parish priest had been won
to the cause of enlightenment. This new priest would teach not su-
persititious "theological religion" but the "religion of the state." He
would perform civil functions, such as registering births and holding

49. To Antoine Jean Gabriel Le Bault, 2 April 1762, Voltaire, *Correspondence* (9604).
See also no. 12912.

50. *Dictionnaire philosophique*, pp. 230–31. Frederick II made a similar distinction between "myth" and "superstition," seeing utility in the former as an approximation and
representation of truth, but none in the latter; see Ronald Grimsley, *Jean d'Alembert*
(Oxford, 1963), p. 170.

51. See the crucial argument of "A" in the dialogue "A, B, C" (1768), *Oeuvres complètes*,
27:399–400.

public festivals, as well as teach morality within a simple set of customs and doctrines.[52] These ideal priests would know the elements of law, agronomy, and medicine as well as their natural religion.[53] The village priest could then cooperate with conscientious seigneurs in ending the neglect of the people.

Voltaire obviously modeled his ideal curé after some of those already ministering to the people of Europe. Intendants such as Turgot already used the curés as extra subdelegates in the country-side; reformers everywhere looked to the local clergy as conduits of information and change.[54] The parish priest of the late *ancien régime* doubled as civil servant and educator. Voltaire aimed not so much to change this structure as to take it over in the name of the public good. He advocated tolerance but appreciated too well the hold of religion over the mass of men to allow the state to leave the matter entirely alone. The state would intervene, much as in Turgot's scheme, to provide a framework within which most people, creatures of habit, would work and pray. The honnêtes gens and whatever religious fanatics remained could then be safely left to their private whims.

Despite his conservatism, Voltaire moved the framework of the double truth toward the theological left. Within his ideal society the people would worship in the manner that the ancient protectors of "pure faith" had done; the new gentlemen philosophes would adore the divine order and do good for its own sake. From the perspective of most exponents of natural religion, Voltaire's social religion would involve no imposture at all. He could easily have argued for his social religion without emphasizing that element of imposture which he perceived from the perspective of his own private beliefs. To be sure, Voltaire genuinely feared the fury of consciences released from re-

52. *Dictionnaire philosophique*, "Religion," p. 361.

53. See the entry in Voltaire's *Notebooks*, 2:528–29; also the supposed words of "Abbé de Saint-Pierre," first published as an appendix to "Le dîner du comte de Boulainvilliers" (*Oeuvres complètes*, 26:559–60), and repeated as an addition of 1769 to *Dictionnaire philosophique*, "Crédo," p. 154. (Voltaire did not substantially distort Saint-Pierre's views; see Merle Perkins, *The Moral and Political Philosophy of the Abbé de Saint-Pierre* [Geneva, 1969], pp. 65–72 on the abbé's proposed civil religion.) Théotime in *Dictionnaire philosophique*, "Catéchisme du curé," pp. 85–89, might be taken as Voltaire's ideal priest for the people. See also W. H. Williams, "Voltaire and the Utility of the Lower Clergy," *VS* 58 (1967): 1869–91, which considers Voltaire's plans in relation to the demands of activist curés.

54. Douglas Dakin, *Turgot and the Ancien Régime in France* (New York, 1965 [1939]), pp. 58–60; Liebel, *Enlightened Bureaucracy*, p. 20.

ligious guilt but uninitiated into the new "mystery," the philosophe's reasonableness. But he chose to argue on the grounds of necessary imposture as much out of peevishness as out of fear.[55] The new radicalism of the Parisian philosophes, with its apparent disregard for soothing powerful, useful men, challenged Voltaire's sense of leadership within the Enlightenment. He chose therefore to play the "realist" opposed to the atheistic "utopian," to appear pragmatic by appealing to the traditional fears of his readers. He openly taunted the Parisians by twice taking Catholic communion and then preaching to his peasants; he took pains to insure that Paris would hear of his clever exploit.[56] In the end, however, he seems to have changed the mind of no one within the inner sanctum of Parisian philosophes. Holbach, Diderot, Helvétius, and Condorcet ignored or rejected his fears and began to explore the fuller implications of a godless society.

## THE FRUIT OF THE ATHEISTIC TREE

Unlike Voltaire, for whom the problem of social religion arose as a curious aside in his polemical career, Holbach had to confront squarely and continually the idea of the supposed utility of religion.[57] In *La Contagion sacrée* he willingly adopted Voltaire's standard of utility:

> Such are the motives and duties which morality announces to mankind; if religion strengthened them and made them more sacred, no matter how incomprehensible its dogmas might otherwise appear, for that reason alone it should not be rejected. It would be madness to want to attack it if it really contributed

55. Compare Voltaire's public declarations on the dangers of destroying useful belief with his private assurances to d'Alembert and Condorcet (11 October 1770, *Correspondence*, 15674): "A powerful man at court [d'Argenson] has sent me a peculiar refutation of the *Système de la Nature*, in which he says that the new philosophy will lead to a horrible revolution if it is not stopped. All of these cries will die out, and philosophy will remain. In the end, philosophy is life's consolation, and its opposite life's poison. Let things pass; it is impossible to hinder thought, and the more people think, the less will men be unhappy."

56. See John Pappas, *Voltaire and D'Alembert* (Bloomington, 1962), pp. 69–73. Chapter 5 provides a good account of the play of personalities in the "civil war" between Voltaire and the Parisian circle.

57. Holbach repeated his convictions many times. For the fullest expressions, see *Le Christianisme dévoilé* (1761), preface; *La Contagion sacrée, ou Histoire naturelle de la superstition* (London [?], 1772), pp. 10–13, 18–22; *Système de la Nature*, 1:260–84, and 2:312–17, 350–53; the essay "Problème important. La religion est-elle nécessaire à la morale & utile à la politique?" published in *Recueil philosophique* (London [?], 1770), pp. 70–112.

to making men better; to seek to destroy it would be to conspire against society.[58]

But for Holbach's ponderous style the words might be Voltaire's. Holbach purposely chose to take the same perspective as the proponents of a social religion. Arguing from that same standard of utility, he arrived at an entirely different judgment—religion had never been and, by its very nature, could never be useful to the legislator.

Holbach's vision of religious history differed markedly from Voltaire's. Voltaire often portrayed public officials as the victims of priestcraft, unwittingly drawn against their interests into a fanaticism created by the people and exploited by its priests. Much more than Voltaire, Holbach had come to see the people as the victim of a lopsided battle between the wealthy few and the poor multitude. In his view, public power and priestly power originated together, partners in exploitation. Religion had continually served the cause of oppressors, priests and laymen alike, and the time had come to eradicate it root and branch. Toward the admirers of ancient Roman religious policies he directed particular scorn. Machiavelli, he argued, outwitted himself in his attempt to prove the wisdom of this manipulative religion in his *Discourses*. "The examples he relies upon," Holbach countered, "unfortunately prove that only the Senate profited by blinding the people to keep it under yoke."[59] The Roman example was but a symptom of a universal phenomenon, the use of religion to serve class interest. Of Voltaire's "irascible God" he wrote that it was useful "only to those who have an interest in frightening men in order to pluck the fruits of their ignorance, fears, and expiations."[60] Holbach looked more deeply than Voltaire into the tradition of the double truth and discovered in the actions of legislators and priests a failure of leadership, not its exercise.

Holbach could not rely entirely upon the damning evidence of history. Although the exponents of a social religion often drew on their own version of history, they made claims primarily on the future, when a purified religion might be taught to all. To counter these claims Holbach adopted Voltaire's favorite pose, the realist.

58. *La Contagion sacrée*, p. 49.
59. *Système de la Nature*, 2:244, note 35. Cf. *Essai sur les Préjugés*, pp. 95–96 and 95 note, where Holbach criticized Cicero for advocating no change in public religious institutions; he did, however, find merit in Cicero's writings against the Roman gods.
60. *Système de la Nature*, 2:262.

All experience showed, he argued, that religious sanctions had no effect whatsoever on the course of everyday life. The human animal is formed in such a way that distant rewards and punishments, no matter how extreme, must eventually give way to present needs and desires. The decrepitude of the most pious nations and the violent acts of the most holy kings bore witness to the inefficacy of the imaginary power of belief in divine wrath. Only the real sanctions of swift justice, he concluded, could sufficiently contain men.[61]

The supposedly pure natural religion advocated by many philosophes seemed sheer fantasy to Holbach. History demonstrated, he believed, that natural religion would always degenerate into fanaticism and superstition. Most philosophes had attributed the degeneration of natural religion into superstition to the people's craving for the miraculous; Voltaire and others hoped that an enlightened and strong leadership could prevent such degeneration. Holbach had less faith in that leadership. Priests and magistrates could never resist the temptations of any cult. There could be no religion without mysteries,[62] he observed; exploiters always walk in the shadows of mysteries. Deism could, therefore, never remain intact; the human mind and human society could never leave it alone. "Most unbelievers and reformers only prune a poisonous tree without daring to bring the axe to its roots," he wrote. "They do not see that the tree will eventually reproduce the same fruits."[63] For Holbach there existed no safe ground of natural religion between the poles of atheism and superstition. Natural religion was only superstition postponed.

Holbach cut through much of Voltaire's wishful thinking with his radical vision. He turned the lessons of history and psychology to his own uses to deny the utility of religion. On one issue alone did his legislative proposals apparently converge with those of Voltaire and Turgot: the transformation of religious institutions into educational ones. Holbach made no compromise with institutionalized religion in *Ethocratie*. Confiscate church lands, he urged Louis XVI, and use the funds to finance a clerisy of state educators to preach a godless moral catechism.[64] Morality without a god could thrive, Holbach thought, as it could not with one.

---

61. *Le Bon sens, ou Idées naturelles opposées aux idées supernaturelles* (London [?], 1772), pp. 143–44, 232.
62. Ibid., p. 112.
63. *Système de la Nature*, 2:353.
64. *Ethocratie, ou le gouvernement fondé sur la morale* (Amsterdam, 1776), pp. 100–03.

The opposition of Holbach to Voltaire set the new boundaries for discussion of social religion. Voltaire defended the utility of religous belief for social containment; Holbach tried to unmask religion as a tool of social exploitation. The more general philosophical speculations raised by Bayle's paradox receded as purely legislative concerns moved to the fore. The problem of tolerance did not enter the debate, which centered entirely on the issue of whether or not the legislator could abandon a technique used since antiquity.

Diderot's long philosophic career reflected the currents and tensions in this debate, and fate eventually brought him to the position of "legislator" for the largest nation in Europe. From the first he nursed strong doubts about the acceptability or utility of a vengeful and cruel god. In "Essai sur le mérite et le vertu" (1745), loosely translated from Shaftesbury, he insisted that fear of punishment eliminated all virtue from a beneficent act, but he conceded that the image of a cruel god might constrain a few men in moments of weakness.[65] Still, his early version of natural religion included an afterlife with rewards and punishments. In "La promenade du sceptique" (1747), the characters Ariste and Cléobule discuss the merits of allowing public religious debate. Ariste voices fears that such debate might shake useful popular prejudice. Cléobule, however, judges all prejudice useless; natural religion will suffice:

> Once a man accepts the existence of a God, the reality of moral good and evil, the immortality of the soul, the future rewards and punishments, what need does he have of prejudices?[66]

Through Cléobule, Diderot voiced what might have been considered a fairly radical position before mid-century, rejecting the idea of "useful prejudice." His minimal religion, however, coincided with the religion naturelle of the *Encyclopédie* and Voltaire. Had his personal belief remained at the level of natural religion, the problem of social religion might not have troubled him further. But Diderot rapidly evolved from Shaftesburian deism to atheism,[67] thus requiring reevaluation of his original answer.

Diderot often professed a hatred almost as deep as Rousseau's of

65. Diderot, *Oeuvres complètes*, 1:54–57.
66. Ibid., p. 182.
67. On Diderot's religious evolution see Aram Vartanian, "From Deist to Atheist: Diderot's Philosophical Orientation, 1746–1749," in *Diderot Studies* 1 (1949):46–63, and Proust, *Diderot et l'Encyclopédie*, pp. 284–93.

lies and artifice.[68] Even as a convinced atheist, he could not tempera-
mentally adopt the cold cynicism of Voltaire. The position of Diderot's *Encyclopédie* remained of necessity moderate[69] and reflected the
general opinion of enlightened circles. But as Diderot emerged from
the constraints of his editorship in the mid-1760s, he soon openly
opposed the idea of social religion. In a remarkable letter written in
1765 to Damilaville, then visiting Voltaire at Ferney, he urged his
friend to stand firmly on the atheist's ground. "Remind him,"
Diderot advised,

> of my fable about the misanthrope who took refuge in a cave
> where he meditated deeply how he might take vengeance in
> the most terrible way upon the human race which disgusted him.
> He said to himself, "I must find some notion to which they will
> attach more importance than their life and on which they will
> never reach agreement," and at that instant he emerged cry-
> ing, "God, God!"

The misanthrope's plan worked well; dispute, hatred, and war
followed. Expanding on his fable, Diderot went on to reason that if
a supposition succeeded in explaining all phenomena the philosophe
would incline toward accepting its truth. "Why then," he continued,
"not take for falsehood a supposition which cannot be applied to any
metaphysical, physical, political, and moral question without obscur-
ing it?"[70] To clinch his argument he then reversed the traditional
wisdom which had long held that philosophers could live without a
god but that the people required one. "Tell him," he concluded,

> that the notion of a supreme being in a Trajan, a Marcus Aure-
> lius, a Cato, and a few other minds equally well formed, who
> walked beneath the eyes of a beneficent being whom they had
> taken for a model, might have been an excellent notion; but if

68. For example, in his dedicatory letter to *Père de famille* (1758), a brief essay on education addressed to the princess of Nassau-Saarbruck, Diderot warned against any lie:
"Lying is always harmful. One error of the mind is enough to corrupt taste and morality.
With a single false idea, one can become barbarous; the brush is seized from the hand of
the painter; the masterpiece from the sculptor; a work of genius is burned; one's soul is
made small and cruel." May or June 1758, *Correspondance* (92).

69. E.g., the article "Philosophe" in which the editor, probably Diderot, eliminated in
the *Encyclopédie* version a specific denial of the utility of religion for social control, an
important message of the original; cf. the versions in Dieckmann, *Le Philosophe*, pp. 48–51.

70. To Damilaville, 12 September 1765, Diderot, *Correspondance* (349).

he inquires into the history which he knows so well, he will see
that for the rest, it has been, is, and will be a fatal idea.[71]

A few weeks later, in a letter to Sophie Volland, he presented a
variation of this argument. Those persons reason backwards, he
maintained, who suppose that belief in a god, rather than belief in
good laws, is the best means of forming honnêtes gens. "With relation to a people," he wrote, "I consider belief in the existence of God,
like marriage. . . an excellent condition for three or four well-
formed heads, but fatal for the multitude." Marriage makes as many
people unhappy as happy; belief in a god makes as many fanatics as
believers. As soon as any worship is allowed, he concluded, "the
natural order of moral duties is reversed and morality corrupted."[72]
The absolute corruptibility of all religious belief impressed Diderot
much as it had his fellow atheist Holbach,[73] and so he opposed
Voltaire in the debate on social religion.

Less than a decade later Diderot received the opportunity to defend
his convictions when the empress of Russia requested his advice on
legislation for the future of her nation. In Catherine the Great he had
to confront a sovereign very much convinced of the wisdom of tradition; the submission of church to state was more complete in Russia
than in any other European state. At first, Diderot remained firm in
his convictions and addressed Catherine in the voice of the Holbachian côterie. Though he promised to deliver, on her request, the
"lovely fantasy" of a just and watchful god (which, he noted, she
shared with Socrates, Phocion, Titus, Trajan, and Marcus Aurelius),
he spilled much ink demonstrating how the admission of any divinity
immediately opened a Pandora's box of cults, priestcraft, intolerance,
and sanguinary conflict, eventually undermining all morality appropriate for this earth. Consequently, Diderot argued, the notion of
God, whether or not one believed it, should be banished from any
legal code: "I would link everything to simple and natural motives

71. Ibid. But cf. the more traditional division of society into those few who might be
atheists and the many who will always believe, in *Oeuvres complètes*, 17:517.

72. 6 October 1765, Diderot, *Correspondance* (351).

73. E.g., Diderot's comment on Helvétius's preference for combining civil and religious authorities in *De l'homme*: "Look here, monsieur Helvétius, God is a bad device with
which you can do nothing worthwhile; the mixture of deception and truth is always
vicious, and neither priests nor gods are necessary." (*Oeuvres complètes*, 2:289.)

as invariable as the human race."[74] Once again Diderot reversed traditional wisdom; whereas Voltaire advised sovereigns to use a god in which they did not believe, Diderot insisted that they should shun a god at all costs, in spite of their beliefs.

At Catherine's insistence Diderot reluctantly agreed to design a religious organization for Russia.[75] The measure of his reluctance can be seen in his witty introduction to the section on morality and religion in "Plan d'une Université." Citing those with whom she disagreed—Bayle, Plutarch, and Hobbes—he wrote of Catherine:

> She thinks that the fear of future punishments has much influence on the actions of men, and that the wickedness which the sight of the gallows does not stop might be contained by the fear of a distant punishment. Despite the infinite harm that religious opinions have done to humanity, despite the inconvenience of a system which puts the confidence of peoples in the hands of the priest, always a dangerous rival of the sovereign, which establishes a superior to the head of society and which institutes laws more respectable and holy than her own; she is persuaded that the sum of the little daily benefits that the belief produces in all stations compensates for the evils occasioned between citizens by sects and between nations by intolerance, a kind of maniacal furor to which there is no remedy.

Such an introduction hardly confirmed the sincerity of his program, nor did his suggested readings in theology, which included Hobbes and Holbach as well as Fénelon and Samuel Clarke.[76]

Diderot tried diligently, nonetheless, to make palatable a distasteful legislative task, providing Catherine with a proposed church, priests, and a catechism. If there must be priests, he insisted, they must absolutely depend on the state. To insure stability the chief of state must subordinate both civil and religious law to natural law and to his authority as sovereign. Tied to the state, Diderot's priest would preach both a civil and a religious catechism. The association

74. *Mémoires*, pp. 105–09. For a nearly identical argument, see "Observations," *Oeuvres politiques*, pp. 346–49.

75. This "consultation" was, of course, largely wishful thinking on Diderot's part since Catherine had no intention of secularizing Russian society to any degree.

76. *Oeuvres complètes*, 3:490–92, quotation p. 492.

of religious sacredness with the civil law might, he hoped, prompt acceptance of that law. To protect the civil interest further, he would require the priest to preach the civil law without commentary. As his ideal model for official religion he proposed the fanciful island of Ternate where the priest merely led the people into the temple, in which stood a pyramid bearing the inscription "worship God, love your neighbor, and obey the law," and then ushered the people out.[77]

To leave nothing to chance Diderot even promoted a catechism for Catherine's state religion—Jacques Barbeu-Dubourg's *Petit Code de la raison humaine* (1774).[78] This catechism admirably suited the purposes of a religious legislator who really wanted no religion at all. Barbeu-Dubourg spent few pages on his godhead, a benevolent being with only a trace of wrath. He concentrated instead on man's duties as defined on the basis of natural law and human need and capacity. Religious sanctions virtually disappear behind human sanctions in the *Petit Code*.

Diderot proposed, therefore, a host of priests educated in deism and atheism and armed with Barbeu-Dubourg's minimal religion. Such a religion might, he thought, do some good; certainly a clergy so educated would command more rightful respect than would an ignorant one.[79] But even as he outlined the means to make the clergy helpful—or at least harmless—he issued one last warning against

77. "Observations," *Oeuvres politiques*, pp. 390–91. On the need to subject the church to the state, see "Entretiens," ibid., p. 322, and "Observations," ibid., p. 389. For earlier formulations of the same notion, see "Pages contre un tyran" (1770), ibid, p. 142, and "Supplément au Voyage de Bougainville" (1772), *Oeuvres philosophiques*, p. 505. The idea of placing the priest under the control of the public power was quite common in Gallican France. Several articles in the *Encyclopédie* stressed this necessity; see "Athée," 1:802, "Législateur," 9:359, and "Prêtre," 13:341.

78. Full title, *Petit Code de la raison humaine, ou exposition succincte de ce que la raison dicte à tous les hommes, pour éclairer leur conduite & assurer leur bonheur* (Amsterdam, 1782; first edition, 1774). Diderot recommended the book even prior to its publication in "Entretiens," *Oeuvres politiques*, p. 323. On his return voyage from Russia he sent a copy to General Betski, advising that "all its paragraphs may enter into the moral catechism desired by Her Imperial Majesty" (9 June 1774, *Correspondance*, [845]). He later pressed his recommendation, though still disowning any personal belief: "It is founded on the existence of a god she recognizes. . . . As for me, paltry creature, I slip away and proceed as if no one were watching me." 13 September 1774, *Correspondance* (853).

79. As evidence Diderot offered what he thought to be the comparatively high respect of the public for the French low clergy and the Spanish high clergy, both groups being better educated than the rest of their respective clergies; see *Mémoires*, p. 167, and *Oeuvres complètes*, 3:512.

expecting any positive results from religion. The Holbachian image of the poisonous tree returned to his mind as he advised Catherine for the last time to temper her enthusiasm for social religion. "The majority of the nation," he wrote,

> will always remain ignorant, fearful, and therefore superstitious. . . . The belief in the existence of God, or the sacred stump, will thus always remain. But who knows what monster this stump might produce if left to grow freely? I would not maintain priests, therefore, as depositors of truth but as obstacles to errors possibly even more monstrous; not as teachers of sensible men, but as guardians of madmen; and I would allow their churches to exist as the asylum . . . for a certain race of imbeciles who might go mad if they were totally neglected.[80]

From religion Diderot thus expected neither the moral health of society, as did Catherine, nor the containment of fear-stricken people, as did Voltaire. He saw value only in a religion acting as both an outlet and a boundary to superstition, and, as he often indicated, he would have preferred no religion at all.

Unlike Diderot, Helvétius proposed legislation in a vacuum, under no pressures from any sovereign to use religion. More than any other philosophe except, perhaps, Montesquieu, Helvétius investigated the full possibilities of the legislator. He despised the spirit of religion but, in the end, found it hard to ignore religion as a shaping force in society. Shrewd legislators, he knew, had used belief in the afterlife to draw out human courage and strength; as an admirer of Spartan discipline, Helvétius could not ignore those qualities. With a certain relish he described how Abyssinian Muslim priests reputedly shaped youths into fanatical killers: drugging their students, the priests would stage an elaborate hoax replete with charming and willing women, and then tell the youths that they had had a "vision" of the future life promised to those who obey the calif.[81] Such powers Helvétius clearly admired, though not the use to which they were put.

In the manner of Holbach and Diderot, Helvétius argued that traditional religion could be of no use to society. Religions could only

---

80. "Plan d'une Université," *Oeuvres complètes*, 3:517.
81. *De l'esprit* in *Oeuvres complètes*, 2:210–12; cf. a similar account of the uses of the Elysian Fields in *De l'homme* (1774), in *Oeuvres complètes*, 3:82.

be more or less an evil and never a benefit, he insisted. To be sure, the Protestant nations of the north and west showed better *moeurs* than Roman Catholic France, Italy, or Iberia. But he attributed no special goodness to Protestantism, only a lack of the more destructive aspects of papal religion.[82] "One must not," he wrote in *De l'homme*, "attribute either the virtues or the purity of moeurs of a nation to the holiness of the cult. Examining the matter further, one sees that the religious spirit is entirely destructive of the legislative spirit."[83]

To use religion in legislation, Helvétius agreed, is to take control out of the hands of the magistrate and place it in the self-serving hands of the priest. Like Diderot and Holbach, he sensed the inevitable destructive force of any established cult. Even containment of popular violence through religion did not appeal to his legislative instincts. To illustrate his fears he related a tale supposedly told by a Hindustani prince to an overeager Muslim priest:[84] The republic of the Castors had been troubled by some robberies of grain warehouses and by several murders. The senate was about to take practical action—open some public depots, improve the main roads, enlarge the police force—when an inspired senator persuaded the members to promulgate instead the doctrine of Michapour, an all-wise being who rewarded good and punished evil. After a period of tranquility, a dispute arose over who first gave Michapour the grains of sand to create the earth; soon, instead of a few robberies and murders, half the nation perished in religious civil war.

The moral of the fable was obvious: religion, far from providing a cure for social violence, would always disintegrate under the pressure of the people's superstitious mind. The creation of any religious cult only invited further trouble.

Not impressed by the legislative possibilities of purely religious sanctions, Helvétius still explored the utility of substitute institutions to satisfy the human impulse to worship and to encourage noble and useful sentiments. In *De l'homme*, therefore, he sketched an outline of a new kind of religion, modeled on what he found best in pagan society.[85] He proposed a religion of public utility with no beliefs or dogmas. The basic principles of the religion would be the sanctity of

82. *De l'homme, Oeuvres complètes*, 3:101, note 32.
83. Ibid., 4:79.
84. For the following account, see *De l'esprit*, in *Oeuvres complètes*, 1:321.
85. For the following account, see *De l'homme*, in *Oeuvres complètes*, 3:70–86.

property, life, and liberty. Famous legislators and benefactors of humanity (such as Lycurgus, Solon, and Sydney) would comprise the pantheon of saints. The distinction between magistrate and priest would disappear, as it had in Rome. Public ceremonies would honor the classical virtues Humanity, Pride, and Fame. In sum, Helvétius envisaged a "divinization of the public good"; in a moment of enthusiasm he exclaimed,

> Let the voice of heaven hereafter be that of the public good; and let the oracles of the gods confirm all laws advantageous to the people.[86]

Through a religion of the public good Helvétius hoped to exploit what he found valuable in the antique pagan deities, stripping the Roman religion of its deception and double truth and bringing its spirit into the open. The magistrate would prevent any move to turn the cult of fame or the public good into dogmatic belief. Helvétius recognized that the public might insist that temples be raised to the various virtues of the Eternal One (the public good), but he charged his magistrates with the responsibility of preventing any further disintegration toward superstition. Eventually, he hoped, the religion of the public good might make equal the potential of all men for healthy moeurs.[87] The new religion might then become not an agent of social control but a means toward one kind of equality.

Helvétius thus moved from atheism toward the political sociology of the religious instinct. His religion of the public good foreshadowed the many nineteenth-century attempts to satisfy a supposed religious function in society with religions of humanity, glory, the people, and the like. Condorcet worked from the same premises toward a different kind of modernity: absolute separation of the religious from the secular power. In an essay suggested by the prize question of the 1780 Berlin Academy[88] he rejected the idea of "useful prejudice" and repeated the familiar conviction of the atheists—that the roots of

---

86. Ibid., p. 79.
87. Ibid., pp. 85–86.
88. "Dissertation philosophique et politique, ou Réflexions sur cette question: s'il est utile aux hommes d'êtres trompés?" in *Oeuvres complètes*, 5:343–89. Written at the time of the contest, it was not submitted. For the background to the contest, see the introduction by Werner Krauss to his edition of the French entries to the contest: *Est-il utile de tromper le peuple? Concours de la classe de philosophie speculative de l'Académie des Sciences et des Belles-Lettres de Berlin pour l'année 1780* (Berlin, 1966), pp. 1–6.

religion will continuously yield dangerous fruit. Even under the watch of the most clever magistrates, he maintained, social religion corrupts all parts of society. The mixture of truth and errors can never be stable. "Either the servile class will become enlightened," he wrote,

> or the ruling class will become stupid with it, or troubles will arise bringing more harm to the oppressors than the servitude of the other class could be useful, or finally both classes might become equally prey to a few tyrants.[89]

Even a purified religion could not serve the purposes of social peace. Eventually, Condorcet thought, the people would discover the errors and discard both truth and error indiscriminately; or, as in Holbach's history, the powerful would not resist the temptation to institute even more vicious errors.[90] No double truth could suit the legislative needs of society as Condorcet foresaw them.

Like Holbach, Diderot, and Helvétius, Condorcet placed his trust in "natural motives." He required of the legislator only "enlightenment and good laws."[91] With purposeful naivete he deemed the truths of morality too simple and self-evident to require any special presentation to the people; bad laws alone had brought the people to their immoral condition.[92] Just laws, he implied, would win the people back to morality.

Condorcet admired Voltaire and could not leave Voltaire's judgments unnoted. He made, however, only one concession to Voltaire: he advised leaders not to attack the belief in a remunerative and vengeful god in nations where morality had always been based on such belief, until that belief had collapsed and a "healthier" moral education established in its place.[93] With this exception, Condorcet considered Voltaire's advocacy of a deceptive social religion a regrettable sacrifice of philosophic principle and legislative wisdom to the pressure of the powerful. In a footnote to the Kehl edition of

89. *Oeuvres complètes*, 5:351.
90. Ibid., p. 353.
91. Ibid., p. 358.
92. Ibid., pp. 360–62.
93. Ibid., p. 382. See also *Oeuvres complètes*, 4:536, a note on Voltaire in which Condorcet advised that the weaning of the people from superstitious belief be accomplished gradually. But regarding the king who stands still and preserves such beliefs, he warned that such a ruler preserves the only sure way to guarantee his eventual demise.

Voltaire's works, Condorcet commented on Voltaire's views with remarkable condescension:

> Notice . . . with what care M. de Voltaire seizes every opportunity to announce to men a god who avenges crimes; and learn to recognize the good faith of those libellers who accused him of destroying the foundations of morality, and made him believe it by repeating it so much.[94]

Condorcet could speak so confidently in opposition to the leader of the Enlightenment because he knew that a wide segment of the advanced thinkers of that movement had, by the 1770s, come to perceive religion as a tool suitable for exploitation, not for enlightened leadership.[95]

94. *Oeuvres complètes*, 4:358.

95. Of the thirty-three entries deemed legitimate for the contest of the Berlin Academy, twenty upheld the negative, and many of the remaining thirteen severely qualified their support of deception; see Krauss, *Est-il utile de tromper le peuple?*, p. 5.

# 6 Instruction

The filtering of light, however feeble, from the upper order of leaders to the lower orders of followers represented for most philosophes the first and best hope of the cause of enlightenment. The editors of the *Encyclopédie* considered this process a worthy goal for their enterprise. Diderot acknowledged in his article "Encyclopédie" that much philosophical and scientific thought would remain forever beyond the reach of common men. Yet he hoped that some advanced knowledge would descend little by little to the lowest orders.[1] Much of the *Encyclopédie* was devoted to the useful arts in the expectation that entrepreneurs and master artisans could understand the most highly developed techniques and transfer this knowledge, if only by rote training, to the worker and peasant. At times there seemed cause for optimism. D'Alembert offered as evidence his view that almanacs which predicted the future had lost their credibility among the lowest orders.[2] And the author of "Multitude" (probably Diderot) insisted that in the long run the judgment of the multitude is right in all matters—"it is an echo which repeats the judgment of a small number of men, who form in advance that of posterity."[3] The hopes of enlightenment rested in the propensity of the people to follow.

Not all were so confident. Voltaire believed that the prospect of enlightening the people almost always seemed hopeless at best and dangerous at worst. In describing the workings of the double truth among the Brahmins of India, he defended their failure to introduce natural religion among the people "who do not want to be educated and who do not deserve it."

> There would even be some risk in wanting to enlighten the people: the ignorant priests would rise up; the women, attached

1. *Encyclopédie*, 5:637.
2. "Almanach," *Encyclopédie*, 1:290.
3. *Encyclopédie*, 10:860. The article is unsigned, but compare the language to that of a letter written by Diderot: "In the long run, my friend, the people is but the echo of a few men of taste; and posterity but the echo of the present rectified by experience." To Falconet, 15 February 1766, *Correspondance* (384).

to their pagodas, their little superstitions, would decry the impiety. Whoever wants to teach reason to his fellowmen is persecuted unless he is the strongest, but usually the strongest redoubles the chains of ignorance instead of breaking them.[4]

Voltaire agreed with the Brahmins that prudence dictated that the philosopher should leave well enough alone and find his audience outside of the people.

Voltaire's correspondence is rife with the expressed distinction between peuple and honnêtes gens. Writing in 1765 to the count and countess d'Argental, he mocked contending church factions, while declaring that reason was penetrating society in spite of them. Soon, he predicted, "they will have empire only over the canaille." "To my mind," he continued,

> the greatest service one can render the human race is to separate forever the stupid people from honnêtes gens; it seems to me that things are well advanced. One should not be able to bear the absurd insolence of those who tell you, "I want you to think like your tailor and your washerwoman."[5]

Voltaire spoke within a wide tradition which associated the philosophe with the gentleman. He found the separation of gentleman from people to his liking and reiterated it often, expecting—with justice—that his readers would readily accept his superficial categories.

Only one philosophe, Etienne Noël Damilaville, pressed Voltaire to clarify and moderate his stance. Voltaire had written to Damilaville much as he wrote to royalty and nobility, hailing the new conquests of enlightenment among the wealthier classes while scorning the canaille. "We are," he told Damilaville, "a body of brave knights, defenders of the truth, who admit among us only well-bred people."[6] But unlike Voltaire's other correspondents, Damilaville raised objections. Damilaville had defended the atheists' cause in discussing the matter of social religion at Ferney, and Voltaire's uncharacteristically defensive response indicates that Damilaville had found his

4. *Essai sur les moeurs*, 1:243–44; see also 2:801.
5. 27 April 1765, *Correspondence* (11722); see as well nos. 11454, 13317, 14239, 14464, 15216, among others.
6. To Damilaville, 19 November 1765, *Correspondence* (12123).

abandonment of the people no more palatable. "I believe we do not understand each other on the matter of the people whom you believe worthy of being educated," Voltaire responded.

> I understand by "people" the populace which has only its hands to live by. I doubt that this order of citizens will ever have the time or capacity to educate itself; they would die of hunger before becoming philosophes. It seems to me essential that there be ignorant wretches. If you were developing an estate like me, and if you had some plows, you would indeed be of my mind. It is not the day laborer who must be educated, it is the good bourgeois, it is the city dweller; this enterprise is formidable and great enough.

The people, he insisted, should hear virtue preached but need not learn to think and dispute about religion. "All is lost when the populace gets involved in reasoning," he concluded, meaning theological reason.[7] Unable to conceive of a form of education which would avoid the pitfalls of superstition or allow the people sufficient time to pursue economic tasks, Voltaire generally distrusted any institutional attempt to bring literacy or "reason" to the people.

Perhaps sensing the inadequacy of even this response to Damilaville, Voltaire later outlined an alternate strategy to institutionalized instruction. Taking note of the many enlightened bourgeois he had met on a recent trip to Montpellier, he speculated, "The low people will certainly be worth much more when the principal citizens cultivate wisdom and virtue; they will be contained by example, which is the most beautiful and greatest of virtues." Pilgrimages and ceremonies can never create a wise man, he explained, but the example of the great can modify the ignorance of the villager. As an example he offered the miraculous liquefaction of the blood of Saint Januarius. Were the lords of Naples to pay more attention to God than to the saint, he thought, the people would soon lose its enthusiasm for supposed miracles. But, he warned, whoever merely announced the truth outright would be stoned.[8] Voltaire thus ended even this optimistic vision on a familiar note of caution: too much, too soon would be dangerous. Still, expanded contacts with Gene-

7. To Damilaville, 1 April 1766, *Correspondence* (12358).
8. To Damilaville, 13 April 1766, *Correspondence* (12376).

van artisans further heightened his optimism. Of Geneva he wrote in 1768:

> The people is most stupid, but light penetrates even its ranks. You may be sure, for example, that there are not twenty persons in Geneva who do not despise Calvin as much as the Pope, and that there are philosophes even in the shops of Paris.[9]

The example of honnêtes gens, reading and understanding the new philosophy, might spread light to the lower classes; Voltaire, however, saw little need or hope to give that dissemination an institutional form. He measured popular enlightenment solely in terms of the tempering of superstition, an end best accomplished by the example of reasonable men, not book-learning.

Voltaire feared attempts to institutionalize this process in the form of public instruction for the people. He envisaged only more priests and fewer workers emerging from a nation of instructed peasants. But in spite of his fears he established a school on his estates as had several other seigneurs in his region. He confessed doubts about his own wisdom to the reading public of France:

> I think it proper that some children learn to read, write, and calculate, but that most, especially the children of laborers, know only how to cultivate, because you need only one pen for every two or three hundred arms.[10]

Ruthless economic calculation notwithstanding, Voltaire educated his peasants. Such inconsistency on his part should not pass unnoted. For all his usual strength of will and disdain for ordinary men, Voltaire could not resist the example of his age and the logic of enlightenment. Both demanded formal instruction for the people.

Popular instruction was a luxury, like philosophes, which the relative prosperity and stability of the eighteenth century could afford. By 1780 monarchs in most European nations had issued decrees that looked forward to some form of universal instruction. The Roman Catholic church accelerated its efforts, begun after Trent, to spread village schools across the countryside of all nations still within its fold. These efforts were matched by the less centralized efforts of Pietists

9. To Jean François Dufour, 20 December 1768, *Correspondence* (14412).
10. *Questions sur l'Encyclopédie*, "Fertilisation," *Oeuvres complètes*, 19:111.

in Germany, humanitarians and evangelicals in England, economic societies in Spain, and seigneurs like Voltaire in France. The concern for reaching the people through schooling had multiple roots. For religious leaders the logic remained the same: to win the minds of the masses. For humanitarians, such as the leaders of the charity school movement in England, instruction might provide economic skills and moral cultivation. For monarchists, the expulsion of the Jesuits in France, Spain, and Austria during the 1760s appeared to open new doors to kings who saw in public instruction a means of political consolidation.

For the philosophes the concern was understandable, though the motives varied. As religion faded as a legitimate social sanction within the thinking of the Enlightenment, instruction took its place as its logical counterpart in the secular world. The new epistemology, stressing the powers of environment and education, naturally enhanced the expectation that instruction could be a means of disseminating lumières to the lowest levels of society. Most philosophes, however, thought that public instruction, within specified limits, offered primarily an economic opportunity to the people and the nation. It is not accidental that within enlightened circles the first agitators for widespread public instruction were the Physiocrats. Their advocacy of free market in grain, however logical from the point of view of theory, defied traditional economic wisdom; the instinct of villagers and townsmen was to keep grain close-by and not to allow it to flow freely. Attempts to institute the free market in grains in France in the 1760s brought widespread, sporadic violence. The Physiocrats then looked to public instruction as a way to reach the people and turn its mind to their way of thinking. Similarly, advocates of public instruction in other nations found economic arguments most compelling, either in the form of curricula geared to work (the "working schools" of England, the "schools of popular industry" in Madrid), or in the more general argument that minimally-educated laborers are more open to new techniques and ideas.[11] Economic arguments often took priority also because many shared the economic fears of Voltaire. Proponents of public instruction tried to turn the tables on their opponents in good debating form, arguing

11. See Andreas Flitner on state-sponsored public instruction in Germany in the eighteenth century: "Education for the state was in its first form education for the political economy of the state." *Die Politische Erziehung in Deutschland* (Tübingen, 1957), p. 17.

that popular instruction would benefit production, not depopulate farms and workshops. For a variety of reasons, both philosophes and the community at large had reached a consensus that some form of public instruction was necessary in an enlightened age. When the academy of Châlons-sur-Marne posed in 1779 its essay question— "what would be the best way to educate the people?"—it allowed no negative answers.[12] Such would hardly have been the case a century before.

During the late 1760s and 1770s, therefore, many members of the philosophic circle advanced schemes for popular enlightenment which reached beyond imitation of the higher orders. The Physiocratic camp initiated this movement. Secular public instruction, supervised by the state and including the basic skills of reading, writing, and arithmetic as well as the elements of morality, became a consistent demand in Physiocratic plans.[13] As early as 1768 Abbé Nicolas Baudeau insisted that "the clearest, most obligatory, most universal *instruction* is the first duty of all government."[14] In 1770 and 1772 Mirabeau hailed the virtues of public instruction in long letters to Karl Friedrich, margrave of Baden.[15] And in 1775 Mercier de la Rivière included a scheme for popular instruction in *De l'instruction publique*, addressed to the king of Sweden.

Several French philosophes quickly followed the lead of the Physiocratic party. In collaboration with Dupont de Nemours, Turgot drew up in 1775 a "Mémoire sur les municipalités" which included provision for the establishment of a council on national education to insure the rudiments of education for all.[16] Condorcet propagandized Turgot's plans, and during the revolutionary years he became a

12. As cited in Harvey Chisick, "Attitudes toward the Education of the *Peuple* in the French Enlightenment: 1762–1789," (Ph.D. diss. Johns Hopkins University, 1974), p. 51. Chisick's thesis provides a valuable, detailed analysis of the numerous contemporary proposals for educating the people. I am indebted to him for providing me with an advance copy.

13. The development of the Physiocratic doctrine of "instruction" is beyond the scope of this essay and still needs a full treatment. For a summary of Physiocratic views, see Georges Weulersse, *La Physiocratie à la fin du règne de Louis XV (1770–1774)*, (Paris, 1959), pp. 94–96, and *La Physiocratie sous les ministères de Turgot et de Necker (1774–1781)*, (Paris, 1950), pp. 113–17.

14. *Avis au peuple sur son premier besoin* (Paris, 1768), p. 123.

15. See especially letters no. 6, 31 March 1770, and no. 29, 20 August 1772, from the Marquis de Mirabeau to Karl Friedrich, margrave of Baden, in Karl Knies, ed., *Brieflicher Verkehr mit Mirabeau und Dupont* (Heidelberg, 1892), vol. 1.

16. See his "Mémoire" in *Oeuvres de Turgot*, 4:578, 620–21.

principal advocate and theoretician of popular education.[17] Diderot's plans for Russia were drawn up after his courtship of Physiocracy but still echoed that movement's concern with universal instruction.[18] Holbach alone seems to have escaped the direct influence of Physiocracy, but his personal vision of a just and peaceable society included provision for universal instruction.[19] Within the space of a decade, therefore, the inner circle of the Enlightenment adopted some form of popular education as a worthy goal for the legislator.

These concerns radiated to other reaches of the Enlightenment. The 1770s saw efforts by Frederick II (despite grave doubts), Maria Theresa, Karl Friedrich of Baden, Maximilian III Joseph, and other central European monarchs to require instruction for their lowliest subjects. French agronomists and their Spanish, Italian, and German counterparts usually required a minimal literacy on the part of all peasants and looked for formal institutional ways to spread new agricultural learning. The economic societies of Spain made popular instruction, in terms of both literacy and working techniques, a central part of their program. Once demands for public instruction had reached both the land of the Basques and the regions of the papal states, no one could doubt that instruction for the people had become a central aim of the mature Enlightenment.[20]

Over much of the continent, however, these reformers did not survey a clear field. The principal advocates of popular instruction during the previous two centuries had been priests, not philosophers. The philosophes had good reason to regard the people as the particular domain of the Catholic church. Since the sixteenth-century Council of Trent, church leadership had placed a high priority on

17. See "Réflexions sur le commerce des blés" (1776), *Oeuvres complètes*, 11:193–94; "Lettre d'un laboureur de Picardie à M. N." (1775), *Oeuvres complètes*, 11:8–9; *Vie de Turgot* (1786), *Oeuvres complètes*, 5:145–46; and a note on Voltaire in *Oeuvres complètes*, 4:253.

18. See especially his "Essai sur les études en Russie," *Oeuvres complètes*, 3:416–18; "Plan d'une Université," ibid., p. 520; "Entretiens," *Oeuvres politiques*, p. 324; "Observations," ibid., p. 387; and *Mémoires*, pp. 129–30, 137.

19. See especially *La Politique naturelle*, 2:267–69, and *Ethocratie*, pp. 100–05, 184, 197.

20. The veritable educational offensive of the eighteenth century throughout Europe requires but lacks a full-fledged study. On the various schemes see Bourde, *Agronomie et agronomes*, 2:986–87, 1056–59; Liebel, *Enlightened Bureaucracy*, pp. 20, 73–75, 90–92; Frederick Hertz, *The Development of the German Public Mind: The Age of Enlightenment* (London, 1962), pp. 296–99, 339–40; Flitner, *Politische Erziehung*, pp. 15–30; Gagliardo, *Pariah to Patriot*, chapter 4; Shafer, *The Economic Societies*, pp. 37–38, 85–89, 95; Venturi, *Italy and the Enlightenment*, pp. 252–54; M. G. Jones, *The Charity School Movement in the Eighteenth Century* (Cambridge, 1937), passim.

reaching the people through schooling.[21] The French monarchy had given royal sanction to mandatory attendance of the so-called *petites écoles* of the church in edicts of 1698 and 1724, and activist bishops were still encouraging the spread of the "little schools" late into the eighteenth century.[22] The actual effectiveness of this parish education varied widely, according to patterns of village settlement, proximity to cities, initiative of diocesan leadership, and vagaries of village custom. The schoolmaster's monthly fees made even rudimentary education inaccessible to many of the poor and, in hard times, a luxury for most villagers.[23] Though concerned with teaching secular skills, the church and the monarchy placed priority less on the transfer of skills than on the inculcation of belief. The leadership of the church had christianized the countryside by 1750 only through extraordinary effort. The temptation to leave the people to the priests represented as much a bow to institutional reality as to philosophical disdain.

In formulating their legislation, many new advocates of public instruction inevitably, therefore, used the church as a model. Far from ignoring the educational success of the priests, the reformers sought to capitalize on clerical efforts. Their plans ranged over a broad spectrum, from Physiocrats who could live comfortably with the church, to Holbach who decidedly could not, but no one could avoid the reality of the petites écoles of the churches. Mirabeau explicitly relied on their pattern of religious instruction. Rebuking those who despaired of ever educating the lower orders, he praised the efforts of religion which "undertook the establishment of this unity of knowledge and, in this way, truly civilized people." Economic knowledge, he argued, should even have an advantage over religious instruction, since it relied on the concrete sanctions of worldly gain

21. On the nature and importance of the "little schools" during the two centuries after the Council of Trent, see Maurice Gontard, *L'enseignement primaire en France de la Révolution à la Loi Guizot (1789–1833)*, (Paris, 1959), part 1. For an excellent study of one region's elementary education in the eighteenth century, see Dominique Julia, "L'enseignement primaire dans le diocèse de Reims à la fin de l'Ancien Régime," *Annales historiques de la révolution française* 200 (April–June 1970): 233–86.

22. See Julia, "Enseignement"; M. Laget, "Petites écoles en Languedoc au xviiie siècle," *Annales* 26, no. 6 (Nov.–Dec. 1971): 1398–1418; and René Tavenaux, "Les écoles de campagne en Lorraine au xviiie siècle; à-propos d'une étude récente," *Annales de l'Est* 2 (1970):159–71.

23. Fees varied according to the skill taught—lowest for reading, more for writing, most for arithmetic.

and loss. "Though religion is entirely spiritual," he told Karl Friedrich, "zeal and wise policies have made its teachings common to all classes of men; so also must it be with the religion of daily bread." To this end he advocated composition of "a formula for public instruction" which a pastor could teach with the religious catechism.[24] For many agricultural reformers the existing church structure seemed an ideal way to channel economic knowledge. No overhaul of existing systems seemed necessary, only recruiting the parish priest to the cause of reform.[25]

Other Physiocratic plans similarly followed the pattern of religious institutions. In his *Première introduction à la philosophie économique*, Abbé Baudeau urged the formation of an "order of instruction"—parallel to the French first estate—which would include public instructors, priests, and philosophers. Although he saw the need for additional lay instructors to spread basic secular skills, nothing in his plans discounted the possibility of priests continuing to assume the dual role of religious and secular educators.[26] The plan of Turgot and Dupont de Nemours was more specific. Their proposed council on national instruction would have taken charge of all educational institutions, including the little schools, and taught social morality using the uniformity of religious instruction as its model. Their schools would also have continued the traditional function of teaching elementary skills.[27]

Those philosophes who could not abide the church as principal instructor of the people sought to take over the structure of church institutions. Consistent if not realistic, Holbach advised the reigning powers of France to seize the educational institutions of the church outright; the state might then substitute secular moral teachings and lay "curés" to provide the people's education.[28] Condorcet predictably echoed Turgot's calls for a nationally supervised public instruction, but, less circumspect than his idol, he also proposed seizure of all church lands not already devoted to instruction. He wished to redirect these possessions toward the support of curés who would

24. Knies, *Brieflicher Verkehr*, pp. 24–25.
25. See Bourde, *Agronomie et agronomes*, 2:1056–57.
26. *Première introduction à la philosophie économique, ou Analyse des états policés* (Paris, 1771), repr. and ed. A. Dubois (Paris, 1910), pp. 17–20.
27. *Oeuvres de Turgot*, 4:578–80.
28. *La Politique naturelle*, 2:267–69, and *Ethocratie*, pp. 100–04, 194.

provide the people with rudimentary secular instruction. This redistribution would, he thought, make possible universal male public instruction along the lines Turgot had envisaged.[29]

Among the Parisian atheists, Diderot proved most moderate and accommodating in his educational program. Though he regarded Russia as a young nation in which the legislator could begin on a proper footing,[30] he still had to deal with the official piety of Catherine. He proposed, therefore, only a modified version of French public education for Russia (and implicitly for France as well). His plans called for a network of schools that would serve the villages and towns, providing elementary education and moral instruction from a combined religious, moral, and political catechism. But, unlike the Physiocratic plans, Diderot's system would provide absolute supervision by secular authority of the content of this instruction. To avoid the economic difficulties which forced many parents to keep their children away from the French primary schools, Diderot—more sensitive than most to the people's needs—insisted that the schools must also provide bread for the people's children. The law could then require all to attend.[31]

One need not be atheist or anticlerical to propose taking the task of education away from the clergy. The issue was taken up by two influential Badenese reformers, both partisans of public instruction and sympathetic to the Enlightenment. The clergyman and administrator Nicolaus Sander used his power in church and state to improve the intellectual level of his clergy, to provide each village within his region of Hochberg with a school, and to enforce mandatory schooling. Sander's efforts were typical of the large-scale clerical and evangelical educational efforts of the eighteenth century. But Johann Schlosser, when he assumed supervision of Hochberg district in 1774, sought to break clerical control of education, with its inevitable emphasis on belief and the skills of literacy. While not denying the need for some literacy and some belief, Schlosser saw a much greater need for practical, vocational education to open economic advantages to the poor of his district. Secular authority must, he thought, assume principal control of the educational process; the

29. *Vie de Turgot, Oeuvres complètes*, 5:145–46.
30. Diderot, *Oeuvres politiques*, p. 224.
31. See note 18 to this chapter.

church, for all its educational zeal, represented an obstacle to the success of public instruction. Still, he proposed control and modification, not elimination, of the clerical village school.[32]

The enlightened circle's plans for public instruction resembled the realities of clerical education in more ways than that of institutional structure, imitating religious instruction in style and substance as well. In the new schools, learning was still to be catechetical. The eighteenth century produced a flurry of activity in the composition of catechisms and primers accessible to the barely literate among the people. The popular *almanachs* of Paris composed for popular consumption gradually changed their orientation from astrology and prophecy to practical advice for the farmer and worker. Madame Villers de Billy's "Historical, religious, and moral instructions for the benefit of laborers and other inhabitants of the countryside" (1746) set the tone for many similar catechisms for rural instruction in France, combining helpful agricultural hints with stern lessons on piety and obedience. These catechisms in turn had their imitators in Germany and Italy. The charity schools of England nurtured a host of primers and catechisms less concerned with economic skills and even more intent on the socialization of the people.[33]

The philosophes were not content to leave the catechizing to clerics and agronomists. On numerous occasions the proponents of enlightened public instruction called for the formulation of moral catechisms to provide the heart of their popular education. Mirabeau proposed an eight-point formula, deduced from the central tenet of the immutability of private property, to be added to the religious instruction in the lands of the margrave of Baden.[34] Mirabeau would have merely placed his own economic creed beside the existing religious catechism, but several philosophes looked forward to an entirely new catechism which would integrate all moral principles into a system comprehensible to the people. Turgot praised the efforts of the duke of Saxe-Gotha who had sponsored the composition of a book of elementary ethics for his peasants. Since that time, Turgot argued, the duke's peasants had become more reasonable than those of any other

32. Liebel, *Enlightened Bureaucracy*, pp. 91–92.
33. Bourde, *Agronomie et agronomes*, 2:985–87, 1058–59; Geneviève Bollème, *Les almanachs populaires au XVIIᵉ et au XVIIIᵉ siècles* (Paris, 1969); Flitner, *Politische Erziehung*, pp. 26–28; Venturi, *Italy and the Enlightenment*, p. 253; Jones, *Charity School Movement*, chapter 3.
34. Knies, *Brieflicher Verkehr*, pp. 25–26.

region.[35] Two years later, in his scheme for national education, Turgot signaled the need for a series of classic works which would spell out the duties of the citizen in a style accessible to all members of the nation.[36] At about the same time, Mercier de la Rivière foresaw the possibility of "a civil and political catechism" which might "clearly and simply set forth natural principles, the fundamental principles of social order and universal morality."[37] In such a way, he thought, all men might be integrated into a single moral framework.

Such visions of a simple, universal moral catechism were not confined to the Physiocratic camp, inclined as it was to exaggerate the pristine clarity of the "natural order" of society. With some enthusiasm Diderot sponsored Jacques Barbeu-Dubourg's little catechism as an ideal text for Catherine's schools; it provided a god (as Catherine insisted) while deriving morality from basic human needs and possibilities (as Diderot preferred).[38] Holbach insisted even more strongly than Diderot on the possibility of, and need for, such a moral catechism, but he saw no need for any concession to religious piety. He often urged the composition of a purely secular moral catechism for all men as a project worthy of the philosophers of his day.[39] Indeed, he eventually took the task upon himself and dashed off his *Eléments de la morale universelle ou Catéchisme de la nature*, published posthumously in 1790. He designed this moral primer—a series of questions and answers—so that morality might "be placed at the doorstep of the simplest men and even of children."[40] Johann Schlosser similarly took the burden upon himself to accommodate truth to the level of the popular mind. His *Catechism of Moral Teaching for the Peasantry* (1771), through the voice of a wise teacher, introduced the "evident" laws of society, property, and economics to the lowest orders. Five years later, in *Catechism of the Christian Religion for the Peasantry*, he combined a simple deism with a mystical Lutheranism

35. Turgot to Dupont, 10 December 1773, *Oeuvres de Turgot*, 3:631. He compared these efforts with those of the Duke of Deux-Ponts who harbored clandestine, atheist presses in his domains.

36. *Oeuvres de Turgot*, 4:579.

37. *De l'instruction publique* (1775), pp. 110–11. Abbé Baudeau saw the same need in *Première introduction à la philosophie économique*, p. 19.

38. See chapter 5 above.

39. *La Morale universelle*, 1:191, and 3:91, and *Ethocratie*, pp. 191–92.

40. "Avertissement" to the work; we cannot be absolutely sure that the words were Holbach's, though they were certainly in his spirit and intention.

in the hope of reaching the emotions of the people. His aims were decidedly more pious than Holbach's but his style quite similar, and his works, unlike Holbach's, enjoyed great popularity in Lutheran Germany.[41]

By 1780, therefore, many leaders of the Enlightenment had fully overcome the temptations of complete separation from the people, much as they had rejected the temptations of deception. The same Enlightenment which in earlier times and in other voices had chosen to speak only to the literate few, now found itself seeking means to speak in the language of the people. This change in goals necessarily entailed a slight increase in the philosophes' estimation of popular capacities. The new advocates of public instruction were forced to attribute to all men some modest ability to comprehend and accept abstract truths. No specific, favorable experiences lay behind this change. Rather, as the legislative nerve of the leading philosophes grew, they perceived the need to reach all men. In turn, they insisted upon the capabilities of the people in order to quiet the fears of men like Voltaire and, one might suspect, to cover their own doubts. In effect, the implications of their expanding program gave them convenient reason to reevaluate the popular mind. As early as his *Essai sur les Préjugés* (1769), Holbach felt compelled to defend the popular mind against the proponents of "useful prejudice." He compared the moral capability of the common man to the intricate actions of the artisan. "Experience and habit," he wrote,

> succeed in facilitating the most complex operations for the common man, the basest artisan. Can we doubt that habit and experience could, in the same way, facilitate the very simple knowledge of the duties of morality and the precepts of reason on which his happiness clearly rests?[42]

The artisan was neither scientist nor inventor, but he performed operations based on the finest accomplishments of science and invention. The common man was not a philosopher, but he could, through habit and indoctrination, perform those actions prescribed by a reasonable philosophy.

Condorcet later neatly developed the logic of this position. "The truths necessary to most men," he wrote,

41. Liebel, *Enlightened Bureaucracy*, pp. 73–75; Flitner, *Politische Erziehung*, p. 28.
42. *Essai sur les Préjugés*, pp. 49–50.

are not complicated in themselves. If they seem so, it is because they present themselves to philosophers only with the host of difficulties which metaphysics has introduced. Philosophers are correct in exploring these subjects; but the people can recognize the truth without examining it.

To Condorcet the basic precepts of sociability seemed virtually self-evident: the evil of hurting one's neighbor; the necessity of obeying the laws; the inviolability of property. "These truths are simple; they are sufficient to rule the conduct of the people, whose actions are no more complicated than its ideas."[43]

Diderot defended the same position but from a very different perspective. While Condorcet sought to increase the Enlightenment's estimate of popular moral capacities, Diderot sought to recall a fellow philosophe, Helvétius, from an exaggerated estimate of those same capacities. Helvétius had argued in parts of *De l'homme* that education could do virtually anything in forming the minds of men. In commenting on Helvétius's work, Diderot appended a caveat to this optimism, warning that the conclusions of genius can be taught to the multitude but the demonstrations of genius remain accessible only to the few.[44] Behind Diderot's caution, however, rested the same estimate as that of Condorcet—the multitude could in its own limited way perceive truth and act on it. So, too, d'Alembert defended popular capacities, in a decidedly backhanded way, against the thorough cynicism of Frederick II of Prussia. The people, he insisted, could be weaned from superstition. Reduce Christianity to its primitive moral principles and then the people might become enlightened in its limited way. "After you have once inculcated these truths firmly in the popular mind," he wrote,

> it should not be, I believe, too difficult to make them forget the dogmas with which you coddled them and which they had seized upon for lack of anything better. No doubt the people is a stupid animal which allows itself to be led into darkness when you don't show it anything better; but if this truth is simple, and especially goes right to its heart like the religion I propose to preach to it, it seems inevitable to me that it will jump at the

43. *Oeuvres complètes*, 5:359.
44. "Réfutation suivie de l'ouvrage intitulé l'Homme," *Oeuvres complètes*, 2:352–53.

chance and will want nothing else. Unfortunately, we are far
from this felicitous revolution in attitudes.[45]

Diderot, Condorcet, and those others who implicitly shared their
views proposed, in effect, a new version of the double truth, or,
rather, a single truth perceived in two ways. The enlightened few
would understand the moral and social order, obey the mandates of
sociability out of enlightened self-interest, and even allow themselves
the luxury of debating issues of great moral complexity. The many
could learn the rules of social order as understood by philosophers
and perhaps even instinctively see their rightness; but they could not
(and need not) understand the intellectual bases of morality. Common usage recognized this distinction. Schooling received at the
*collèges*, (the secondary level) and from tutors was often called "education"; for the people, the philosophes usually spoke of "instruction,"
a term often reserved for religious indoctrination. The educational
reformers of the Enlightenment—Locke, Rousseau, Condillac, La
Chalotais, and others—sought to create active, critical intelligence
among those with the leisure to cultivate their reason. They wanted,
in effect, to nurture more philosophes. Their program took logical
and temporal priority in the unfolding of the Enlightenment. The
advocates of reformed popular instruction sought only the means to
bring the simplest conclusions of philosophy to the level of the people.
The posited success of their instruction relied not on the critical
capabilities of the few but on the imitative faculties of the many.

The aim of the new catechisms differed little from their clerical
models: to provide the people a set moral and social framework in
which to function. Whereas religious catechisms had tried to orient
the people's actions to heavenly ends, the new catechisms would
emphasize the structure of a secular society and the place of the
people in that structure. For the Physiocrats the immediate goal was
concrete and impelling; they must indoctrinate the people to accept
their new economics. Not surprisingly, therefore, the Physiocrats
first perceived the need for reformers to speak to the people in
language which would soothe its fears. To this end they urged
monarchs to use all possible means, from common pamphlets to
universal instruction, to spread the new doctrines. From this limited

45. Frederick II, *Oeuvres* (Berlin, 1854), 24:517.

aim, the hopes of the proponents of instruction rapidly expanded toward integrating the man of the people into the nation as some form of "citizen." In proposing his council on national instruction, Turgot expressed astonishment that while human wisdom had found means to train grammarians, geometers, doctors, and painters, it had failed to establish ways to form citizens.[46] La Rivière proposed to the king of Sweden that his entire government become "a public school where all citizens might learn to flee vices, detest crimes, and cherish and practice virtues."[47] Formal instruction in the schools would provide only part of a systematic effort to make government a means of educating the populace into a system of sociability and citizenship.[48] Diderot and Holbach similarly sought, with their catechisms, to integrate the whole range of civil, political, and moral duty, and give the man of the people a sense of his place in the general order of things.

As much as these philosophes wanted to induct the common man into a unified moral universe, their plans in no way ignored existing social differences. They wanted to reconcile the man of the people to his estate rather than create the critical intelligence which might give him the desire and means to escape it. Their instruction would, they hoped, offer the skills and moral perspective by which the people might perform its designated social functions more peaceably and productively. Reading, writing, and arithmetic would provide an adequate and necessary background for all occupations. Beyond that point, instruction would emphasize performance of one's function. "As there are schools to teach the truths of religion," Dumarsais wrote in the *Encyclopédie*, "there should also be schools where the people would be shown the exercises, practices, duties, and virtues of its estate, so that it would act more knowledgeably."[49] The various plans for public instruction fulfilled this basic design.

Holbach is typical, emphasizing, in the moral philosophy that he sought to catechize, the series of duties particular to each estate and social function. To the poor he preached the duties of obedience and

46. *Oeuvres de Turgot*, 4:579.
47. *De l'instruction publique*, p. 14.
48. Ibid., p. 20.
49. "Education," *Encyclopédie*, 5:397. See also "Législateur," *Encyclopédie*, 9:360, for a similar view.

labor; to the rich, those of *bienfaisance* and economic leadership.[50] He spoke of the child as already belonging to an estate; a student was already an "owner" or an "artisan" (or destined to be such) even as he was being schooled. Holbach's system stipulated that each pupil would compete for prominence within his destined world. Those marked by birth and upbringing for the magistracy, the army, or letters would seek status within their professions. The children of the people, on the other hand, would be encouraged to excellence by small prizes.[51] Pupils would not, therefore, choose their roles on a basis of their blossoming abilities; they would instead assume roles designated from childhood and largely determined by birth. The child would be educated toward his role.[52]

Not all of the plans were as explicit as Holbach's in seeking to educate and reconcile the people to its lot. But all agreed on one matter: in almost all cases the people's education would terminate at the level of the little schools. Though the philosophes wanted public service open to competition, their educational schemes left very limited access for the people's children to the secondary education that might make them viable competitors. Turgot proposed a secondary education "more developed according to the functions which the students' rank puts them in a position to fill in society,"[53] thereby recognizing rank as a precondition for training to public service. Others were more circumspect but allowed little more real opportunity. Diderot sternly warned Catherine that the odds were a thousand to one that genius, talent, and virtue would be found in the cottages of the people rather than in the palaces of the great. To nurture those potential resources among the people, he advised that a limited number of scholarships to secondary schools be made available to graduates of the little schools;[54] most men, however, would return to

50. E.g., his description in *Ethocratie*, p. 196: "A catechism of human morality, tailored to each order of citizens, would show them from infancy the qualities appropriate to their station, the virtues they should become accustomed to, the vices they must fear and flee for their own good."

51. *Ethocratie*, pp. 184–85.

52. Cf. the plans of Schlosser (Liebel, *Enlightened Bureaucracy*, pp. 73–75) and Mirabeau (Knies, *Brieflicher Verkehr*, p. 65). See also the many schemes described in Chisick, "Attitudes Toward the Education of the *Peuple*," passim.

53. *Oeuvres de Turgot*, 4:580.

54. *Mémoires*, pp. 131–32, 133 note, 137 note; "Entretiens," *Oeuvres politiques*, p. 325; *Oeuvres complètes*, 3:421–22, 426.

their labor. Diderot specified that the number of colleges should remain few in order to avoid draining the resources of the countryside. Too many would be a calamity for the nation's economy.[55] He lauded the virtues of an open society with an open education, but, at the same time, recognized an economic need to limit the outlets which education might provide.

Diderot was not alone in expressing a wish to discover unusual ability among common men. Mirabeau urged Karl Friedrich to find among the people "those privileged spirits [*génies*] who, by their competitiveness, ability, and breadth of mind, might become very useful men in the principal functions of society."[56] The new instruction would serve, therefore, a twofold purpose: to instruct most men in their duties and basic skills and to discover the exceptional man among the multitude. Condorcet voiced both these demands in 1776. Society needed, he insisted,

> a public education . . . to instruct everyone in what is useful to know in his station, in what his needs permit him to learn; an education such that no man of genius, in whatever station fate has placed him, could escape the knowledge, the art for which nature formed him.[57]

By speaking primarily of the génie—the man of exceptional talent[58] —Diderot, Mirabeau, and Condorcet underscored the infrequency with which their popular instruction would lead to further education and higher social station. The potentially outstanding leader or man of letters, they thought, should be found among the people. But the moderately intelligent man of the people would necessarily share the same fate as his less able neighbor—he was destined to return, better trained, to the labor by which most men must live.

Effectively distinguishing instruction for the people from fuller education for those of higher station, the philosophes followed both

---

55. "Plan d'une Université," *Oeuvres complètes*, 3:519.
56. Knies, *Brieflicher Verkehr*, p. 26.
57. "Réflexions," *Oeuvres complètes*, 11:193.
58. The word *génie* did not have the full connotation of the nineteenth-century *genius*, but it did imply at least exceptional talent. On the idea of "genius" in France and Diderot's part in redefining it, see H. Dieckmann, "Diderot's Conception of Genius," *Journal of the History of Ideas* 2, no. 2 (April 1941): 151–82.

the demands of economic reality and the general sway of literate and administrative opinion. They realized that it was optimistic to expect the people to spare their sons and daughters from household and field labor to receive even the most basic education. Condorcet spoke of an education for the common man providing "what his needs permit him to learn." The exigencies of rural life kept a large number of poor children from attending the existing schools. Even the most elementary instruction on a universal scale remained a visionary hope for the church as well as the philosophes.

Traditional ideology strongly reinforced the implications of the people's limited time and resources. Clerical educational enterprises in France had long evoked substantial opposition from the elite. The parish schools had multiplied largely without protest. But as clerical orders began to give free access to a considerable number of secondary schools (the *petits collèges*), many feared that the people would be tempted from the fields and shops to less productive occupations, especially occupations within the church. Apprehensions that the nation might become overpopulated with priests and pensioners impelled Colbert to institute an inquiry into the state and extent of the collèges early in the reign of Louis XIV. Ordinances designed to check the spread of teaching orders remained, however, largely without effect. The petites écoles received royal favor while the petits collèges remained suspect.[59]

In the eighteenth century, this opposition to widespread secondary education continued strong.[60] Montesquieu considered the multitude of collèges "one of the great abuses of the kingdom," estranging children of artisans and merchants from their economic order without providing them any new calling.[61] The expulsion of the Jesuits in the 1760s revived the discussion of the value of so many small, free collèges, and provoked an upsurge in the traditional opposition.[62]

59. On seventeenth-century opposition to easy access to collèges see François de Dainville, "Collèges et fréquentation scolaire au xviiie siècle," *Population* 3 (July–Sept. 1957): 474–76, 479–80, 486, 492–94.

60. On eighteenth-century opposition see Gontard, *Enseignement primaire*, pp. 52–56; J. Delvaille, *La Chalotais, éducateur* (Paris, 1911), pp. 117–20; and P. Ariès, *Centuries of Childhood*, trans. R. Baldick (New York, 1962), pp. 309–11. See also d'Alembert's article "Collège," *Encyclopédie*, 3:637.

61. "Pensées," *Oeuvres*, 2:61–62, 65. Montesquieu's educational notions were those of the Renaissance gentleman; see his comments on the College of Modena in "Voyages," *Oeuvres complètes*, 2:1215, and in *De l'esprit des lois*, book 4, chapter 2.

62. For the opinions of those who would separate the instruction of the people from the

The Breton parlementaire La Chalotais expressly excluded the sons of the people from the reformed educational system he envisaged in his *Essai d'éducation nationale* of 1763.[63] In an oft-cited reaction to this proscription, Voltaire lauded La Chalotais's conservatism. Adopting his favorite pose, that of the wise seigneur, he wrote, "I who cultivate the earth present you with a request to have laborers and not tonsured priests."[64] Voltaire saw no other possible result from institutional popular instruction than more priests and more fanaticism. He extended his fear of the small collèges into opposition to all institutionalized instruction for the people, but his fears were exceptional. The general current of French opinion favored little schools to bring rudimentary moral and intellectual training to the people, while it opposed easy access to any education beyond that state.[65] The advocates of a new form of popular instruction generally retained that opinion.

Elsewhere in Europe pedagogical reformers faced substantial opposition from those fearing social and economic dissatisfaction among the people. While nowhere else were there even the limited opportunities which the collèges offered in France, still some charity schools in England deliberately excluded writing from their curriculum; even after 1800 Hannah More would warn against the dangers of a "literary education"—the ability to write—among the poor. For all their limitations, the charity schools were looked upon with a a great deal of hostility and suspicion among a hierarchy-conscious British elite. Frederick II officially sanctioned universal instruction for the people, but only grudgingly and with Voltairean fears for the effects, envisioning an exodus away from the farms into sterile, urban occupations. Maria Theresa similarly moved toward sanctioning general education, but her minister of state, Count Anton Pergen, limited that education to the minimum necessary for the

education of the higher classes, see La Chalotais, *Essai d'éducation nationale* (Paris, 1763); Guyton de Morveau, *Mémoire sur l'éducation publique, avec le prospectus d'un Collège* (n.p., 1764), pp. 42–48; the anonymous *De l'éducation. Ouvrage utile aux pères, aux gouverneurs, . . .* (Amsterdam, 1768), pp. 127–28; [Abbé Coyer], *Plan d'éducation publique* (Paris, 1770), pp. 255–56, 345–46; and the proposals of Rolland d'Erceville and Philippon de la Madeleine, discussed in H. C. Barnard, *Education and the French Revolution* (Cambridge, 1969), pp. 35–52. Even Diderot saw danger in the multiplication of small colleges: see above, pp. 110–11.

63. Pp. 25–29.

64. Voltaire to La Chalotais, 23 February 1763, Voltaire, *Correspondence* (10238).

65. See Laget, "Petites écoles," p. 1404.

efficient work of the laboring orders. More than that, he feared, would breed discontent unprofitable to the state.[66]

In the face of this opposition, and sharing some of its fears, the reformers proposed neither radical nor revolutionary changes in the social order. They sought not a nation of Emiles, but a nation of minimally-educated, virtuous, peaceable laborers. Holbach concurred with Plutarch in defining the art of government as "making men capable of being well-governed."[67] The proponents of enlightened instruction saw their plans as an essential step toward that goal. An instructed people, they thought, would understand and accept its station in life. Raised on the reasonable morality of the state, it would avoid the pitfalls of fanaticism and superstition. It would be able to read elementary pamphlets and instructions issued by the government to improve productivity and health. In sum, instruction might create a people far removed from the fanatical mob of the *Henriade*.

Occasionally philosophes saw beyond their imposed limits on public instruction to some higher ends. Adam Smith vigorously advocated the state's underwriting of public education, with a view toward requiring all citizens to acquire basic skills in reading, writing, and accounting. Such skills would, he knew, bring economic rewards. But beyond these economic rewards, acknowledged by all persons favorable to public education, he saw the potential of giving texture and meaning to minds threatened by the rote work of the division of labor. Smith, like most philosophes, considered common labor morally debilitating. The "torpor" of the laborer's mind, he wrote in *Wealth of Nations,*

> renders him not only incapable of relishing or bearing a part in a rational conversation, but of conceiving any generous, noble, or tender sentiment, and consequently of forming any just judgment concerning many even of the ordinary duties of private life.

Neither members of the upper classes nor barbarian tribesmen faced the dangers of monotony in the way that the worker did in Smith's

66. Jones, *Charity School Movement*, chapter 1; Robert Webb, *The British Working Class Reader* (London, 1955), p. 16; Flitner, *Politische Erziehung*, pp. 20–23. Kann, *Austrian Intellectual History*, p. 132.

67. *La Morale universelle*, 2:41.

society. It was therefore the duty of the state, Smith proposed, to provide sufficient economic support so that basic education might be available to all men.[68] Smith was more sensitive than most to what education might mean psychologically to the common man. His fellow philosophes at times grew callous in their habit of speaking to economic realities; perhaps it took an economist to see beyond economics.

While most educational reformers stressed the need to maintain class differences, Mirabeau saw in educational plans a way toward a type of unity. The morality and citizenship brought to all men through universal schooling might help unify a fragmented society. In 1770 he expressed this need in terms of a shared vision which could unite the efforts of men:

> This unity can rise to its fullest extent and work in a lasting way only by means of a unity of perceptions [*conformité dans la façon de voir les objets*]. If knowledge differs in any way from ignorance, then to educate some and to abandon others to ignorance within the same society is to establish a principle of disunion or civil war.[69]

While Mirabeau and other reformers honored many of the social divisions within society, they thought they saw the means by which to unify the vision of the philosophe and the people at the most basic level. In proposing their plans they expressed faith not so much in the people (who, as always, would be led) as in the legislative capabilities of a public power understanding its own best interests and employing the resources of enlightenment.

Above all one should remember that these programs of instruction did not exist in isolation in the minds of these reformers. Though they perceived little chance for education to provide a pathway out of a life of labor, and though they explicitly sought to teach the people to accept its lot, they also sought means to improve that lot. The Swiss Physiocrat Isaac Iselin warned that under prevailing conditions education of the peasantry might only lead to discontent and unhappiness. He did so not to deny the utility of educational reform but to underscore the need for accompanying economic and social re-

---

68. *Wealth of Nations*, 2:267–70, quotation p. 267.
69. Knies, *Brieflicher Verkehr*, p. 23. Cf. La Rivière, *L'ordre naturel et essentiel des sociétés politiques* (London, 1767), 1:86–91.

forms.[70] In that sentiment he was at one with most of the philosophes. All wanted a contented laboring class; none wanted a class content with misery and oppression.

70. Gagliardo, *Pariah to Patriot*, p. 99, note 20.

# 7 The Laborer's Share

## Discipline and Charity

The French philosophes and their contemporaries often spoke of the people as gens des bras much as later generations referred to workers as so many "hands." The verbal reduction of men to their arms reflected the perspective of those interested in the people primarily as producers of society's wealth and hence concerned with keeping those arms in steady motion. Idleness seemed the greatest sin against society, and stern discipline often seemed its only cure. In the analyses of the British "political arithmeticians" of the seventeenth century, low wages provided a convenient answer to the disciplinary and economic needs of society, keeping the people constantly at work to avoid starvation while maintaining a low competitive price of goods for export.[1] Even as opinion shifted from the necessity of controls toward the virtues of the open market, British writers such as Bernard Mandeville, William Temple, and Arthur Young still found much to recommend in wages depressed by the indirect actions of the labor market and the growth of population.[2] Some mercantilists found virtue in wages above subsistence but the consensus remained that men were disinclined to labor and that discipline, rather than incentives, held the key.[3] French political economists usually followed the British lead, and throughout the seventeenth and eighteenth centuries many would find the "utility of poverty"

1. On mercantile wage theory and the need for low wages—controlled if necessary—see Edgar S. Furniss, *The Position of the Laborer in a System of Nationalism* (Boston, 1920), pp. 157–77; Michael Wermel, *The Evolution of the Classical Wage Theory* (New York, 1939), pp. 3–22; and Eli Heckscher, *Mercantilism*, trans. M. Shapiro (London, 1955), 2:153–72. Furniss, pp. 177–85, does indicate a few exceptions—men who objected on economic or moral grounds to the idea of the "utility of poverty."
2. Furniss, *Position of the Laborer*, chapter 6.
3. For corrections to the view that all mercantile writers disregarded social welfare for the sake of state power, see Jacob Viner, "Power Versus Plenty as Objectives of Foreign Policy in the Seventeenth and Eighteenth Centuries," and Charles Wilson, "The Other Face of Mercantilism," chapters 3 and 5 respectively of D. C. Coleman, ed., *Revisions in Mercantilism* (London, 1969).

an appealing notion.[4] François Quesnay could still exploit this common opinion to persuade *Encyclopédie* readers of the advantages of free trade in grain and the consequent rise in prices. "It is . . . a great inconvenience," he wrote,

> to accustom the people to buy grain at too low a price; it consequently becomes less laborious, feeds itself at little cost, and becomes lazy and arrogant; farmers find workers and servants with difficulty; they are quite badly served in years of abundance. It is important that the masses earn more, and that they be pressed by need to do so. In the previous century, when grain was much more expensive, the people was accustomed to it, worked proportionately harder, and was forced to be more laborious and more prosperous.[5]

Quesnay thus used common prejudice, though he turned the argument around and insisted that the people might benefit financially from the discipline of high prices. But when he later fully analyzed his policy of free trade and high grain prices, he explicitly denied any desire to reduce real wages as a form of economic discipline. In "Hommes," an article intended for the *Encyclopédie*, Quesnay argued at length against "the maxims of those cruel men who insist that you must reduce the people to misery to force it to work."[6] The man beset by oppressive taxes and servile duties, Quesnay argued, no longer strives to better his lot; he reduces his labor to provide the barest necessity and becomes an economic cipher, consuming exactly what he produces. Only the hope of economic ease could encourage the people to more productive labor.[7] An economy which promised rewards for hard labor could provide the jobs and economic demand which would elicit the riches that nature offers through cultivation of the land.[8] Ten years later, in 1767, the strength of this argument still seemed evident to Quesnay, by then the architect and defender of a highly developed and codified economic model. His twentieth "general maxim" of Physiocracy read simply:

4. E.g., see Henri Hauser, *La Pensée et l'action économiques du Cardinal de Richelieu* (Paris, 1944), pp. 144–46. The phrase "utility of poverty" is Furniss's.

5. "Grains," *Encyclopédie*, 7:831.

6. Institut National d'Etudes Démographiques, *François Quesnay et la Physiocratie* (Paris, 1958), p. 541 (hereafter cited as I.N.E.D.).

7. I.N.E.D., pp. 540–41.

8. Ibid., pp. 541–42.

> *That the ease of the lower classes should not be diminished*; because they
> will not be able to contribute enough to the consumption of
> those foodstuffs which can only be consumed in the nation, thus
> diminishing the reproduction and revenue of the nation.[9]

The dynamics of Physiocratic economics now allowed for a well-paid, secure laboring population as most mercantile ideals had not.

Though the leading philosophes continued to debate many aspects of Physiocratic theory, they too rejected poverty as a useful legislative instrument. "Those who argue that the peasant should not live at ease," De Jaucourt wrote in the *Encyclopédie*, "spout a maxim as false as it is contrary to humanity."[10] In 1770 Turgot compared the wages of the people to the working of a machine. All machines need a little play, he argued; any clock built so that all parts fit to perfection will soon grind to a halt. The wages of the people need, therefore, a margin above bare necessity to guard against economic changes. A little excess became, in Turgot's view, "a very necessary thing."[11]

Turgot's observations were neither isolated nor idiosyncratic; they represented the growing consensus of the enlightened community. The humanitarian mood of the era, coupled with the sharpening perception of economic reality, motivated many economic writers to look more deeply into the assumptions of the "utility of poverty." They found the theory unsatisfactory. As the initial panic of the early eighteenth century over rising poor rates in Britain subsided, emphasis in economic writings shifted from the need for discipline to the need for incentives, chief among which were consistent employment and high wages.[12] By the time Adam Smith published *Wealth of Na-*

9. Ibid, p. 954. "Reproduction" was a key concept in Quesnay's economic model. Physiocratic arguments revolved about the need for sufficient agricultural profits to insure that a certain amount could be reinvested into the land which, in turn, would reproduce the nation's annual agricultural product.

10. "Impôt," 8:602. For a similar statement see also his article "Peuple," 12:476. Rousseau argued the case against oppressive taxation justified by the utility of poverty in "Economie (Morale & Politique)," 5:347. The economist J.-J. Graslin rejected the idea of reducing the peasant to misery on the grounds that the loss of every peasant to death or begging cost the nation a man who produced ten times what he received in wages; see *Essai analytique sur la richesse et l'impôt*, p. 164. Holbach voiced objections similar to Quesnay's in *La Politique naturelle*, 1:184. Cf. also Thomas More's rejection of poverty as social policy in *Utopia* (1516), ed. Edward Surtz, S.J. (New Haven, 1964), pp. 45–47.

11. *Oeuvres de Turgot*, 3:288. See also his letter of 25 March 1767 to David Hume in E. Rotwein, ed., *David Hume: Writings on Economics* (Madison, Wis., 1970), pp. 210–13.

12. See the articles of David Coats, "Changing Attitudes to Labour in the Mid-Eigh-

*tions* (1776) the talk of need for subsistence wages to drive men to labor was increasingly rare among economic writers, though still a common theme in society at large.[13] Smith reacted to the proponents of low wages with decisive cogency, unmasking both their cruelty and the fallacy of their theory. Citing the apparent rise in the standard of living among the lower orders during the eighteenth century, he asked rhetorically, "Is this improvement in the circumstances of the lower ranks of the people to be regarded as an advantage or an inconveniency to the society?" The answer, which should have been clear to all but was still regarded with suspicion by those who favored the discipline of low wages, he spelled out concisely:

> Servants, laborers and workmen of different kinds, make up the far greater part of every great political society. But what improves the circumstances of the greater part can never be regarded as an inconveniency to the whole. No society can surely be flourishing and happy, of which the far greater part of the members are poor and miserable. It is but equity, besides, that they who feed, clothe and lodge the whole body of the people, should have such a share of the produce of their own labor as to be themselves tolerably well fed, clothed and lodged.

Moving beyond simple logic to what he and his age considered good economic standards, he embroidered on the case for high real wages: they increase population, a constant worry of eighteenth-century social observers concerned with population as a measure of power and prosperity; they encourage industry, making the worker healthier, more content, more diligent in pursuing labor which brings ample rewards; they prevent the sickness, death, and decreased productivity caused by bare subsistence wages. Employers of labor had often insisted, Smith noted, that high food prices made the worker more productive. Behind this supposed concern for productivity, Smith discerned the greed of men who knew that hard-pressed workers would agree to work at low wages. But what is profitable to the profit taker, Smith broadly implied in *Wealth of Nations*, has little

teenth Century," *Economic History Review,* 2d ser. 11, no. 1 (Aug. 1958):35–51, and "Economic Thought and Poor Law Policy in the Eighteenth Century," *Economic History Review,* 2d ser. 13, no. 1 (Aug. 1960):39–51. See also Marshall, *The English Poor,* chapter 1.

13. For the continuing theme see Malcolmson, *Popular Recreations in English Society,* pp. 96–98.

to do with the profit of the nation as a whole. From that wider perspective, high wages, symbols of a growing demand for labor and hence a healthy economy, were to be the aim of legislation.[14] Though Smith and other philosophes never convinced themselves that most people could ever rise dramatically above the level of subsistence, they insisted that enforced poverty could never serve as an economic whipping rod or a social policy. The idea of making a nation wealthy by impoverishing most of its inhabitants lost any logic it might once have had. Instead, the philosophes went about trying to find economic solutions by which virtually everyone might win.

Still, the theme of discipline for the lower orders did not disappear. The people need not exist on the edge of misery, the philosophes thought, but the people must work steadily to produce the nation's wealth. The issue of religious holy days provided a convenient focus for a continuing sense of social discipline. Since the early seventeenth century, many administrators in Catholic nations had considered the prohibition of labor on regional and national holy days a great disadvantage in economic competition with Protestant neighbors. Many argued for the limitation or suppression of holy days.[15] Even in Protestant England popular holidays and amusements faced severe opposition, though more from moralizing evangelicals than calculating economists.[16] The philosophes readily picked up this theme, which combined motives of anticlericalism with contempt for the manners of the people. Abbé Mallet insisted that holy days had turned into "occasions of debauchery and licentiousness, often even assaults and murders." He offered in their place a detailed plan for telescoping all holy days into Sundays, thereby limiting the days of rest and license.[17] Like Mallet, most philosophes associated popular

14. *Wealth of Nations*, book 1, chapter 8, 1:66–88, quotation p. 80.
15. Heckscher, *Mercantilism*, 2:302–03.
16. Malcolmson, *Popular Recreations in English Society*, passim.
17. "Fêtes des Chrétiens," *Encyclopédie*, 6:565–71, quotation p. 566. On the fear of Protestant competition, see also "Maîtrises" (Faiguet de Villeneuve), 9:914. Mallet's proposal was not as radical as might appear at first glance. Both Turgot and Voltaire reported that several bishops had already undertaken such plans by the 1760s. See Turgot, *Oeuvres de Turgot*, 2:226, a letter (11 November 1762) to the controller general, requesting his intervention to persuade the bishop of Angoulême to extend a five-year suppression of many holy days; Turgot claimed the support of no less than the bishop of Paris. For Voltaire's views, see his "Requête" of 1770, *Oeuvres complètes*, 28:347, and his article "Fertilisation" in *Questions sur l'Encyclopédie, Oeuvres complètes*, 19:110.

leisure with popular drunkenness; Voltaire swore that tavern keepers had invented the holy days.[18] The life of the taverns appalled the genteel philosophes, who preferred more refined forms of *libertinage*; considerations of public manners held as much sway as considerations of economics in their criticism of church festivals.

Some philosophes naively insisted that they spoke for the people in calling for this reform. Voltaire addressed the monarchy in 1770 in the name of "the most useful part of the human race": "We ask your permission to live; we ask your permission to work."[19] With a similar pose of paternal compassion Condorcet noted approval of Voltaire's sentiments. "To forbid a man to work for his family's subsistence is barbaric," he wrote, "to punish a man for having worked . . . is an injustice."[20] But the social bias implicit in Condorcet's program emerged soon after, as he argued for freedom to work as a replacement for forcing men "on certain days to give in to the laziness, the debauchery which necessarily follows a large gathering of base men." Eliminating holy days and establishing Sunday as a time of public instruction and business appealed to his instincts for social order.[21] No one asked the laborer if he wanted his holy days suppressed; paternal discipline, much more than paternal compassion, was at work in the philosophic attack on the holy days.[22] The policy of curtailing festive days found eager followers among reformers and monarchs throughout Europe.[23]

18. The attack on fêtes and popular drunkenness was widespread. See e.g., Holbach, *La Morale universelle*, 1:243–45; Helvétius, *De l'esprit, Oeuvres complètes*, 1:144, note 1, and *De l'homme, Oeuvres complètes*, 3:239, note a; Condorcet, "Lettre d'un laboureur de Picardie," *Oeuvres complètes*, 11:3; Voltaire, articles "Catéchisme du curé," *Dictionnaire philosophique*, pp. 88–89, and "Fêtes," *Questions, Oeuvres complètes*, 19:114–17; *Encyclopédie*, "Cabaret," 2:487, and "Société," 15:354–55; and Diderot, on the Dutch populace, *Oeuvres complètes*, 17:377.

19. "Requête," *Oeuvres complètes*, 28:312; see additionally his supposed letter from a worker of Lyon in his article "Fêtes," *Questions, Oeuvres complètes*, 19:115–17.

20. Condorcet, *Oeuvres complètes*, 4:407.

21. Ibid., pp. 407–08. For a similar suggestion see also "Lettre d'un laboureur de Picardie," *Oeuvres complètes*, 11:3.

22. Voltaire did, however, argue the people's cause on the matter of fasting during some holy days and Lent, calling for abolition of a custom which deprived the people of the little meat and meat products in their diet, while the rich had easy access to fish and other substitutes. See "Requête," *Oeuvres complètes*, 28:342–45. Abbé Mallet appended a similar proposal—excluding Lent—in his article "Fêtes," *Encyclopédie*, 6:569–71.

23. See, e.g., Hertz, *The Development of the German Public Mind*, p. 333; Gagliardo, *Pariah to Patriot*, p. 46; Liebel, *Enlightened Bureaucracy*, p. 67; Kann, *A Study in Austrian Intellectual History*, p. 128; Venturi, *Italy and the Enlightenment*, p. 276.

This spirit of mercantile discipline carried over into the philosophes' attitude toward the begging population. Bands of beggars and brigands—numbering perhaps as much as one million in France in times of crisis—[24] roamed the countryside and crowded the city gates and marketplaces of Europe. The demands of the begging population, both of the pitied "true poor" (*vrai pauvre*) and the despised "healthy beggar" (*mendiant valide*),[25] far outstripped the capacity and will of royal administration and private charity. The debate on poor laws in England virtually swallowed up other talk about popular welfare until late in the century. The philosophes joined in the continuing debate on how best to provide for the needs of the deserving poor while forcing the healthy beggar to work. Diderot summed up the philosophes' project in the *Encyclopédie* when he noted, "*Hôpitaux* should not frighten the unfortunate, but the government should frighten the lazy."[26]

The philosophes showed little compassion toward that reputed healthy beggar whom royal administration had tirelessly sought to eliminate by threats of the galleys and confinement. Though reformers often blamed bad administration for the great number of beggars, they still assumed that many begged out of sheer laziness. The most obvious solution for involuntary poverty was to make the nation prosperous,[27] but for the *fainéant* the philosophes held out the rod of harsh laws strictly enforced. Voltaire wrote, with predictable directness, "Beggars are a parasite which latches on to opulence; it

24. The number fluctuated greatly with economic conditions, since so many lived on the edge of subsistence. Voltaire estimated the number of healthy beggars at 100,000, while the Physiocrat P. J. A. Roubaud estimated 300,000. (See the exchange of letters, Voltaire to Roubaud, 1 July 1769, and Roubaud to Voltaire, c. 1 August 1769, in Voltaire, *Correspondence* [14740, 14810].)

25. Trying to sort out the true poor from healthy beggars, pilgrims, poor people on a necessary trip, brigands, and the like was a monumental task. On the various categories of poor, of which the division *vrai pauvre* / *mendiant valide* was only the beginning, see Jean-Pierre Gutton, *La société et les pauvres: L'exemple de la généralité de Lyon, 1534–1789* (1970), book 1, chapters 1 and 2, and Olwen Hufton, "Begging, Vagrancy, Vagabondage and the Law: An Aspect of the Problem of Poverty in Eighteenth-Century France," *European Studies Review* 2 (1972): 97–123.

26. "Hôpital," 8:294. The eighteenth-century *hôpital* did not resemble our modern "hospital"; the poor, the sick, the insane, the old—in short, most of society's outcasts— were gathered together under the same roof. I have therefore retained the French untranslated in the text.

27. See Montesquieu, *De l'esprit des lois*, book 23, chapter 29; Roubaud to Voltaire, in Voltaire, *Correspondence* (14810), opposing Voltaire's advocacy of forced labor for beggars; Condorcet, *Oeuvres complètes*, 4:484–85; and Diderot, *Encyclopédie*, "Hôpital," 8:293.

must be shaken off; opulence must make poverty work; let hôpitaux be for sickness and old age; workhouses for . . . vigorous youth."[28] He even once proposed that seigneurs be allowed to stop beggars and force them to work.[29]

Many like Voltaire saw coercion from above as the only cure for the healthy beggar. De Jaucourt traced the series of harsh but ineffectual laws which marked the path of the royal battle with vagabondage in his article on "Mendiants" in the *Encyclopédie*. As an alternative to the threat of the galleys, he proposed a system of workhouses, overseen by entrepreneurs in search of profit and offering perhaps a small wage to laborers. For the hard-core vagabond he recommended deportation to the colonies. This program, he thought, would cut down the number of healthy beggars while allowing funds to flow to the true poor.[30] Even Condorcet found the need to discipline the healthy beggar imperative. In a letter written in 1781 he described a Dutch punishment—a machine on which a beggar had to peddle continuously to save himself from drowning beneath rising waters, designed to instill a preference for honest labor. Such treatment Condorcet judged "a little cruel," but the principle did not repel him at all.[31]

The desire to substitute work for idleness could betray great harshness. The English workhouse, originally designed to cure underemployment, rapidly degenerated into a grab bag of society's outcasts little different from most French hôpitaux. But in the plans of many philosophes, work was designed to provide a welcome solution for the man of the people who was temporarily or chronically underemployed. Turgot and others considered the public workshop a measure of charity to those without work. The reformers chose to emphasize the predominance among the begging population of those who desired work but could not find it. From that perspective, generating work became the perfect embodiment of bienfaisance,

28. *Questions sur l'Encyclopédie*, "Gueux," *Oeuvres complètes*, 19:322–23.

29. To Roubaud, 1 July 1769, Voltaire, *Correspondence* (14740). Voltaire made the same suggestion in *Questions*, "Fertilisation," *Oeuvres complètes*, 19:112, where he added a provision for a "reasonable wage" for those forced to work.

30. *Encyclopédie*, 10:331–32. The idea of workhouses, both as agents of discipline and a measure of charity, had a long history in France. On early seventeenth-century proposals, see Hauser, *La pensée et l'action économiques du Cardinal de Richelieu*, pp. 158–61.

31. Condorcet to the secretary of the Academy of Châlons, on a proposed prize topic on the means to eliminate mendicity; see *Oeuvres complètes*, 1:297–98.

providing work for the true poor while isolating the unwilling. As intendant of Limoges, Turgot integrated the public workshop into a full system of aid to the true poor, and as controller general he continued to sponsor this idea as the best means of reducing the begging population.[32] His proposed first step, as in all plans of the time, was to sort out the deserving poor from the fainéants and then to determine the most appropriate kinds of aid for those deserving poor. The homeless vagabond would be subject to arrest, but the state would take responsibility for providing useful work to the healthy and willing.[33] Turgot envisaged a broad program of public works. Most men in need of work would be committed to road building, an activity which would have the added benefit of replacing the much-despised royal corvée. In some cases artisans might require only advances from allocated funds to begin work again.[34] Women and children might also join in the public works, though Turgot preferred that they continue spinning, the traditional work for women, with training provided if needed. He hoped that eventually these public enterprises would become self-perpetuating companies under the supervision of private businessmen.

Some motives of discipline did enter Turgot's schemes. On road-building projects he proposed payment by the task to discourage idleness. He insisted in 1770 that wages be kept below normal to prevent those already employed from entering public workshops. (He did, however, suggest in 1775 that any profits be divided among grown men and women, and that the state purchase artisan production above market value to stimulate work.)[35] Much of the funds for his projects would come from the self-taxation of the wealthy who would, one might expect, keep wages at a minimum. He also advised payment in kind, to discourage squandering of wages at the tavern.

32. See Turgot's instructions to the assembly of charity of Limoges, 11 February 1770, *Oeuvres de Turgot*, 3:205–19, and his memorandum of 1775, in vol. 4, pp. 499–515. As controller general, Turgot encouraged royal sponsorship of *ateliers de charité*, begun by his predecessor, Abbé Terray.

33. As controller general, Turgot tried to reduce as much as possible the number of vagabonds under arrest, preferring to return them to their homes and to local charity and *police*; see his memorandum of 1775, *Oeuvres de Turgot*, 4:515–18.

34. *Oeuvres de Turgot*, 4:501.

35. *Oeuvres de Turgot*, 3:214–15, and 4:511–12. Competition of public with private industry was a major drawback. Roubaud rejected Voltaire's schemes for forced labor on this basis, arguing that an experiment in public industry in Lyon had merely lowered demand for labor from those outside; see Voltaire, *Correspondence* (14810).

Nonetheless, the workshops seemed more a gift than an imposition, and the proposals along the lines of Turgot's appealed to a large number of philosophes and reformers.[36]

For the poor unable to work—the young, the old, the ill—the reform proposals of the philosophes emphasized the appropriateness of care and the proper allocation of resources. Reform of the hôpitaux took first priority. The indiscriminate gathering of poor, sick, old, and insane in the crowded institutions of the cities often made charity a nightmare for the city dweller, while villages and small towns often had no institutions at all. Diderot and Voltaire endorsed and propagandized the administrative and sanitary reforms advanced by the philanthropist Chamousset, designed to make the Hôtel-Dieu of Paris endurable to its residents and a model for other institutions.[37] More important, the philosophes sought to take many of the unfortunate out of the hôpitaux entirely. The proposals of Nicolas Baudeau, a leading French Physiocrat, were typical of reform attitudes. Under his scheme, the blind and the old would no longer enter hôpitaux but rather would receive care at home at public expense. Invalids would work and function to their capacity at specially designed homes. Foundlings would still be placed in country homes, as was the practice in Paris at the time, but the state would provide sanctuaries for abandoned children in order to discourage the practice of exposing infants. Laws would ban begging pilgrims, but the state would provide passports to poor people forced to travel, entitling them to lodging at villages and towns along their way. The so-called *pauvres honteux,* for whom poverty marked a drastic fall in social standing, would receive funds for minimum upkeep of their homes and educa-

36. In addition to the harsh versions of Voltaire and De Jaucourt see the support given Turgot's ideas by Condorcet, *Oeuvres complètes,* 4:484–85, and 5:31; and Holbach, *Ethocratie,* pp. 145–48, 234. Turgot's committee on mendicity understandably endorsed public works projects in 1774; see Ira Wade, "Poverty in the Enlightenment," in H. Friedrich and F. Schalk, eds., *Europäische Aufklärung* (Munich, 1967), p. 322. Abbé Pluche, in *Le Spectacle de la Nature, ou entretiens sur les particularités de l'histoire naturelle* (1770 [1746]), pp. 350–53, proposed a system of work-charity involving road work, small loans, and fallow lands as resources.

37. See Diderot, "Hôpital," *Encyclopédie,* 8:293–94, and his praise for the reform efforts of Madame Necker, 1 March 1781, *Correspondance* (923). For Voltaire, see *Dictionnaire philosophique,* "Charité," (addition of 1770), pp. 133–37. When the Hôtel-Dieu in Paris suffered a major fire, Voltaire contributed to its rebuilding, while d'Alembert led the drive among Parisian intellectuals for funds. Voltaire's plans to contribute profits from his play *Lois de Minos* were foiled by a pirated edition; see Voltaire, *Correspondance* (17055, 17062, 17071, 17135).

tion for their sons at a collège.[38] Only the sick would then remain for the care of the hôpitaux. To finance this broad program, Baudeau insisted upon large contributions from the church. Medieval canon law, he argued, required that one-fourth of all church revenues go toward care for the poor. In addition, he insisted that all foundations once dedicated to the care of the poor must return to their chartered purpose. Private charity and public revenues might supplement these funds as required and a hierarchy of officials, ranging from a central commission to the village syndic, would administer the revenues.[39]

Though only one of many schemes, Baudeau's plan embodied much of the spirit and substance of the ideas of the enlightened circle. Turgot, Holbach, and a royal committee under Turgot's ministry supported outdoor relief wherever possible and eventual decentralization of the huge urban hôpitaux.[40] Both Diderot and Voltaire proposed extensive and humane programs for the care of foundlings.[41] Designs on church revenues for the care of the poor quite naturally appealed to men who despised the social and religious role of the Catholic church but who appreciated the need for public services under its domain. Diderot proposed nationalization of funds dedicated to the hôpitaux so that they might be distributed fairly according to the needs of institutions.[42] Helvétius and Condorcet sketched plans to confiscate church revenues and direct them toward charities or tax relief for the poor.[43] The Spanish philosophe

38. Baudeau's concern for this special category of poor was not unusual. Turgot provided for a special fund for the pauvres honteux in his instruction of 1770, *Oeuvres de Turgot* 3:212. See also Olwen Hufton, "Toward an Understanding of the Poor of Eighteenth-Century France," in J. F. Bosher, ed., *French Government and Society, 1500–1850* (London, 1973), pp. 158–59.

39. [Nicolas Baudeau], *Idées d'un citoyen sur les besoins, les droits, et les devoirs des vrais pauvres* (Amsterdam, 1765), passim.

40. Holbach, *La Morale universelle*, 2:180–81. On the Turgot committee of 1774, see Wade, "Poverty in the Enlightenment," p. 320. Outdoor relief already was a significant part of assistance to the poor in some urban areas. For a detailed description of the workings of such relief, see Philippe Loupès, "L'assistance paroissiale aux pauvres malades dans le diocèse de Bordeaux au xviiie siècle," *Annales du Midi* 84 (1972):37–61.

41. Voltaire approved of the scheme of François Moreau to establish an agricultural school for foundlings and regretted that his own lands were too poor to support such an establishment; see Moreau to Voltaire, 20 May 1767, Voltaire, *Correspondence* (13296) and Voltaire's reply, 1 June 1767, *Correspondence* (13312). Diderot proposed state care and instruction for foundlings in Russia, followed by entry and trading in the home of a craftsman (the craftsman might receive freedom after rendering such service a few times) and finally a shop and house in the capital for the young adult; see *Mémoires*, pp. 187, 226.

42. "Hôpital," *Encyclopédie*, 8:293–94.

43. *De l'homme, Oeuvres complètes*, 3:74–76, note a. See also Condorcet's proposals for

Bernard Ward envisioned a secular national commission to coordinate all charitable activities, effectively taking over much clerical revenue and supplementing it with funds from a lottery.[44] Even the relatively moderate Turgot used his leverage as controller general to initiate inquiries to insure that all funds once donated for the support of the poor still served that purpose, and, if necessary, to prepare a plan for redistribution of these funds among foundations within a region to insure proper care for all.[45]

The philosophes were not innovators on matters of economic discipline or charity reform. But their awareness of the victimization of some poor and their sense of the responsibility which must fall upon the rich moved them to give more precedence to the humane side of their paternal perspective, less to the impulse toward discipline. They rejected the threat of misery as a legitimate legislative tool, and promised those unable to escape centralized charity that their needs would be filled adequately and efficiently.

## LEADERSHIP AND RESPONSIBILITY

The evolving paternalism of the Enlightenment brought with it a heightened sense of economic leadership and responsibility. In 1775 Voltaire wrote to Nicolas Baudeau, describing the feats of an unnamed hero in the Physiocratic mold. "I have before my eyes a great example of what an honest and moderate liberty can create in commerce as well as agriculture," he began.

> In one of the prettiest settings of Europe this side of Constantinople, but one of the most ungrateful and unhealthy soils,

state takeover of ecclesiastical revenues in his notes to Voltaire, *Oeuvres complètes*, 4:373–75, and in *Vie de Turgot, Oeuvres complètes*, 5:145–46.

44. Sarrailh, *Espagne éclairée*, pp. 527–28.

45. See his letter to the Bishop of Fréjus, 18 November 1774, *Oeuvres de Turgot*, 4:264–65. Turgot's opposition to permanent foundations which had ceased to serve legitimate purposes was longstanding; see his article "Fondation," *Encyclopédie*, 7:72–76. For Condorcet's support, see his *Vie de Turgot, Oeuvres complètes* 5:23–24. For an explication of Turgot's views in the context of general opposition to clerical foundations, see Jack A. Clarke, "Turgot's Critique of Perpetual Endowments," *French Historical Studies* 3, no. 4 (1964):495–506. The reformers drew on a large reservoir of public resentment toward the extent of ecclesiastical property. On this subject see John McManners, *French Ecclesiastical Society Under the Ancien Régime: A Study of Angers in the Eighteenth Century* (Manchester, 1960), pp. 117–28, and Joseph Dedieu, *Montesquieu* (Paris, 1913), pp. 241–42. Voltaire shared Turgot's views on perpetual endowments; see "Remarques sur l'Essai" (1763), *Essai sur les moeurs*, 2:923.

there was a little hamlet inhabited by forty unfortunates, rav-
aged by scrofula and poverty. A man of respectable fortune
bought this frightful territory expressly to change it. He began
by draining plague-infested marshes. He cleared land. He
brought in foreign artisans of all kinds, especially watchmakers,
who knew neither master artisans nor guilds, nor *compagnon-
nage*,[46] but who worked with marvelous industry. . . . Finally,
in a few years, a little spot with forty savages has become an
opulent little town inhabited by 1,200 useful people.[47]

The veil of anonymity was thin indeed, for anyone would know that
the man of modest wealth but great determination was Voltaire
himself. Voltaire took great pride in his role as seigneur of Ferney
and leader of the region. Huber's paintings of Voltaire in his later
years often portray him in the pose of the benevolent patriarch,
watching over the work and play of his peasant and artisan community. More than merely endorsing the Physiocratic doctrine of
free trade, Voltaire pointed, in the letter to Baudeau and elsewhere,
to a broader theme of enlightened economics—the need for leadership. When he jotted down some observations on agriculture for
*Questions sur l'Encyclopédie*, he included in almost every remark the
simple injunction that the seigneur should oversee his own lands.
Only the seigneur, he argued, had the funds, initiative, education,
and foresight to bring production and prosperity to their fullest possibilities.[48] In an age and a country where most large landowners
lived away from their estates, leasing their land in a manner to discourage long-term investment, Voltaire could point with some justice
to his own career at Ferney as an example of economic leadership in
a moribund economy.[49]

In the writings of the Physiocrats, the search for leadership found
its hero in the *fermier*, the relatively well-to-do peasant who normally
rented from large landowners and who had sufficient capital to farm

46. Unofficial organizations of journeymen and apprentices, largely in reaction against
the increasingly closed clique of master artisans who controlled the guilds.

47. March or April 1775, Voltaire, *Correspondence* (18281).

48. "Fertilisation," Voltaire, *Oeuvres complètes*, 19:107–12; see also, "Economie,"
*Oeuvres complètes*, 18:453–64.

49. On the role of moeurs among landholders as a significant barrier to economic development, see Robert Forster, "Obstacles to Agricultural Growth in Eighteenth-Century
France," *American Historical Review* 75 (1970):1600–15. On patterns of leasing and their
effects, see the same author's *House of Saulx-Tavanes* (Baltimore, 1971), chapter 2.

efficiently for profit.[50] To this entrepreneurial initiative Quesnay and
his followers counterposed both the absentee landlord, who settled for
traditional revenues without concern for increasing production, and
the poor sharecropper of the south and west, who barely earned his
subsistence while the landowner exacted his half of a minimal crop.
Only the yeoman farmer, the Physiocrats argued, could elicit nature's
maximum agricultural offering by striving to increase the margin of
revenues over his lease. These leaders would in turn mobilize the
resources of the countryside and bring the benefits of prosperity to
the day laborer, the owner, and the state.[51]

Within the Enlightenment the idea of economic leadership worked
in more varied ways than it did in the visions of Physiocracy. Like
many agronomists of his day, Holbach rejected the virtues of the
large agricultural entrepreneur, preferring instead a multitude of
small farms to large holdings on the English model. Such small farms,
he argued, gave subsistence to more families than large estates.[52] The
rich landowner would still, however, have much to offer to the countryside. Holbach pictured his ideal society much as later historians
and storytellers would idealize the Old Regime:

> The good citizen is useful to his country in whatever class he
> finds himself: the poor man fills his social task by honest labor,
> from which a solid and real benefit results for his fellow citizens;
> the rich man fulfills his task when he aids the poor man to ful-
> fill his own; in aiding active and laborious poverty, in paying
> for his work, in helping give him the means to subsist, in a word,
> by good deeds [*bienfaisance*], the rich man can pay his debt to
> society.[53]

Holbach portrayed the rich man as he ought to be and recognized
full well the gap between this ideal and the real world. He knew the
poor to be victims of the rich but saw a cure not in the victory of poor

50. On the status of the higher level peasant, see Pierre Goubert, *Beauvais et le Beauvaisis
de 1600 à 1730* (Paris, 1959), pp. 170–75.

51. On the economic doctrines of the Physiocrats, the work of Ronald Meek, *The
Economics of Physiocracy* (Cambridge, Mass., 1963), is indispensable. The works of Georges
Weulersse (see bibliography) provide the historical background and development of the
theories and theoreticians.

52. *Ethocratie*, p. 122, note 52. On the continuing debate on the benefits of small and
large farms, see Bourde, *Agronomie et agronomes*, 2:1005.

53. *Ethocratie*, p. 140; similarly *La Morale universelle*, 2:170.

over rich but in the assumption by the rich man of the duties of leadership.

In the rather simple moral world of Holbach, the burdens of economic leadership fell on the "rich man" in general; within the more complex world of the *Encyclopédie* the theme of economic leadership was much more varied but still very much alive. The large farmer received his due in the Physiocratic articles "Agriculture," "Blé," "Fermiers," "Grains," and others. The author of "Généreux" praised the efforts of the duke of Lorraine, who reportedly established an ongoing public corporation to maintain a continuous supply of grain at a stable, moderate price.[54] Diderot lauded the philosophe, who acted as Socrates' midwife to the artisan mind, bringing the processes of the arts into the light.[55] And the entry "Alsace" offered a detailed set of proposals to improve the conditions and production of Alsatian mines, requiring state supervision and initiative on a broad scale.[56] No specific economic doctrine united the proposals of the *Encyclopédie*. The Physiocratic articles preached the virtues of free trade in grains while Diderot pointed to the necessity of supervision and controls in the trades of butchers, bakers, and meat vendors.[57] But the spirit of economic activism and leadership—the idea that both the state and the wealthy man can create prosperity—pervaded the approach of the *Encyclopédie*.

Diderot's personal support shifted from Physiocracy, during the years of his editorship, to anti-Physiocracy (*Apologie de l'Abbé Galiani*, 1770), to the Turgotian liberalism of his later years.[58] But throughout his career he maintained his belief that the power of leadership could create wealth for a nation. In proposing legislation for Catherine the Great he once fantasized that he had received the royal crown and had taken it upon himself to transform luxury in Russia and France from a "mask of misery" to a "sign of public well-being and general happiness."[59] "King Denis" became an economic leader of major

54. *Encyclopédie*, 7:574.
55. "Discours préliminaire," *Encyclopédie*, 1:xxxix.
56. *Encyclopédie*, 1:301–02.
57. *Encyclopédie*, 2:350–52, 359–60; 3:12. He still favored state supervision of quality, weights, and measures two decades later; see *Mémoires*, p. 252.
58. On Diderot's evolution on the matter of grains, see Georges Dulac, "La question des blés," *Europe*, nos. 405–06 (Jan.–Feb. 1963): 103–09.
59. *Mémoires*, p. 149.

proportions. He sold royal domains to increase tax revenues and improve production; he drastically reformed the royal household; he reduced pensions; he gradually eliminated monastic holdings and lowered clerical revenues to those needed for social services; he streamlined the collection of taxes and eliminated most tax agents; he eliminated privilege and shifted tax burdens onto the rich.[60] In other memoranda, he proposed additional duties: building roads, creating cities, fostering the growth of a third estate of artisans and shopkeepers.[61] All these goals, he determined, rested within the reach and responsibilities of leadership.

The program of "King Denis" captured the philosophes' sense of economic activism. While laissez-faire has survived as the supposed economic injunction of the eighteenth century, the animus of enlightened economics was quite different. Much power rested with the leaders of society, private and public, to generate wealth which all could share. They addressed their plans primarily to monarchs, not from any theoretical belief in "enlightened despotism" but from a knowledge of where power lies and a sure sense that economic reform would inevitably precede social and political reform. They looked to holders of power, from landowner to king, to think in terms of generating wealth through action in the spirit of both the new technology and new sense of social justice. Different milieus dictated different policies. The Badenese economic reformer Reinhard saw two goals within reach of his activist margrave, Karl Friedrich—emancipation of the peasant from all personal servitude, tithes, feudal dues, and similar burdens, followed by the conversion of a free peasantry to the newest agricultural methods. These he regarded as the sine qua non of Badenese growth and prosperity.[62] Joseph von Sonnenfels, Austrian cameralist and advisor to Maria Theresa, also looked to the freeing of the peasant as the beginning of prosperity, but he looked to freedom within an economy which offered a stable living. To achieve this goal, he urged, among other measures, restriction of Catholic holy days, dissolution of guild monopolies to open more employment, land grants to peasants whenever possible, export premiums on grains, and a tax-exempted minimum income for the

60. Ibid., pp. 145–60. Also found, almost verbatim, in "Entretiens," *Oeuvres politiques*, pp. 289–300.
61. *Mémoires*, pp. 55–58, 187, 197–98, 257.
62. Liebel, *Enlightened Bureaucracy*, pp. 43–45.

people.[63] The Neapolitan reformer Giuseppe Palmieri urged upon his impoverished nation a wide-ranging program of change, including state-supported credit for the provinces and their farmers, incentives to convert feudal barons into English-style agricultural entrepreneurs, and destruction of privileges and monopolies responsible for maldistribution of income.[64] And Jeremy Bentham, though he lived in an economy that many on the continent regarded with envy, proposed a number of legislative projects designed to further improve that economy. Among his proposals were the nationalization of the Bank of England, providing for supervision of all banking executives; the initiation of government activity and supervision in matters of research, education, health, transportation, and communication; and the assumption by the state of responsibility for most forms of insurance. He thus looked favorably on most measures that would promote a stable and more egalitarian economic order for the mass of men.[65] The policies thus differed widely, but the spirit of activism with special concern for the masses remained paramount throughout the proposals of economic reformers.

The new kind of economic leader proposed by the reformers stood in opposition to the predictable figure of the well-entrenched villain who had failed to use his position of private wealth to produce public prosperity. The list of villains had become traditional by mid-century: monks who supposedly lived in idleness and leisure; tax agents who harassed peasants and merchants and acted as parasites on the nation's tax revenues; monopolists who sought to control the flow of goods, especially grain, and reap windfall profits from the sufferings of the people; holders of feudal dues and privileges that represented taxes on the labor of the people with no recompense.[66] As their sensitivity to the victimization of the people grew, some philosophes added to the villainous company the idle rich who failed to generate prosperity through proper expenditure. In the first half of the eighteenth century, most reformers had agreed that expenditure by the rich—in virtually any form—helped produce economic

63. Kann, *Austrian Intellectual History*, pp. 174–91.

64. Venturi, *Italy and the Enlightenment*, pp. 208–09.

65. T. W. Hutchinson, "Bentham as an Economist," *Economic Journal* 66, no. 262 (June 1956):288–306, esp. pp. 302–03.

66. On the broad-ranging attack on feudal dues and privileges, see J. Q. C. Mackrell, *The Attack on "Feudalism" in Eighteenth-Century France* (London, 1973). The movement he describes was seconded across the continent.

prosperity and brought indirect benefits to the laboring classes. Voltaire's famous poem "Le mondain" captured the mood of an Enlightenment at once hostile to the Christian ascetic spirit and comfortable in the aristocratic society of the Parisian salon.[67] Voltaire never abandoned his faith in the utility of all expenditure and luxury; he continued to defend his poem as late as 1770.[68] Even while ridiculing the Lenten "fast" of the rich Parisian—delicacies brought from the coast—Voltaire could not resist preaching the old notion of the utility of luxury. This expenditure, he wrote,

> gave a living to the messengers, to the horsedealers who sold the horses, to the fishermen who furnished the fish, to the netmakers . . . to the boat builders, etc., to the grocers where one bought all the exotic chemicals which make fish taste better than meat.[69]

To the many supporters of Voltaire's position, such as Samuel Johnson, luxury expenditure represented bienfaisance, rewarding the working poor by providing work and revenue.[70] But by the 1770s Voltaire appeared more than a bit old fashioned on the problem of luxury. Diderot described "Le mondain" as the "apology for the fever of a dying man, which I'd never take for a good thing, though perhaps once the sick man's fever stops, he will die."[71] Condorcet attributed Voltaire's "errors" to his education in an age still under the spell of Colbert.[72]

Instead of accepting all luxury, the reformers of the mature Enlightenment began to try to distinguish its proper and improper forms. Nicolas Baudeau codified the Physiocratic position by defining two types of ostentation—that of consumption (*faste de con-*

67. On the generally favorable attitudes toward *luxe* as they crystallized after the age of Colbert, see André Morizé, *L'apologie du luxe au xviiie siècle et "Le mondain" de Voltaire* (Paris, 1909), pp. 25–129, and Spengler, *French Predecessors of Malthus*, chapter 4, "Cantillon and the Theory of Luxury." In a striking short article, Hans Kortum has linked the defenders of *luxe* (e.g., Fontenelle, Perrault) with the defense of the "moderns," and the opponents of *luxe*, (e.g., Fleury, Fénelon) with the defense of the "ancients"; see "Frugalité et luxe à travers la querelle des anciens et des modernes," in *VS* 56 (1967):765–75.
68. Voltaire, *Oeuvres complètes*, 10:94–96.
69. *Questions*, "Carême," Voltaire, *Oeuvres complètes*, 18:53.
70. Voitle, *Samuel Johnson the Moralist*, pp. 98–100.
71. *Mémoires*, p. 145, and "Entretiens," *Oeuvres politiques*, p. 284.
72. *Oeuvres complètes*, 4:384.

*summation*) and that of decoration (*faste de decoration*). The former involved foodstuffs and encouraged increased production from the land, either by direct demand for food or by expenditure for roads, canals, irrigation, and the like. The latter, true *luxe*, drew expenditures away from the heart of the economy toward mere show and worked to the detriment of society.[73] The author of "Luxe" in the *Encyclopédie*, Saint-Lambert, distinguished between a luxury based on honest and fruitful activity and one based on the abuses of tax collectors, monopolists, and financiers. Large-scale expenditure by the possessors of ill-gotten wealth in part cured unfair inequality by spreading wealth, but enlightened reform to prevent such wealth seemed a much healthier physic.[74] Diderot, Helvétius, Holbach, and Condorcet similarly saw in the luxury of the rich a sign of excessive inequality and an obvious signal to the legislator that society needed reform.[75] In 1776 Condorcet attacked most strongly the economic and social imbalances symbolized by excessive luxury. "It is not the grain trade, it is not the perfection of the art of working the earth that causes depopulation; it is luxury," he wrote,

> which, in poor and oppressed nations, trades the subsistence of the poor man's children for the extravagant toys with which the rich man caters to his boredom or vanity; it is luxury which has produced the destructive art of having a single man devour the subsistence of a hundred families; it is luxury which has changed into parks and pleasure gardens the fields which should

73. For Baudeau's central statement of the Physiocratic doctrine on luxe, see *Principes de la science morale et politique sur le luxe et les lois somptuaires*. Baudeau considered only the second real "luxe" and called for the legislator to educate the rich in the "natural and essential order of national expense" so that they might direct their expenditures in useful directions (p. 31).

74. *Encyclopédie*, 9:765–71.

75. Helvétius's somewhat muddled views appear in *De l'esprit*, *Oeuvres complètes*, 1:139–58, and in *De l'homme*, *Oeuvres complètes*, 4:14–53. Diderot clarified his own views primarily in his commentary on *De l'homme* in *Oeuvres complètes*, 2:414–18. Whereas Helvétius tried to distinguish "good" and "bad" luxury in the manner of Saint-Lambert, Diderot would term only the latter "luxury" at all, and in need of correction. (For an earlier statement of Diderot's views, see his Salon of 1767 in *Oeuvres complètes*, 11:84–89.) Holbach distinguished *commerce utile*, which increased the supply of foodstuffs, from *commerce de luxe*, which exchanged necessities for objects of men's vanities; see *Ethocratie*, pp. 125–53 for an extended discussion. Holbach, more of a moralizer than most philosophes, condemned luxury on numerous occasions; see also *La Politique naturelle*, 2:242–65, and *La Morale universelle*, 2:166–77.

have nourished men; it is luxury which covers with useless pro-
ductions the lands which should have yielded grain.[76]

Luxury at the highest levels no longer seemed, as it had to Colbert
and Voltaire, the outward glow of inner economic health.

Philosophes and reformers discerned other villains, at a much lower
level of society, but still above the people. These were the guilds,
with their system of masterships. Motives for opposition to guild
institutions were numerous, generated in part by social bias, in part
by the legitimate perception of the cramping effect of guilds on prices
and employment. The critics argued rightly that most *maîtrises* had
become hereditary possessions, blocking entry for those below.[77]
Those men concerned with the supply and price of foods saw in the
monopoly of the guilds one cause of inflated prices for the lower
orders. To religious sceptics the heavy guild investment in church
rituals represented a misallocation of resources; and to others the
guilds appeared a primary cause of underemployment.[78] Those who
supported suppression of the guilds could and did, therefore, argue
that the measure would bring relief to the people. In the 1776 edict
suppressing the guilds, Turgot wrote in the king's name:

> We must assure all our subjects the full and entire enjoyment of
> their rights; above all we owe this protection to that class of
> men who, having no property but their work and their industry,
> have, all the more, the right and need to employ to the fullest
> extent the only resources they have for their subsistence.[79]

76. "Réflexions sur le commerce des blés" (1776), *Oeuvres complètes*, 11:159. See also his
denunciations of Colbert in his notes to Voltaire, *Oeuvres complètes*, 4:375–85. He did,
however, accept luxury expenditure as an interim cure for gross inequality since it allowed
funds to flow down to artisans; see ibid., pp. 234–35.

77. On guilds and maîtrises as agents of oligarchy, see the urban studies of Goubert,
*Beauvais et le Beauvaisis*, pp. 270–73, Pierre Deyon, *Amiens au xviie siècle* (Paris, 1967),
chapter 25, and Maurice Garden, *Lyon et les Lyonnais au xviiie siècle* (Paris, n.d), pp. 559–61.
The Grand Fabrique in Lyon seems to have been an exception, where major divisions
existed only between the *maîtres* and the *marchands* above them; maîtrises were accessible
to most journeymen. See Garden, pp. 572–82.

78. For criticism of the guilds in the 1760s and 1770s, see especially the indictments of
Faiguet de Villeneuve in the *Encyclopédie*, "Maîtrises," 9:911–15, and Turgot's project
for and edict of suppression in *Oeuvres de Turgot*, 5:158–60, 238–55. Diderot voiced opposition to guilds on several occasions. See *Oeuvres politiques*, pp. 295, 432; *Oeuvres complètes*,
17:7; and Diderot to Abbé Galiani, 10 May 1776, *Correspondance* (869). On Voltaire's
opposition to guilds, see R. Charbonnaud, *Les idées économiques de Voltaire* (Paris, 1971
[1907]), pp. 154–57; Voltaire enthusiastically endorsed Turgot's reforms of 1776.

79. *Oeuvres de Turgot*, 5:238–39.

Diderot's judgment of a year earlier was even less circumspect. The guilds and maîtrises were "an exclusive privilege which condemns him who knows how to work to do nothing, to be a brigand, to die of hunger," and Diderot recommended their elimination in the growing nation of Russia.[80] These attacks on the guilds were echoed by philosophes, economists, and monarchs throughout Europe.[81] The guilds and guild masters took their place beside other monopolists and privileged orders as abusers of wealth and power.

Enlightened economic leaders would, therefore, encourage general prosperity and bear the responsibilities of wealth and authority. In most matters, however, the state would exercise only indirect supervision, creating a climate of moral opinion and a set of market structures which encourage responsible expenditure and entrepreneurial activity. But on one issue the philosophes unanimously insisted that there could be no evasion of responsibility—the fiscal burden of the state. Enlightenment investigation of economic issues had begun with the problem of fiscal abuse and privilege, and reformers had quickly recognized fair and proportionate taxation as the only measure which could both save royal finances and bring some measure of equity to the people.[82] Though the reformers differed markedly on fiscal methods, the spirit of fairness underlay all of their proposals.

The *Encyclopédie* offered several variations on the theme of equitable tax reform. Rousseau channeled his animus against luxury into a program for reform outlined in his article "Economie (Morale & Politique)." Though Rousseau recognized capitation as the fairest tax method in an ideal world, he characteristically thought that this

80. *Oeuvres politiques*, "Observations," p. 432.

81. See *Wealth of Nations*, chapter 10, part 2; Sarrailh, *Espagne éclairée*, pp. 557–61; Liebel, *Enlightened Bureaucracy*, p. 67; Shafer, *Economic Societies*, pp. 104–08; Hertz, *German Public Mind*, p. 331.

82. To be sure, in many ways, direct and indirect, the wealthy and privileged had borne some of the financial load of the French state since the emergency capitations and vingtièmes of the age of Louis XIV. In times of military crisis, mostly after 1660, the monarchy had levied theoretically universal taxes as temporary measures; noble owners of non-noble lands had paid taxes on substantial parts of their estates; landowners had often absorbed tax burdens of farmers and sharecroppers; the privileged were subject to many of the duties on commercial goods. The wealthy also underwrote state finances as farmers general, holders of royal *rentes*, and purchasers of offices. Still, royal capitations and emergency taxes remained temporary and often worked from the rolls of the arbitrary taille, assumption of tax burdens by the landowner was voluntary and yielded much leverage, and, whatever the risks, investment in state finances usually produced profits and status.

ideal could not work in a world which had always found ways to rob the poor. The workings of fraud, the failure to exempt necessities, and the inability to compensate adequately for the poor man's losses had worked to the advantage of the rich. Since the existing taille taxed subsistence at its heart, Rousseau proposed instead a massive program of taxation on imports, exports, and luxuries. In addition to producing revenues based on the ability to pay, these taxes would place many goods under the state's moral *police*, allowing some control of luxury consumption.[83]

De Jaucourt offered a more balanced reform approach, though he too emphasized the need for "distributive justice" in all taxation. To avoid exploitation by tax farmers, he insisted that taxes flow directly into state coffers, without unnecessary overhead. A progressive capitation, with rates increasing with income, would provide the bulk of revenues; he offered the fourfold social division of Athens after the legislation of Solon as a successful precedent.[84] A tax on luxuries would bring additional revenues and might, he suggested elsewhere in the *Encyclopédie*, provide a fund with which to buy out manorial dues and obligations.[85] A moderate proportionate tax on land and a modest sales tax on foodstuffs would complete the state's revenues.[86]

In a different vein, the article "Vingtième" offered a close approximation of the Physiocratic proposal of a single tax on land. Echoing Mirabeau, the authors suggested that labor itself was the people's tax and that the wealthy should bear any additional burdens in the form of monetary taxes.[87] In this plan all taxes would fall on landowners whose property and revenues would be determined by cadastral survey. The proportional vingtième would replace all

83. *Encyclopédie*, 5:346–49. J.-J. Graslin proposed very similar views some years later in his *Essai analytique sur les richesses et sur l'impôt* (1767). Graslin argued that a progressive capitation would have to rise so steeply to be really fair that, in fact, it could never work in society. He too proposed, therefore, principle reliance on taxes on goods, ranging from no taxes on objects of primary necessity to very high taxes on luxury objects. For Graslin's views, see the edition of A. Dubois (Paris, 1911), pp. x-xxx and 121–210.

84. *Encyclopédie*, "Impôt," 8:601–03.

85. "Taxe," 15:947.

86. The tax on foodstuffs was no doubt regressive but had some appeal even to Diderot, who saw it at work in Holland and appreciated its "hidden" workings; see *Oeuvres complètes*, 17:393–94. By the prevailing Physiocratic theory, such a tax fell, in any case, on the landowners who would have to raise wages to meet the increased cost of subsistence.

87. *Encyclopédie*, 17:874. See Mirabeau, *Théorie de l'impôt* (Paris, 1760), pp. 19–21, 415–16, for the source of this idea.

duties, including the highly lucrative but regressive duties on wine and salt. The laborer would contribute his labor to society; the landowner—on whom in theory all taxes eventually fell[88]—would give a proportionate share of his income to the state as part of his obligation.[89]

The alternatives offered in the *Encyclopédie* captured the contemporaneous spirit of fiscal reform in Europe. Though the Physiocratic "single tax" on the land drew only a small following outside Quesnay's circle, the idea of a proportionate tax on wealth won wide acceptance among reformers. Holbach favored a proportionate tax on income, set at a fixed rate, collected in nature, and supplemented by taxes on luxuries.[90] Voltaire considered proportionality the very essence of taxation and applied that principle in his support of Machault's vingtième, his opposition to the Physiocrats' *impôt unique*, and his crusade against the regressive salt tax and *aides* in the region of Gex.[91] For this sentiment Voltaire could have found ample support in *Wealth of Nations*, where Smith made proportionality his "first maxim" on taxation. Throughout his discussion Smith consistently weighed the effect of various kinds of taxes against fairness to the laborer and his standard of living. On this basis he systematically ruled out any taxes on the essential possessions of the poor, returning to luxury taxes as the fairest measure, though not without difficulties.[92] David Hume had similarly looked to luxury taxes as most equitable and "least felt by the people"; poll taxes, he argued, are

88. This theory could seem to contradict the Physiocrats' contention that they worked in the interest of fairness, since taxes supposedly fell on the landowner in any case. Miromesnil tried to argue this case against Turgot in 1776. Turgot did not argue that the worker would benefit directly from tax reform, since workers' wages basically varied with subsistence. But he did argue that tax reform would make a big difference in distribution of the tax burden as privileges and arbitrariness were eliminated from the contemporary taille and capitations. He did also argue that the tax set-up allowed the large landowner to pick up the sharecropper's taille at his discretion, allowing him to cut the sharecropper's income to the barest subsistence. (See Turgot's memorandum responding to Miromesnil's objections to tax reforms in *Oeuvres de Turgot*, 5:164–73.) Condorcet argued that the *tax annuelle* did fall entirely on the landowner through the workings of the market, but that extraordinary taxes during wartime squeezed the wage earner. He also argued that high taxes, inefficiently collected, put unnatural limits on the amount of work available to the people; see *Oeuvres complètes*, 4:432.

89. *Encyclopédie*, 17:874–77.

90. *La Politique naturelle*, 2:142–44.

91. On Voltaire's ideas on taxation, see M. Goubard, *Voltaire et l'impôt: Les idées fiscales de Voltaire* (Paris, 1931), pp. 123–44.

92. *Wealth of Nations*, 2:310.

open to great arbitrariness and massive inequities.[93] So, too, many French reformers, such as Graslin and Forbonnais, realistically saw great obstacles to the establishment of any truly fair personal or property tax, and proposed instead heavy reliance upon taxes on consumption, with rates varying inversely to the relative necessity of objects taxed.[94] Diderot did not come to specific conclusions on taxation in his advice to Catherine, but he expressed support for any tax which met the tests of proportionality and consistency.[95]

To be sure, entrepreneurs like Voltaire also saw personal advantage in reform of the general farm, and administrators like Forbonnais saw great benefits to the crown in taxes which soaked the rich and privileged. But the idea that the poor could and must not bear any heavy fiscal burdens provided both a common denominator and a strong rhetorical appeal. Complex Physiocratic models which attempted to explain how all taxes fell on the landholder could convince only a very few of the wisdom of a direct, proportionate tax. Awareness of the people's misery, however, was widespread. Against that background, the logic of a taxation which forced those who benefited most from the social order to bear the responsbility for its maintenance seemed clear.

## FREEDOM AND STABILITY

Beyond the leadership and responsibility of the wealthy and powerful, the philosophes offered the people a much more controversial gift—the open market. After matters of taxation, no issue agitated economic speculators of the Enlightenment more than the merits of a free market, especially in grain. In France so many restrictions hedged the grain market, from the village level upward, that trade in grain often remained effectively limited to the village or town and its vicinity. The impulse of early modern society was to try to insure that no food would flow away from the local community.[96]

93. "On Taxes," in Rotwein, *David Hume: Writings on Economics*, p. 85.
94. On the proposals of these and other similar reformers, see Jean Airiau, *L'opposition aux Physiocrates à la fin de l'Ancien Régime: Aspects économiques et politiques d'un libéralisme éclectique* (Paris, 1965), pp. 63–86.
95. "Observations," *Oeuvres politiques*, pp. 446–49.
96. For an account of how one village regulated its food supply and food dealers, see Thomas Sheppard, *Lourmarin in the Eighteenth Century: A Study of a French Village* (Baltimore, 1971), chapter 4.

Encouraged by English and Dutch experiments with the open grain market, the Physiocrats propagandized views counter to traditional wisdom. Far from creating stability, they argued, the closed grain markets tied the fate of a district to the vagaries of its local harvest. The open market seemed then to offer the prospect of an even flow of grain to areas of need from areas of surplus. As exports expanded, the Physiocrats predicted, the price of grain would settle at a moderately high price, the so-called *bon prix*, which would yield increased agricultural investment, expanded production, and a larger fund of wages.

Most philosophes and reformers accepted the virtues of the open market of grain, especially in internal trade. Turgot and Condorcet were enthusiastic supporters of this aspect of Physiocratic theory. Voltaire fully accepted the virtues of the open market, all the while ridiculing Physiocratic tax theories.[97] Diderot supported Physiocratic market policies throughout most of his career. Even such outspoken critics of Physiocracy as Abbé Galiani and Jacques Necker proposed only modifications of free trade to guard against excessive exports at the expense of internal supplies.[98] Throughout Europe free internal markets gained support from numbers of philosophes and administrators. The reasons were varied. For Antonio Genovesi the Neapolitan famine of 1764 marked the final condemnation of strictly regulated grain markets. For Justus Möser free trade in grain was only part of a larger program for a free peasantry able to own land and interested in expanding production. For Adam Smith the free market in corn represented primarily a means of efficient allocation of grain in scarce and plentiful years. For the Madrid Society freeing agriculture represented one step in breaking down guilds, monopolies, and other restrictions which seemed to cramp and limit Spain's wealth.[99] Whatever the logic it should be noted that eigh-

97. On Voltaire's support of free trade in grain, see Charbonnaud, *Idées économiques de Voltaire*, pp. 138–49. Voltaire ridiculed the Physiocrats' "impôt unique" in his tale "L'homme aux quarante écus," *Oeuvres complètes*, 25:305–68.

98. For Galiani's views, see his *Dialogue entre M. Marquis de Roquemaure et Mˢ le Chevalier Zanobi*, ed. P. Koch, in *Analectica Romana*, 21 (Frankfurt am Main, 1968), passim. For Necker's views, see part 4 of his *Sur la législation et le commerce des grains*, in *Oeuvres complètes* (Paris, 1820–21), vol. 1.

99. Venturi, *Italy and the Enlightenment*, pp. 208–09; Smith, *Wealth of Nations*, 2:25–29; Shafer, *Economic Societies*, p. 83; Gagliardo, *Pariah to Patriot*, p. 53.

teenth-century reformers did not perceive the open market in grain and other goods as the ferocious and manly competitive war that it would seem to nineteenth-century ideology, constantly generating new advances, weeding out the weak, disregarding individual welfare. Rather, they saw the open market as a necessary and humane experiment, stabilizing allocations, generating a higher level of annual production, moving when necessary toward greater personal freedom for the laborer.

The reformers could substantially agree that open internal markets would help stabilize the supply of grain. But the problem of wages, raised by the grain issue, presented greater difficulty. The Physiocrats' bon prix would apparently cut real wages unless other forces impelled a simultaneous rise in money wages. Even a temporary dislocation in prices could cause widespread misery. Consequently, to defend themselves against charges of inducing starvation among the people, the Physiocrats had to approach the problem of wages.

Wage theory in the eighteenth century lacked any semblance of sophistication.[100] The reformers denied that wages should be kept at bare subsistence as a matter of state policy, but they often lacked the conceptual tools or the social will to see the means to raise wages. Traditional wisdom held that wages would vary with the price of subsistence, but wage theory went little beyond that wisdom. The reformers concentrated primarily on production and revenue, assuming that the benefits would fall to society in general. The most sophisticated economic model of the day, Quesnay's *Tableau économique*, ignored problems of distribution and wages entirely. But fears that the bon prix might squeeze the day laborer forced Quesnay to deal with wages, if only in a cursory way.

At times Physiocrats appeared to accept a temporary squeeze on the worker.[101] But Quesnay normally assumed that wages would rise

100. On the general poverty of Enlightenment wage theory—largely attributable to an overwhelming concern with production—see Spengler, *French Predecessors of Malthus*, pp. 372–81, and Jean-Louis Guglielmi, *Essai sur le développement de la théorie du salaire* (Nice, 1945), "Chapitre préliminaire."

101. See note 5 of this chapter above, and the remarks of Mirabeau, quoted by G. Weulersse, *Les physiocrates* (Paris, 1931), p. 289. Weulersse concludes that though the Physiocrats tried to find benefits for the people in their schemes, they really accepted a lower standard of living for the gens des bras. The conclusion seems unjust. Except for a few isolated remarks, the economists assumed that the lot of the people would become more stable under the new regime and that wages would at least rise to meet the new price of grain. They had every reason to want that stability, since instability had brought urban

automatically with the money price of subsistence and, in more optimistic moments, saw some possibility that the wage earner might share in the new prosperity. He assumed that if his reforms were instituted, the fund of wages (the demand for labor) would expand, bringing fuller employment to the countryside. Still, since his economic model did not assume a continuing expansion of the economy with consequent upward pressures on wages, he relied on the arbitrary supposition that wages would stabilize at a level above mere subsistence. In his "General Maxims" of 1767, Quesnay argued that the high price of grain would bring a higher living standard, since wages were pegged to the price of grain. If the daily wage usually equalled one-twentieth of the price of a *setier* of grain, then a higher natural price would leave more above subsistence than before. For example, were the current price of grain and the current wages such that 100 *livres* served for subsistence and 30 livres for objects beyond pure necessity, a doubling of the natural price of grain would leave 200 livres in wages for subsistence and 60 livres beyond.[102] Quesnay provided no mechanism for this adjustment, assumed prices of other articles would not rise, and postulated a margin above subsistence to begin with. In the end, therefore, he relied primarily on his instincts, on the supposition that a prosperity born of higher agricultural production and stable prices would fall to the benefit of the laborer.

Both Turgot and Condorcet expressed similar expectations of a rise in the living standard for the laborer. Turgot has been accused of originating the idea of the "iron law" of wages according to which competition always reduces wages to minimum subsistence, and there is no doubt that he judged the case substantially in that light.[103]

---

violence. While they did not argue exclusively or mainly from the perspective of the people, they also did not have in mind a progress bought at its expense.

102. See I.N.E.D., maxim xix and note, pp. 954, 973.

103. H. Grange, in "Turgot et Necker devant le problème du salaire," *Annales historiques de la révolution française* 29 (1957):19–33, tries to portray Turgot as an unfeeling liberal in the nineteenth-century Manchester mold and Necker as the friend of the working man. I think he both underestimated Turgot's concern for improving the life of the people and overestimated Necker's paternalism. Turgot advocated a free market in grain, but saw benefits for the people in that open market, and he advocated reforms in taxation, the corvée, and charity clearly aimed at improving the people's lot. Necker can best be described as a "social pessimist," finely attuned to the illegitimacy and injustice of the social order but unable and unwilling to see a way out. Instead, he recommended giving the people "le pain qui le nourrit, la religion qui le console," as the most society could offer. (See Necker, *Oeuvres complètes*, 1:126.) Necker argued that given the injustice of the social order, the best one could do was to guarantee the people its bread through restrictive

But "subsistence" is an elastic term, and Turgot thought he perceived some margin of comfort for the manual laborer. In a healthy economy, as we have seen, Turgot thought that a little excess constituted a "necessity" for the wage earner.[104] In the stable grain market of the Physiocrats he thought he perceived a mechanism to give that modicum of comfort. Turgot argued that the price of a day's labor was pegged to the normal price of grain in an area, not its higher average price. Real wages would rise as the normal price of grain approached the average price, a result of a stable grain market.[105] Condorcet found the argument congenial and often expressed confidence that the new economies would bring a higher standard of living for the common day worker.[106] Like Quesnay, Turgot and Condorcet ignored problems of market mechanisms and the difference between real and money wages; their analyses betray worthy hopes more than solid reasoning.

Their easy assumptions did not pass unchallenged. Though common wisdom among political economists assumed that wages rose and fell with the costs of subsistence, the new political economy was becoming increasingly aware of labor as a commodity and wages as its price, determined by market laws of supply and demand. In a letter of 1766 Hume questioned Turgot's assumptions that higher taxes on consumption would automatically bring higher wages. Wages, he argued, depend on "quantity of labor" and "quantity of demand," implying that only increasing demand or decreasing supply could raise wages to meet new costs of living. Turgot had understandable difficulty meeting Hume's objections.[107] Adam Smith expanded on Hume's intuitions, opening up wages for the first

---

legislation and, as he argued at great length in 1788, maintain popular religious belief as a consolation and sedative. (See *De l'importance des opinions religieuses*, in *Oeuvres complètes*, vol. 12.) Condorcet—a social optimist as well as an opponent of social religion—sensed the conservatism in Necker's "realism," arguing against him that reformers thought that the people wanted and deserved more: equality before the laws, the end of oppressive luxury, the abolition of corvées and gabelle, reform of taxes, a reformed and free criminal justice, abolition of the *droit de chasse*, better transportation, and public instruction. (See "Réflexions," *Oeuvres complètes*, vol. 11, chapter 3.) Condorcet's perspective might have been in part naive, but I think he correctly perceived the false compassion in Necker's observations.

104. *Oeuvres de Turgot*, 3:288.
105. Ibid., pp. 286–89.
106. "Réflexions," *Oeuvres complètes*, 11:132–43; "Monopole, monopoleur," in vol. 11, p. 44; and *Vie de Turgot*, in vol. 5, pp. 40–41.
107. Rotwein, *David Hume: Writings on Economics*, pp. 208–13.

time to full-scale analysis. He correctly saw that only an expanding economy could sustain a high standard of living for its wage earners.[108] The stable economy of agricultural reproduction envisaged by the Physiocrats could not. All philosophes looked to some improvement in the people's lot under reformed economics, but none could foresee that sustained growth which could give the laborer significant leverage in the competition for a share of the wealth. Even a man of the sensibility of Condorcet conceded that, though sustained growth might dramatically raise the standard of living, the future appeared to hold for the laborer wages only slightly above subsistence even in a reformed economy.[109] Without having experienced a burgeoning economy the reformers could only suppose that as a reformed economy prospered, benefits would filter down to most at the base of the economy. Adam Smith looked to an increase in production leading to "that universal opulence which extends itself to the lowest ranks of the people."[110]

The philosophes' goals for the economic future were, therefore, modest by modern standards, though still most optimistic by those of the Old Regime. Condorcet defined his aims in 1775:

> That all members of society have assured subsistence in all seasons, in all years, and in all places that they live; that above all he who has only his wages may buy the subsistence which is necessary: such is the general interest of the whole nation; such must be the goal of all legislation on food.[111]

Similarly, Holbach opposed the current order of society to an ideal one in which the majority of men might "without excessive work, procure the needs nature has made necessary."[112] Helvétius judged a man happy when, by a moderate amount of work, he could easily provide both a generous diet and a home for his family.[113] And Diderot objected to Helvétius's standard only by insisting that a man should also be able to save enough over subsistence to have both a margin in times of crisis and independence in old age.[114]

108. *Wealth of Nations*, 1:72–79.
109. *Oeuvres complètes*, 11:103–05.
110. *Wealth of Nations*, 1:12.
111. "Réflexions," *Oeuvres complètes*, 11:111.
112. *Système de la Nature*, 1:348; see as well *La Politique naturelle*, 2:151–52.
113. *De l'homme, Oeuvres complètes*, 4:191, note 6.
114. *Oeuvres politiques*, "Réfutation," p. 473.

To the philosophes, poverty appeared the necessary and acceptable condition of most men. To indicate the economic enemy, they and their contemporaries often spoke not of "poverty" but of "misery"—that condition in which economic burdens put subsistence in jeopardy. Diderot defined both *pauvreté* and *misère* in the *Encyclopédie*, and the difference is striking. "Poverty is a condition opposed to opulence," he wrote; "in it one lacks the pleasant things of life; one cannot emerge from it by one's own efforts; it is not a vice in itself, but it is worse than that in the opinion of men. . . . A poor man with a little pride can do without aid."[115] Poverty was an unenviable condition, inevitable within existing technology. "Misery," however, was something abnormal, deserving and capable of legislative correction:

> There are few souls so strong that *misery* does not humble and degrade them in the end. The masses are unbelievably stupid. I cannot conceive what magic spell closes its eyes to its present *misery* and to the even greater *misery* which old age holds for it. *Misery* is the mother of great crimes; sovereigns create miserable men, and they will answer both in this life and in the next for the crimes which *misery* will have committed.[116]

Dependence and instability marked the laborer in the eighteenth century. Adam Smith observed that, unlike the merchant, farmer, and manufacturer, "many workers could not subsist a week, few . . .

---

115. *Encyclopédie*, 2:213. The full title is "Besoin, Nécessité, Indigence, Pauvreté, Disette." In a world where most people were "peuple," the need to distinguish within that mass was necessary, much as the French police had to try desperately to sort out types of beggars: vagabonds, brigands, poor transients, begging pilgrims, begging orders, etc. The full text is interesting and runs as follows: "*Poverty* is a condition opposed to *opulence*; in it one lacks the pleasant things of life; one cannot emerge from it by one's efforts; it is not a vice in itself, but it is worse than that in the opinion of men. *Indigence* is nothing more than extreme *poverty*; in it one lacks necessities. *Famine* [*disette*] refers to food; *need* [*besoin*] and *necessity* [*nécessité*] are terms which would be completely synonymous to *poverty* and *indigence*, respectively, if they did not have some relation to the help one can expect from other men; *need* impels less than *necessity*; the *poor* are despised; the *indigent* are pitied; one avoids those in *need*, and one serves those in *necessity*. A *poor* man with a little pride can do without aid; the *indigent* must accept it; *need* forces one to ask for it; *necessity* makes one accept the smallest gift. If the delicate nuances in the different conditions are examined, perhaps one will find the reason for the strange feelings that they elicit in most men."

116. *Encyclopédie*, 10:575. The distinction was, of course, not absolute. Within many contexts, especially in the parlance of the church, *pauvre* meant "in need of help." The *Encyclopédie* defined *Pauvre* in this sense (12:209), but identified this use as Scriptural. More often, however, the philosophes spoke of pauvres as synonymous with peuple. They almost never spoke of *misère* without indicating that it was an unnatural and unacceptable con-

a month, and scarce any a year without employment."[117] The cure to misery rested in a stability which relieved those pressures driving the people to the thin edge of starvation. These pressures—the injustice of laws, the myopia of seigneurs, the treachery of nature—fell within the province of the able and vigorous legislator. The elimination of corvées, militia service, arbitrary tax burdens, feudal dues, and closed markets would bring predictability to the life of the peasant. Government and entrepreneurs would bring new techniques and higher productivity to the countryside. Reform of most taxes would relieve the downward pressure exerted by an unfair tax structure. A healthy economy, supplemented by public charity workshops, would provide a stable fund of work. A sane, discriminating charity would meet unforeseen misfortunes. Some eighteenth-century utopians offered much more to the people. But from the philosophes' reformist perspective, the end of misère and the advent of stability seemed reward ample enough for the gens des bras.

---

dition, normally linked to some abuse. On the use of *pauvre* as a person who has only his labor, see J.-P. Gutton, *La société et les pauvres*, pp. 8–11.

117. *Wealth of Nations*, 1:68.

# 8 Equality

As one aside in a novel of asides, Diderot's fatalist Jacques and his master engage in a debate on equality.[1] The master has scorned his servant's mistress for desiring a *Jacques*, a mere peasant. The dialogue continues at cross-purposes:

> *Jacques*: A Jacques! A Jacques, sir, is a man like any other.
>
> *Master*: Jacques, you're wrong, a Jacques is hardly a man like any other.
>
> *Jacques*: Sometimes he's better.
>
> *Master*: Jacques, you're getting carried away. Resume the story of your loves, and remember that you are and always will be only a Jacques.

Jacques, of course, will not leave the matter alone and offers in his own defense ten years as equal and friend to his titular "master." The master insists in turn that he has given the name "friend" to Jacques only as a superior does an inferior. The friends nearly come to blows before their kind hostess offers to arbitrate. Her decision betrays a wisdom so typical in Jacques's fatalist world:

> Having heard the statement of monsieur Jacques; and from facts which seem to prove that his master is a good, a very good, an overly good master; and that Jacques is not a bad servant, though a bit prone to confound absolute possession with a free and temporary gift; I declare null and void the equality established between them by the passage of time, and I immediately reestablish that equality. Jacques will descend, and having descended, will ascend.[2] He will return to all the prerogatives which he has enjoyed until today. His master will extend his hand and say in friendship, "Hello Jacques, so good to

---

1. *Oeuvres romanesques*, pp. 659–66.
2. Her solution seems to parody the paradoxical structure of Rousseau's social contract in which everyone, having given himself up to everyone else, gives himself to no one.

see you again." And Jacques will reply, "And I am, sir, enchanted to see you again." And I forbid that this matter ever come in question again, or that the prerogatives of master and servant ever be weakened in the future; and I order that the matter of what one can and the other must do be left in the same obscurity as before.

Jacques first accepts his fate, then insists on his superior utility in the social order, then cites scripture to predict his ultimate victory, and then gives in.[3]

The confrontation thus ends with no decision, or at least a decision not to decide. The desire of the hostess—and, implicitly, Diderot—to leave the matter in obscurity is extraordinary in the literature of the philosophes, who normally demanded clarity, not obscurity. The conscious ambiguity of the hostess's decision mirrors an ambiguity in the minds of Diderot and the philosophes. They sensed and experienced the inequity and dangers of a hierarchical society and sympathized with the people's misery, but they also enjoyed and appreciated the benefits of a society which allowed the luxury of arts, literature, and philosophes. They could not, as had Jacques, take solace in the biblical promise to make the last first, nor would they have especially wanted to see such a turn of events. But in the end they could not leave the matter of equality entirely in the shadows, if only because their opponents constantly accused them of leveling differences and undermining right order. They rarely proposed legislation in the name of "equality"; to do so would have been impolitic. More often than not they dealt with the deeper ambiguities of equality at the level of myth and "natural history."

The oldest such myth the philosophes had at hand was the legend

---

3. The motif of the temporary confusion of orders appears elsewhere in Diderot and held some fascination for him. Most significantly, he reported on his Holland trip: "I am told that for a long time in the scigneury of Warmonde they used to celebrate a type of saturnalian holiday where valets became masters and masters valets. The valets, magnificently attired, were served by the seigneur and his lady, covered by the simplest of clothes. The next day everyone returned to his condition and took up his tasks." See *Oeuvres complètes*, 17:417. One is tempted to see in this remark the germ of the incident in *Jacques le Fataliste* or at least a similar fascination with the motif. See also Diderot's description of the fête at La Chevrette in a letter to Sophie Volland, 13 or 14 September 1760, *Correspondance* (178), for his appreciation of the social harmony at the castle fête. (I owe this reference to J. Proust, "La fête chez Rousseau et chez Diderot," *Annales Jean-Jacques Rousseau*, 39 [1968]:175–96.)

of "natural equality," expressed in tales of golden ages or primitive tribes where a beneficent Nature allowed equality among all men. Antique historians had left a legacy of nostalgia for uncomplicated, virtuous ages that existed before the advent of such corruptions as money and property. Herodotus's Scythians, Plutarch's Spartans, and Tacitus's Germans reemerged in the philosophes' writings as paradigms for the present, corrupted age. The author of "Scythes (philosophie de)" in the *Encyclopédie* held up the virtues of these primitive men to evoke shame in his contemporaries. Arguing that these simple men knew more happiness than their civilized Greek neighbors, the author anticipated the "outrage" of his reader:

> What! can ignorance of vice be preferable to knowledge of virtue; and do men become wicked and unhappy as their minds improve and as the semblance of divinity emerges among them?

Recognizing fully the barbarian ferocity of the Scythians (they blinded their slaves to eliminate all distractions), the author still cast his lot with their simplicity. "I prefer," he wrote, "a momentary atrocity to a permanent, civilized corruption; a violent attack of fever to spots of gangrene." Still, his account of the contacts of Scythian heroes with Greek philosophers and legislators indicates that the exchanges were fruitful for both sides.[4]

One man's Scythian was another's Spartan. For Helvétius, as for Rousseau, the myth of Spartan virtue provided a measure of the corruptions of modernity. Sparta represented a past eternally lost. The virtue of the egalitarian warrior band had something to tell the world many centuries later, but the ancient society remained irreconcilable with an order based on property and wealth. Helvétius discussed the cause of this change—money—with consistent emphasis on its degrading effects. In the end, however, there could be no escape; the abolition of money would now bring poverty and chaos into a world dependent on gold. Only a republic of landholders could, he thought, resurrect a part of that antique virtue.[5] Most philosophes indulged in these excursions into the myth of natural equality. They often portrayed lands without an impoverished peuple, where primitive economy either allowed or forced a virtuous equality. "In a sparsely populated society," Turgot noted in 1748, "there is no

4. *Encyclopédie*, 14:849.
5. *De l'homme, Oeuvres complètes*, 4:14–59.

*populace*; equality reigns and drives away despotism; kings cannot live apart from their subjects; their people is their guard and their only court."[6] Rare is the nation without a populace, and that is the point. By placing this reign of natural equality far distant from the corrupted world of eighteenth-century Europe, the philosophes absolved the legislator of any duty to reestablish it. These myths were moral fables, not legislative prescriptions.

The idea of natural equality allowed the philosophes to hold up a radically different social order against their own. But to deal with the realities of the eighteenth century, much more often they chose the tactic of "natural history," explaining the given order in terms of the natural flow of human events and passions. Men might be, in some vague sense, equal by nature; they were also very unequal by that same plastic standard. The philosophes met any attempts to take natural equality at face value with a strong assurance that inequality played a natural and essential role in the ordering of any civilized nation. "Barbarism makes all men equal," Turgot once remarked,[7] and the philosophes chose the inequalities of civilization over the equality of barbarism, knowing that they effectively had no choice. In his long reply to the sentimental egalitarianism of Madame de Graffigny's *Lettres d'une péruvienne* (1747), Turgot became the first of the philosophes to oppose a natural history of inequality to the fantasies of primitive equality and happiness. The differences in human conditions, he wrote in 1751, arose naturally from differences in ability among individuals and families. Without inequality everyone would live at the level of subsistence agriculture, and no one can rightfully ask for that. Rather, according to Turgot, justice and utility recommend that those not fortunate enough to be born with great ability or rank place their labor at the disposal of others, trading their fruitless natural independence for their subsistence. The man of leisure then has time to create even more general wealth. Rejecting any hopes for an unwise and unjust equality, Turgot advised that one accept the differentiation of function and ranks and appreciate its advantages.[8]

6. *Oeuvres de Turgot*, 1:134; repeated similarly on p. 296. Cf. Smith, *Wealth of Nations* 2:205: "The first period of society, that of hunters, admits of no such inequality. Universal poverty establishes there universal equality."
7. *Oeuvres de Turgot*, 1:217.
8. Ibid., pp. 241, 243.

Some years later Voltaire offered a much less sanguine version of Turgot's story, again responding to an apparently false egalitarianism. In *Du Contrat social* Rousseau had dramatically posed the problem of the legitimacy of inequality. "Man is born free," he declared, "and everywhere he is in chains."[9] Rousseau, then, found legitimacy only in the elaborate egalitarian structure of the social contract. Voltaire probably had Rousseau in mind when he raised the same dilemma in the opening words of the entry "Egalité" in his *Dictionnaire philosophique*:

> What does a dog owe a dog, and a horse a horse? Nothing; no animal depends on his fellow; but man has received the Divine light called "reason," and what is its fruit? To be enslaved over practically all the earth.

Rather than seek to legitimize the social order, Voltaire explained its inevitable illegitimacy. If all goods were readily available, he wrote, there could be no servitude. Once land becomes scarce, however, the strong steal from the weak and oppress them. There are only two classes, oppressors and oppressed, with many grades between. The oppressed are born into their condition and learn to accept it; when pressed too hard they revolt and die. The present state of society depends on millions of propertyless men who must work the land and make shoes for others. "Equality," Voltaire concluded, "is . . . at once the most natural and most chimerical of things."[10]

Voltaire used exaggerated rhetoric here much as he had on the issue of social religion, this time to play Thrasymachus to Rousseau's Socrates. The "natural histories" of the philosophes generally found their place somewhere on the spectrum between Turgot's optimism and Voltaire's apparent resignation. Holbach echoed Turgot's optimistic formulations on numerous occasions. "Diversity among individuals of the human race puts inequality between them," he wrote, "and this inequality supports society. If all men were equal in bodily strength and mental talents, they would have no need for one another."[11] Adam Smith was less approving, more analytical of the natural roots of inequality. Property causes inequality; the greater the property, the greater the inequality. Property accentuates all

---

9. *Oeuvres complètes*, 3:351.
10. *Dictionnaire philosophique*, pp. 175–77.
11. *Système de la Nature*, 1:119; see also *Politique naturelle*, 1:173–74 for similar arguments.

causes of rank and subordination—personal abilities, age, riches, noble birth—giving them concrete form. Civil government, largely instituted to protect property, "is in reality instituted for the defence of the rich against the poor, or of those who have some property against those who have none at all."[12] An artificial institution, then, cements a natural and inevitable evolution toward subordination. Hierarchy found its place in the Enlightenment's "nature."

Whereas myths of natural equality emphasized the dissatisfaction of the philosophes within the political and social order, these natural histories of inequality testified to their essential comfort within the economic order. Yet a measure of criticism and frustration inhabits even these myths. The philosophes cast the hierarchical world in economic terms. The Christian myth of inequality resulting from original sin (forming a hierarchical society within a hierarchical universe) had no place in the philosophes' writings, though the myth remained very much alive among their contemporaries.[13] Even the more empirical formulation of Pufendorf—that inequality originated with government—found no admirers among the leading philosophes.[14] Turgot and Holbach saw naturalness in a hierarchy of economic service, but they left implicit the standard of utility by which to test its legitimacy. Voltaire seems to have been resigned to severe forms of inequality, but his division of society into oppressors and oppressed could give little comfort to those at the top who preferred much more dignified titles. Helvétius made clear in his account of the workings of money and property that no matter how inevitable they might be, they had no claims to higher moral legitimacy. Adam Smith analyzed the "natural" workings of property, capital, profit, and labor with a view toward control and reform. The philosophes' natural histories, therefore, gave only limited sanction to the existing economic hierarchy; they accepted its inevitability but did not sanctify it by a cosmic or sacred order. With utility as the measure of a just society, the door remained open to some form of legislative inter-

12. *Wealth of Nations*, 2:203–07, quotation p. 207.

13. E.g., see the essay of Abbé Talbert which captured the prize in the famous Dijon essay competition of 1754 on the origins of inequality, in Roger Tisserand, ed., *Les concurrents de J.-J. Rousseau à l'Académie de Dijon pour le prix de* 1754 (Paris, 1936), pp. 138–51. The essays of Banlos Bournan (ibid., pp. 63–75), M. Etasse (pp. 153–62), and M. de la Serre (pp. 181–90) followed similar lines of argument.

14. See the entry of Dr. Monteau to the Dijon competition, in ibid., pp. 98–113, which combines Pufendorf and Montesquieu to justify social inequalities.

vention. Despite his apparent resignation, even Voltaire could not refrain from actively supporting measures to relieve his "oppressed." All hierarchies have a bottom rung, and his rested above the level of mere miserable survival.

For the philosophes who had acknowledged this ambivalent framework of "natural equality" and "natural inequality," the temptation remained to ignore altogether the problems of those below themselves. A third tradition of long standing advised men that equality and inequality were ultimately irrelevant to happiness, the most important goal of life. Just as the Christian promise of eternal salvation to the virtuous poor might have allowed some to forget the poor, the stoic consolation that, regardless of social rank, all men face the same pleasures, the same pains, and the same ultimate fate provided a similar justification. Each condition has its pleasures, according to this tradition, and each is subject to equal psychological anguish. "Nobility is moved by tales of battles and victories, just as peasants are moved by having beautiful bells," Montesquieu once observed,[15] and no doubt he found satisfaction in that prospect.

Diderot gave the theme more stoic solemnity some years later in a letter to Sophie Volland. In the fall of 1759 proposals for heavy luxury taxes and forced loans on royal officeholders had caused anxiety among the aristocratic côterie at the Holbach household and directed discussion toward the terrors of poverty. Diderot reported these fears to Sophie, but then placed himself above such concerns. "As I saw it," he wrote to her,

> I thought that for a man who has neither wife, nor child, nor any of those attachments which make wealth desirable and leave nothing superfluous, it would be almost indifferent to be rich or poor. Were I poor, I would go into exile and submit to the ancient condemnation brought by nature upon the human race—to earn bread by the sweat of the brow.
>
> This paradox is connected to the equality which I have recognized among conditions and to the little difference, in matters of happiness, which I see between the master of the household and his doorman.

Virtue and knowledge alone distinguish men, he reasoned, and, in any case, the needs of life are few. He described the workers beneath

15. *Oeuvres complètes*, 2:422.

his window, who had labored since sunrise with only a piece of black bread to eat, and yet who sang and told coarse jokes. "At night," he concluded, "they go home to naked children around a smoky hearth, to an ugly and dirty peasant woman, and to a bed of dried leaves; and their fate is neither worse nor better than mine." Like Ecclesiastes he described his vain search for pleasure and distraction, but all attempts had ended in despair.[16]

The theme could be pressed to extremes,[17] and no philosophe indulged in its consoling power more than Holbach. The apparently equal potential of all, regardless of rank or station, for the happiness of life, consecrated his version of a hierarchical society:

> Enlightened policies insure that every citizen will be happy in the rank where birth placed him. There exists a happiness for all classes; where the state is properly constituted, there emerges a chain of felicity extending from the monarch to the farmer. The happy man rarely considers leaving his sphere; he likes the profession of his ancestors to which education has accustomed him since childhood. The people is satisfied as long as it does not suffer; limited to its simple, natural needs, its view rarely extends beyond.[18]

To the contentment of the people's limited life Holbach counterposed the anxiety of the rich. "Boredom . . . is a hangman," he wrote, "who continually punishes in the name of nature those who have not learned to rule their passions, occupy themselves usefully, or moderate their amusements."[19] Holbach thus asked his reader neither to pity automatically the poor laborer nor to envy the wealthy. Within a framework of properly limited desires, each could form a link in the "chain of felicity."

The conservative motives within this consolation cannot be denied. Despite his perception of the possibility of happiness in poverty, no philosophe was ready to give up wealth and comfort,

16. Diderot to Sophie Volland, 3 November 1759, Diderot, *Correspondance* (156). The theme is a familiar one in Diderot's correspondence; see nos. 150, 268, 348.

17. Robert Mauzi has chronicled a host of such observations in his *L'idée du bonheur dans la littérature et la pensée française au xviiie siècle* (Paris, 1960), chapter 4. Though the notion was indeed "threadbare," as Peter Gay has noted with respect to Voltaire (*Voltaire's Politics*, p. 24), I have tried below to show that it was not without nuance in some contexts.

18. *La Politique naturelle*, 2:165–66.

19. *La Morale universelle*, 1:168.

with all their pitfalls, for the laborer's "contentment," any more than Bossuet's listeners sought poverty to gain salvation. A tradition which saw felicity in the limitations of the people's lot threatened to justify a callous disregard for the misery of poverty. The historian of the idea of happiness in the eighteenth century, Robert Mauzi, has seen just such a function in this consolation, serving as a balm to the consciences of "bourgeois" moralists.[20] But whatever its function as conservative ideology among most writers, the myth did not pass entirely unquestioned among the philosophes nor did it always serve to gloss over the plight of the poor.

Two sharp refutations testify to the willingness of the philosophes to see through the mask of universal felicity. In an attack on Pascal appended to his *Lettres philosophiques* (1733), Voltaire challenged the wisdom of emphasizing the pains of the great. Pascal had compared society to a wheel, with the people near its center and the powerful near the rim. The same movement of the wheel, Pascal noted, shakes the great man on the unstable edge much more than the people near the stable center. Voltaire responded sharply:

> It is false that the lowly are less shaken than the great; on the contrary, their afflictions are more violent because they have fewer resources. Of a hundred people who commit suicide in London and elsewhere, ninety-nine are from the base people, and barely one from a higher condition. The comparison with the wheel is ingenious and false.[21]

Though Voltaire occasionally indulged in the same moralizing as had Pascal, his instinct for hard-headed realism remained strong.

Four decades later Diderot found it necessary to take a fellow philosophe to task for ignoring the real misery in the people's condition. Helvétius had discoursed at some length in *De l'homme* on the pleasures of anticipation supposedly experienced by the artisan who works with joy during the day in expectation of his reward—a

20. Mauzi, *L'idée du bonheur*, chapter 4. Though thoroughly researched, Mauzi's account of the problems of ideology in the idea of happiness founders on his own ideology. To make his account work, Mauzi deems Voltaire a "bourgeois" (p. 159), Diderot a "bourgeois" of another kind (p. 159), Montesquieu a "rich bourgeois" (p. 160); while Condorcet's attempts to fit the stoic consolation into a pattern of legislation that would narrow the gap between rich and poor are seen as a prefiguring of Marx's ideal type of the "petit-bourgeois" (p. 151, note 2).

21. Voltaire, *Oeuvres complètes*, 22:48.

day's wages and a warm hearth. To these pleasures Helvétius juxtaposed the fleeting joys and omnipresent boredom of the rich.[22] He presented this myth in his usual manner of bald overstatement; Diderot saw his myopia and rebuked him for his excesses. Diderot appreciated the tradition of stoic consolation, but he realized that the former farmer-general had a poor perspective from which to know the joys or pains of the laborer. The pleasures of anticipation he judged fragile and unfounded:

> The fatigue from his work is such that he is much more aware of the end of his work than the advantages of his wages. . . . What he utters at the day's end which takes the spade from his hand is not "Now I'll get my money" but rather "Finally I'm done for the day."[23]

Fatigue reduces the pleasures of financial rewards and marriage; most children, Diderot argued, are conceived on Sundays and holy days.[24] Against Helvétius's equation of the pains of boredom to those of indigence, he insisted upon the disabling effects of much labor. He considered comparison of physical misery to the voluntary decrepitude of the rich unfair and callous, whatever its superficial psychological truth. And where Helvétius had hailed the superior pleasures of a man who by moderate work could provide for the needs of his family, Diderot added the need for security in times of trouble; he found no joy in conditions where sickness and old age inevitably brought despair. "If the common man forgets the frightful specter of the hôpital, or if he looks at it without being frightened by it," he wrote, "it is only because he has been brutalized."[25]

Diderot properly recalled Helvétius from a position in which psychological truisms threatened to obscure awareness of the people's misery. But neither Diderot nor later historians have given Helvétius enough credit. No doubt he falsely estimated the effects of labor, but he continually tied any happiness for the common man to conditions of stability and relative ease. The chapter of *De l'homme* in which he discusses the worker's pleasures bears the title, "What constitutes the

22. *Oeuvres complètes*, 4:132–36.
23. *Oeuvres politiques*, p. 468.
24. Ibid.
25. Ibid., p. 441; cf. his brief entry "Misère" to the *Encyclopédie*, quoted on p. 146 above.

happiness of individuals; the basis on which one must build national felicity, necessarily composed of all the individual felicities." He points his entire discussion, therefore, to the instruction of the legislator. "There is no society where all citizens can be equally wealthy and powerful," he acknowledges at the outset. "But are there," he asks, "any societies where all can be equal in happiness?" This question he answers with a qualified yes, setting specific economic conditions:

> Wise laws could no doubt bring about the miracle of universal happiness. If all citizens have some property; if all have a certain amount of ease; and if they can abundantly provide for their needs and those of their family with seven or eight hours' labor, they are as happy as they can be.[26]

Work is regarded as an evil, he argues, because under most governments the people can earn the necessities of life only with excessive labor, bringing both physical ruin and mental anguish.[27] Helvétius considered his model of the happy artisan not a reality but a realistic legislative goal in the world of inequality. He resisted the notion that, since all can be happy within their conditions, the legislator need not care and pointed instead toward the encouragement of universal happiness as a goal within the reach of human legislation, as opposed to literal equality which can never exist.

Ironically, therefore, the man who seemed most to forget the condition of the poor worker also insisted on an economic goal as radical as that of any of the philosophes. Helvétius accentuated the possibility of legislation and change by adopting a myth supposedly designed to mask social difference. Holbach similarly held up his "chain of felicity"—whatever its naivete—not as a reality but as a legislative goal. Like the myths of natural inequality, the myth of equal happiness served varied purposes. One cannot define the philosophes' perspective on equality with one myth alone, nor even distill one "meaning" from any of these traditions. Still, taken together, these myths expressed congruent impulses, pointing toward a certain kind of social order. For Helvétius and the other philosophes these ideas pointed the way toward a stable and equitable society, allowing great economic inequality but providing for enough of life's

26. *Oeuvres complètes*, 4:130; repeated similarly, ibid., p. 136.
27. Ibid., pp. 133, 137.

needs to give equal access to pleasures. It remained for the legislator to turn these impulses into law.

### The Legislative Solution

To explain the unequal structure of society, Montesquieu used not natural history but an analysis of the "spirit" of governments. Noble privilege and civil inequality are, he maintained, essential to the most common form of political society, a monarchy.[28] In a monarchical society, he wrote in *De l'esprit des lois*, criminal laws must fine the nobleman more heavily than the commoner but must exact harsher corporal punishments from the latter, though the crimes be identical. The nobleman loses his honor with the first blow of corporal punishment, which causes him pain enough in a society where honor is all-important; the common man by definition has no honor, and his body must therefore suffer more.[29]

Though appreciative of the shrewdness and eclecticism of Montesquieu's sociological approach, the philosophes who succeeded him could not accept an analysis of what is as a prescription for what ought to be. Montesquieu's apology for civil inequality in a monarchy disappeared rapidly from the canons of the Enlightenment. Soon after mid-century, the demand for civil equality became standard in the philosophes' writings. Condorcet expressed the impatience of his comrades when he asked, "Why, in *De l'esprit des lois*, did Montesquieu never speak about the injustice or justice of the laws he cites, but only about the motive which he attributed to these laws?"[30] For Montesquieu law had to give concrete form to the proper spirit and structure of a society. For most other philosophes, law served a very different function: to provide a structure of fairness within which real inequalities—those of intellect, ability, opportunity—might justifiably work.

Of all the philosophes, De Jaucourt followed Montesquieu most closely, accepting the principle of ranks, distinctions, prerogatives, and subordination in all governments, especially monarchies.[31] But

28. *De l'esprit des lois*, book 5, chapters 9–12.

29. Ibid., book 6, chapter 10. Montesquieu perceived something of the spirit of monarchy in the laws of imperial Rome which increased punishment as the criminal descended in social rank.

30. *Oeuvres complètes*, 1:365; referring to Montesquieu's *De l'esprit des lois*, book 29, chapter 4.

31. See above, p. 52.

he recognized, in the entry "Egalité naturelle" in the *Encyclopédie*, the need to balance inequality with institutions embodying the truth of natural equality. He drew five conclusions from the common humanity of men: dependence can only be legitimate if it contributes to general happiness; one must obey rules of justice and equity in dealing with others; whatever does not incontestably belong to one man belongs to all; any object held in common must remain so or be divided equally; and one must treat men with a charity born of the universal susceptibility to suffering. De Jaucourt thus used the elastic principle of natural equality to justify his perception of what men owed one another. But he offered one further conclusion: the illegitimacy of civil or political slavery. He defined this slavery as any arbitrary power—in the hands of ministers, courtiers, financiers, or the like—which leads to unjust wealth and unacceptable poverty. Laws, he insisted, must in some way reinstate the moral equality of all men and compensate for the natural equality lost in the transition to civil society.[32]

Though De Jaucourt stopped short of a direct demand for civil equality, his friends within the Encyclopedic circle seized on it as a partial solution to their ambiguous feelings about inequality. As early as 1752 Diderot adopted the cause of civil equality, tracing in "Apologie de l'Abbé de Prades" a brief natural history of early society. Men first lived in a herd, unencumbered by any law; the discovery of differences in strength and talent brought on the rule of the strongest; but then enough men felt the inconvenience of arbitrary rule to institute laws eliminating its abuse.[33] The passage of time—and with it the appreciation of inequities within the Old Regime—only strengthened Diderot's conviction of the proper role of law. In 1774 the prospect of relative equality in Holland exhilarated him. In this land, he wrote,

> each is master of his home; civil liberty places each inhabitant at the same level; the great cannot oppress the small, nor the rich oppress the poor. In upholding the privileges of the citizens, the magistrate defends his own.[34]

The Dutch example, including its provision of prompt, free justice

32. *Encyclopédie*, 5:415.
33. *Oeuvres complètes*, 1:466–67.
34. *Oeuvres complètes*, 18:406.

to all, remained vivid in his mind as he formulated his legislation for Russia. He urged many measures on Catherine, but "above all" he insisted upon "laws so general that they except no one." "The universality of the law," he continued,

> is one of the greatest principles of the equality of subjects.
> Let no one be able to strike or mistreat or seriously injure another without punishment.
> The most common of men takes on loftiness, courage, and pride when he knows he has a defender in the law.
> Use your commission above all to establish this kind of legal equality; it is so natural, so human, that only wild beasts could resist it.[35]

Though Diderot's insistence on justice that was prompt and free as well as equal was unusual,[36] his concern for civil equality was common among philosophes in the 1770s. Civil equality fit neatly into every perspective from which the philosophes chose to view society. Arbitrary distinctions had always seemed to bring chaos in political, economic, social, and intellectual matters, and the rule of universal law would spell the apparent end to arbitrariness. The relative order of England, codified by liberal theorists, exemplified success within the framework of civil equality. Even nature seemed to counsel this change, as the traditional hierarchical universe gave way to the scientific one of matter and motion governed by blind laws.

But the ideal of civil equality appealed most for another reason— it was limited and safe. Whatever implications the reign of civil equality held for the social values of the Old Regime, the reformers recognized that their solution allowed room for economic differences on a broad scale. Mercier de la Rivière noted this advantage:

> The law of society is certainly the same for all men; the rights which it gives are all of equal justice, but they are not all of

35. *Mémoires*, p. 63; for similar statements see "Observations," *Oeuvres politiques*, pp. 366, 379.

36. See, however, *Encyclopédie*, "Chambre de justice," 3:53, which describes without comment an experiment of 1610 where each parlement established a chamber where the poor could plead their cases without expense. Condorcet also endorsed free justice in *Vie de Turgot* (1786), *Oeuvres complètes*, 5:18, implying that this was Turgot's opinion as well. Adam Smith explored fair means to finance the system of justice in *Wealth of Nations*, book 5, chapter 1, part 2.

equal value, because their value is totally independent of the law.

Ability, inheritance, misfortunes, and other factors would, he recognized, leave the economic ordering of society outside of the consideration of law.[37] Voltaire accepted this economic reality in a harsh moral tale in *Dictionnaire philosophique*, casting the early history of society in much bleaker terms than had Diderot fifteen years earlier. He recounted an Indian fable: Adimo, the father of all Indians, had two sons and two daughters. One of the sons was a giant, the other a hunchback. The giant kept his entire family in his service, maintaining a monopoly on sexual relations. When he tired of one of his sisters he gave her to his brother. The sons of the hunchback proved less weak than their father, and the sons of the giant less strong. When the giant's eldest son attempted to rule as had his father, the family leagued against him and formed a republic. According to Voltaire, others give a different genealogy, placing the republic first. But all philosophers agree, he wrote, that the rule of law was a late invention and that earliest times were ruled by force alone. In the end, however, Voltaire dismissed his fable as beside the point. "I do not know," he concluded,

> what has happened in the order of time; but in the order of nature, it must be admitted that all men being born equal, violence and cleverness made the first masters; laws have made the last.[38]

Voltaire did not reject the ideal of civil equality,[39] but he recognized that equal laws did not end the dominance of an elite. Laws could only place that rule within a more predictable order of stability and fairness. Justice must be blind to economic and social standing, for better *or* worse.

Economic competition would thus decide who was master, and civil equality would spread an umbrella of fair play over that competition. Still, much as the philosophes insisted on the absolute sanctity of private property, they did not entirely deny the legislator a role in determining a fair distribution of wealth and social power.

37. *L'ordre naturel*, 1:24–25.
38. "Maître" (1767), *Dictionnaire philosophique*, pp. 294–95.
39. E.g., his insistence, at about the same time, on the need for civil equality in *Essai sur les moeurs*, 1:666 and 2:26.

Behind the myths of natural equality and the natural histories of inequality stood a feeling that movement toward equality brought health to society. All sensed that some amount of redistribution, if only through fairer taxes, would add much more happiness to the life of the people than it subtracted from that of the rich. Voltaire's mythical Scythians were, after all, only a thin disguise for very real Genevans. Diderot's Dutch displayed some of the appealing equality of his Tahitians. And though Turgot criticized Madame de Graffigny's Peruvians and condemned Lycurgus's Sparta, he could not resist finding an ideal in contemporary America:

> There the uncultivated land becomes fruitful under industrious hands; laws faithfully observed forever uphold tranquility in these fortunate climes; the ravages of war are unknown; equality banishes poverty and luxury, and conserves, with liberty, virtuous and simple moeurs; our arts spread there without our vices.[40]

Europe could never duplicate the conditions of even these not-so-mythical lands, but they represented a direction toward which she might move.

Though a more equal distribution of property seemed a worthy prescription for their age, the philosophes rarely argued for reform on that basis. To do so was impolitic, even dangerous. Turgot's moderate reforms of 1776 brought accusations that he was leading a dangerous assault on the hierarchy of society.[41] Furthermore, the philosophes' own sense of the sanctity of property made argument from the need for greater equality difficult. Instead they chose other tactics to argue for measures which would help reduce economic differences within society. They wrote of the need for fair taxation, the "inconvenience" of feudal distinctions and dues,[42] the illegitimacy of some feudal prerogatives as infringements on the public sphere, the need to encourage so-called natural forms of production and consumption, the injustice of one man tying down future genera-

40. "Discours sur les avantages . . . "(1750), *Oeuvres de Turgot,* 1:205; on Sparta see ibid, p. 207.

41. See e.g., the remonstrances of the Parisian Parlement against Turgot and Boncerf, in Lester Mason, *The French Constitution and the Social Question in the Old Regime, 1700–1789* (Bonn, 1954), pp. 61–63.

42. See the pamphlet of 1776 by Boncerf, *Les inconvéniens des droits féodaux.*

tions through a perpetual endowment. These plans and criticisms all implied some form of redistribution, perhaps more significant from top toward the middle than middle toward the bottom, but still in the direction of more equality. But the value itself of equality generally remained hidden behind other arguments.

Only very late in the Enlightenment did Condorcet support the impulse toward equality as a viable justification for making laws. He accepted the common wisdom that a certain amount of inequality encouraged talent and industry, but he also remarked that "the less marked this inequality, the happier society."[43] He considered the traditional radical alternatives—community of property or sumptuary laws—dangerous and inadequate. The Sparta of Lycurgus preserved equality at the expense of numbers of slaves, and its virtue resembled "honor" among thieves and inquisitors.[44] Sumptuary laws undermined the benefits of free commerce and, in Geneva, even personal liberty.[45] Condorcet argued that other laws might indirectly strike at the foundations of unnatural inequality: new laws relating to marriage, equal partition of estates, free trade and the end of privileges, taxes without exemption and profiteers, and the end of legal distinctions which psychologically depress the people.[46]

Helvétius pushed the impulse toward equality in yet more radical, but less legislatable, ways. To recapture antique virtue in an age of money and property, he at times envisioned a republic of landholders, encompassing as broad a spectrum of the nation as possible.[47] Not all philosophes had accepted wholeheartedly the Physiocratic ideal of large landholders. Holbach saw the possibility of moral regeneration through the growth of small peasant properties;[48] Diderot urged Catherine to spread the landed wealth of Russia among a large number of small proprietors.[49] Condorcet admitted in the 1780s that the preference of large to small properties remained open to debate.[50] But most philosophes foresaw only indirect measures to divide and spread proprietary wealth. Helvétius, however, proposed several

43. *Oeuvres complètes*, 4:234, commenting on Voltaire's "Le mondain."
44. Ibid., p. 453.
45. Ibid., pp. 463–65; see also *Vie de Turgot, Oeuvres complètes*, 5:197.
46. *Vie de Turgot, Oeuvres complètes*, 5:196.
47. *Oeuvres complètes*, 4:139–41, 213.
48. *Ethocratie*, p. 126, note 52.
49. "Observations," *Oeuvres politiques*, p. 406.
50. *Oeuvres complètes*, 4:392–93.

more direct alternative measures to reach this goal that went beyond the traditional legal and social reforms of the philosophic party:[51] a reform of moeurs which would encourage landowners to reward faithful service with grants of land;[52] confiscation of church lands and their redistribution to the people, the original owners;[53] making the nation an inheritor of its inhabitants or at least heavily taxing lands above a certain size to force their sale.[54] None of these schemes seemed in the offing; Helvétius's plans always showed more of the moralist's good intentions than the legislator's realism. But he, more than any other philosophe, brought the value of closing the ranks between rich and poor into the open and argued on that basis. Within the limits of the sanctity of property, the philosophes preferred this direction whenever the legislator had a clear choice.

The philosophes thus hoped that the wise legislator could close the gap between rich and poor. They were certain that society could afford to grant the people civil equality. But in all their discussions they barely considered the possibility of giving the people political responsibility. The search for a just public order, immune from the twin evils of instability and arbitrariness, shaped the political speculations of the Enlightenment. Solutions ranged across a broad spectrum; the pluralism of Montesquieu's *De l'esprit des lois* mirrored the pluralism of the age. All governments had to meet the tests of stability and equity, but within these perimeters the political order of Walpole's England, Voltaire's Geneva, or Catherine's Russia might seem to meet the standards of enlightenment. Still, across this range of possibilities, the people played virtually no role. "One can affirm," Diderot wrote, "that all government tends toward despotism or anarchy."[55] In the eyes of the philosophes the people had the unique and unenviable distinction of furthering both: the children of Discord were also the pawns of Caesar.

The passions of the mob seemed real enough to the philosophes, to whom urban violence remained a sporadic threat. Turgot received word of the Gordon riots in England six years after the *guerre des*

51. See *Oeuvres complètes*, 1:144, note 1, for his attack on the corvée.
52. Ibid., and vol. 4, p. 31.
53. *Oeuvres complètes*, 3:74–76, note a.
54. *Oeuvres complètes*, 4:42–43. See also pp. 139–41, where Helvétius turned around the traditional wisdom that only the propertied should be citizens and argued that to make men citizens the nation should give them some property.
55. "Anarchie," *Encyclopédie*, 1:407.

*farines* of 1774 that had helped undermine his position as controller general. The news brought despair, not anger. The riots proved, Turgot wrote to a friend, "what we already knew, that men are far from being enlightened, and what many do not know so well, that there is no greater enemy to liberty than the people."[56] The riots revived the lesson of history—popular power destroys the hope of stability and the foundations of liberty.

Holbach commented at length on the prospects of popular power in his *Politique naturelle* of 1773. In keeping with classical political theory, he included democracy as a possible form of government, but ancient experience proved to him that popular power had no place in a realist's perspective. Holbach discussed democracy as a natural stage in the growth of society after the rule of kings. "Sovereignty rested in the whole of society," he wrote, "but the confusion which soon followed usually turned it into merely modified anarchy." The "idol of equality" drove the people to expel its best leaders and accept those who catered to its whims; eventually all men of exceptional virtue or wealth felt the wrath of the people.[57] Holbach discovered insupportable dangers even within the supposedly safe confines of mixed government. The people, "susceptible to frenzy, fanaticism, and passion, and usually deprived of foresight,"[58] drove such governments to precipitous acts. The judgment of Holbach was absolute, and typical of his fellow philosophes:

> In a word, wherever the people possesses power, the state carries within it the principle of its destruction. Liberty degenerates into license, and anarchy follows. Furious in adversity, insolent in prosperity, proud of its power, surrounded by flatterers, a multitude knows no moderation; it is ready to receive the impressions of all those who make the effort to deceive it; barely held back by the bonds of decency, it acts without reflection or shame; it inclines toward the most shameful crimes, the most shocking excesses.[59]

Popular political action in no way seemed to differ from the grain mob, at worst a leaderless anarchy, at best a tool of vicious deceivers.

56. *Oeuvres de Turgot*, 5:628–29, Turgot to Dupont de Nemours, 28 June 1780.
57. 1:62–63; for similar judgments see 1:68–69, 2:65–66, 238–39.
58. *La Politique naturelle*, 2:235.
59. Ibid., p. 240.

In an *Encyclopédie* article, Nicolas Boulanger traced the history of republicanism back to a revolt against theocracy among nations of independent spirit. The populace took it upon itself to limit the power of priests and placed true mastery only in the hands of an invisible god. The result was anarchy. "Each one wanted to be the master and the center, and the center, being everywhere, was nowhere."[60] Unable to live without a leader, the jealous and despotic crowd soon became the tool of tyrants.[61] The arbitrary rule of the despot thus stood as the historic inheritor, as well as the logical counterpart, of the arbitrary rule of the people.

Montesquieu had placed great emphasis on the people's love of tyrants in his accounts of the rise and fall of Rome, especially in *Considérations sur les causes de la grandeur des romains et leur décadence* (1734). To the aristocrat of La Brède, the senatorial party represented the spirit of moderation and equity in the Roman republic, and the popular party embodied the spirit of jealousy, rivalry, and bloodthirstiness. Even in its days of glory, the senate succumbed to the spirit of the people, making constant war to satisfy its desires.[62] Territorial expansion brought large armies and ultimately legions independent of the control of the senate. Rome faced its demise when both Caesar and Pompey ignored the senatorial order and curried favor with the populace. Pompey's repentance came too late for him to play Sylla to Caesar's Marius, and the senatorial tradition of moderation all but died.[63]

Montesquieu's Roman history reflected the accepted wisdom of the time. In an early *pensée* he had noted, "All the ancient republics perished at the hands of the people who empowered one man against the senate."[64] His ancient history was a long gloss on that text. Though Montesquieu's deep respect for hereditary aristocracy disappeared from Enlightenment canons, his perception of the tyrannical, tyrant-loving crowd remained.

Most philosophes proposed some variation of a senatorial order to

60. "Oeconomie politique," 11:380. He parodied part of a pensée of Pascal (no. 72 of the Brunschvieg edition): "[The universe] is a sphere with its center everywhere and its circumference nowhere."

61. Ibid., p. 381.

62. *Oeuvres complètes*, 1, part 3, p. 355; see also the "Dialogue de Sylla et Eucrate," ibid., pp. 557–58.

63. Chapters 9–11.

64. Pensée no. 194, *Oeuvres complètes*, 2:72.

serve, advise, and correct those with authority. Property rather than heredity would allow access to full citizenship with its consultative and legislative powers. Turgot and Dupont de Nemours outlined the most complete plan for creating this order in their *Mémoire sur les municipalités* of 1776, proposing a hierarchy of assemblies, beginning at the parish level. The unit which defined one vote would be 600 livres of annual landed revenue, by no means unsubstantial. Men would vote in proportion to their revenues; one man might cast several votes while several might have to combine their lots to produce one. These provisions effectively disfranchised almost all of those called "people." The reformers feared the tumult of large assemblies and saw a distinct probability that the money of the very rich might buy the votes of the very poor. With elitist logic they therefore denied power to the corruptible poor in order to protect society from the corruption of the rich. Dupont and Turgot estimated that in a parish of a hundred families, only five or six might actually exercise the *voix du citoyen*. The weight of decision would then fall on the wealthy, educated few, making the assemblies much more "reasonable" than if the illiterate and uneducated had control.[65] Not surprisingly, they associated wealth with political stability, education, and a sense of the wider public interest. In their optimism they assumed that the uneducated and volatile people without land and without a voice could expect equitable treatment within a reformed political order.

Turgot's association of property with citizenship was frequently echoed throughout the Enlightenment period. Holbach insisted on the virtues of the wealthy as representatives of the nation in the *Encyclopédie* and in *Politique naturelle*.[66] Helvétius compared ownership of land to participation in the antique Spartan armed band, producing a much lower kind of virtue, but nevertheless the only public virtue available in corrupted modern times.[67] Diderot professed admiration for "the spirit of democracy" to Catherine, but he saw no possibility of initiating anything like democratic rule in Russia. The special advantage of democracy, he wrote, is "the cooperation and

65. *Oeuvres de Turgot*, 4:583–88.

66. "Représentans," *Encyclopédie*, 14:45 and *La Politique naturelle*, 1:182–97. In the later work he seems to imply, though very vaguely, that the people might legitimately have some say in choosing from among the aristocracy of wealth, but in the end the people would have to rely on the wisdom of magistrates. these

67. *Oeuvres complètes*, 4:212–13.

opposition of general wills to individual wills."[68] Russia might harness that spirit through a permanent *nakaz*, an assembly of the wealthy.[69] The possibility of popular control played no part in his speculations, nor, we might suspect, did he ever give it serious consideration.

Even when presenting theoretically acceptable versions of democracy, the philosophes undercut its possibility by stipulating very strict, rare conditions—the small city-state, cut off from powerful neighbors, inhabited by virtuous men of relatively equal economic stature. Montesquieu codified these conditions in *De l'esprit des lois*, and other philosophes followed closely.[70] But geographic and social limitations alone did not satisfy Montesquieu. When he chose to describe acceptable democracies, he selected Rome after Servius Tullius and Athens after Solon. Both legislators had devised schemes which placed effective voting power in the hands of an oligarchy while preserving the forms of democracy. Montesquieu appreciated their efforts.[71]

Ironically, Voltaire, among the leaders of the mature Enlightenment, came closest to giving democracy a full endorsement as a viable alternative. His involvement in the political affairs of Geneva had brought him to the side of disfranchised *natifs* in their dispute with the Genevan oligarchy. In 1768, in the midst of these activities, he composed the dialogue "A, B, C" in which he gave a stature to "B," as defender of democracy, equal to that of the defender of British moderate government. "I could accommodate myself quite well to a democratic government," the spokesman "B" remarked, and proceeded to endorse a government in which all property holders in a territory, from merchants to farmers to masons and carpenters, had a voice in the making of laws.[72] The sentiments of "B" did not pass unchallenged within the dialogue, but Voltaire's willingness to give solid arguments to a spokesman for democracy represented a dramatic personal step. This endorsement, however, was not without ambiguity. "B" offered a "voice" to all property owners, thereby

68. "Entretiens," *Oeuvres politiques*, p. 276.

69. "Observations," *Oeuvres politiques*, pp. 352–71.

70. Book 3, chapter 3, and book 5, chapters 1–7. For examples of repetition of Montesquieu's provisions, see *Encyclopédie*, "Démocratie" (De Jaucourt), 4:816–18, and Voltaire, p. 170 below.

71. Book 2, chapter 2.

72. Voltaire, *Oeuvres complètes*, 27:347–48.

excluding the unpropertied and leaving implicit the possibility of a weighted vote in the manner of classical democracies. The spokesman for British moderation within the dialogue, "A," identified "B" as speaking like a resident of North Holland, a political body still far from offering a universal male franchise.[73]

Three years later, in an entry on "Démocratie" for *Questions sur l'Encyclopédie*, Voltaire again defended the legitimacy of democracy, this time in light of the criticism of Bayle. Against his predecessor he maintained that democratic principles, liberty and equality, did not necessarily lead to violence and rapine. The ambitions of great men, he insisted, caused greater havoc. But he still accepted the traditional geographic and economic limitations on the real possibility of popular rule.[74] In 1773 he could write simply to Frederick II, referring to ancient Athens, "I don't like the government of the canaille."[75] In that judgment he could expect the consent of his fellow philosophes as well as that of the king of Prussia.

The idea of the full participation of all men in government remained a myth, useful as was the myth of natural equality, but like the latter most properly related to nations remote in place and time. It was in this sense that d'Alembert could praise the oligarchical government of Geneva for having all the advantages of democracy and none of its inconveniences.[76] Likewise, Voltaire could write to d'Argental in 1765 that he inclined toward the "democratic" side of the Genevan disputes, intending not an endorsement of democracy as a form of government but a declaration of his sympathy with the more popular "bourgeois" side.[77] A decade later Voltaire again appealed to the spirit of democracy when defending his leadership in the cause of tax relief for his region of Gex. Writing to d'Argental he admitted that some might find the spirit of the tax proposals from the leadership of Gex "too popular." "We would answer," he wrote, "that in ancient Rome, and even still in Geneva, Basel, and in the small cantons [of Switzerland], plebeians make the laws."[78] Democracy thus balanced the spectrum of governments, keeping the

73. Ibid., p. 348.
74. Voltaire, *Oeuvres complètes*, 18:331–35.
75. 28 October 1773, Voltaire, *Correspondence* (17510).
76. "Genève," *Encyclopédie*, 7:576.
77. 14 October 1765, Voltaire, *Correspondence* (12070).
78. 30 March 1776, Voltaire, *Correspondence* (18895).

weight of opinion from falling too heavily on the side of absolute
monarchy or feudal privilege without, however, providing a realistic
alternative.

The philosophes could preach equality before the law because civil
equality required only recognition of a common humanity. The much
larger leap to political equality presupposed a common intelligence.
Except under very rare conditions, the people appeared cut off from
the education and spirit supposedly requisite for participation in the
processes of politics and administration. The philosophes thought of
politics in the classical manner as a solemn process requiring leisure,
education, and stature. Bentham alone was stubborn enough in his
utilitarianism to follow its logic to political democracy. Politics, he
thought, is the weighing of happiness; the happiness of each man is
equal to that of another; hence, all should have a vote in the process.[79] To other philosophes it seemed that the people by definition
could bear no public responsibility; the monarchy could not be
trusted with arbitrary authority; the aristocracy of wealth would
have to do. In the end, Jacques would have to trust his master.

79. Mack, *Jeremy Bentham*, pp. 412–20.

# Conclusion: Dominance and Responsibility

## ROUSSEAU: THE LOGIC OF DIGNITY

The philosophes followed an elitist logic of economic and social realism, tempered by their sympathy for the lot of the people. They perceived society as a hierarchy justified not by sacred order but by its inevitability and its potential utility. Within this hierarchy, established by economics and talent, they saw both great possibilities for fairness and ability and great realities of oppression and misery. Theirs was hardly the only social vision of the period. Most seigneurs still perceived the world in legal distinctions of privilege and service. Charity sermons still spoke of Christian stewardship—a sense that poverty represented an eternal, God-given reality, an opportunity for the poor to enter heaven through patience, an opportunity for the rich to earn heaven through charity. Utopians like Morelly and Godwin looked to ideal orders of social equality without seeing the means to get there. Pessimists like Linguet and Necker perceived exploitation in terms so stark that reform seemed useless at best. "Cosmic tories" like Pope and Jenyns saw the social order, with all its suffering, justified in a universal theodicy in which all worked for the best.[1] And most men in the eighteenth century, like men in all centuries, did not think much at all about society.

The philosophes dealt more or less fully and successfully with each of these alternatives. But the social vision of one from their midst—Jean-Jacques Rousseau—plagued them more than most, precisely because he moved from many of their assumptions to a quite different vision of the people and its needs. Of the major voices of the Enlightenment, Rousseau alone professed to speak for the people as one of the people. In a reflective note of 1768, he sketched his tragic relationships with all orders of society. The people warranted two entries: "The people, which was my idol, sees in me only an old fogey and an outlaw. . . . The leaders of the people, hoisted on my

---

1. The phrase is Basil Willey's; see *The Eighteenth Century Background* (London, 1940), chapter 3.

shoulders, would like to hide me well enough so that they alone could be seen."[2] Both his admiration for the lowly and his feeling of betrayal mark the perspective of the man who promised to be a courtier of the people.[3] For all his links to the Enlightenment—its interests, tactics, opinions—Rousseau remained an outsider to the company of Voltaire, Diderot, and Holbach. A lonely and complex man, he feared with good reason that no one would understand him, not even his "idol" the people.

Each reader has his own "Rousseau," fashioned out of the tangled web of insights, judgments, and misperceptions that make up the body of Rousseau's writings. His contemporaries were no exception. But out of the multitude of personal and philosophical judgments the philosophes passed on their wayward companion, one Rousseau intrigued them above all—the moralist.[4] Whenever the philosophes tried to label the protean Genevan, the names and titles of ancient moralists—dissectors of motives and weavers of paradox—came to mind. To Diderot in 1759 Rousseau was "the great Sophist." To d'Alembert he was a man "who thinks he is a cynic, but who is only inconsequential and ridiculous." Voltaire often referred to Rousseau as various facets and relations of Diogenes, the paradigmatic Cynic. By June, 1762, Rousseau seemed to Voltaire no better than "Dio-

2. "Sentimens du public sur mon compte dans les divers états qui le composent," *Oeuvres complètes*, 1:1184.

3. In *Du Contrat social* Rousseau criticized Grotius and Barbeyrac for being courtiers of their monarchs: "If these two writers had embraced true principles, all of their difficulties would have been lifted and they would always have been consistent; but it would have been most painful for them to tell the truth and pay court only to the people. Truth never brings fortune, and the people gives neither ambassadorships, nor professorships, nor pensions." (*Oeuvres complètes*, 3:370–71.)

4. As all readers must, I went back to Rousseau to try to disentangle his thoughts. I have found several useful and persuasive guides. On Rousseau as moralist, C. W. Hendel, *Jean-Jacques Rousseau, Moralist*, 2 vols. (New York, 1934), though discursive, gets the main points essentially right; Ernst Cassirer, *The Question of Jean-Jacques Rousseau*, trans. Peter Gay (Bloomington, Ind., 1963), links Rousseau to the moralism of Kant, and Gay's chapter "Jean-Jacques Rousseau: Moral Man in Moral Society," in *The Enlightenment*, 2:529–52, synthesizes the tradition of those who see unity in Rousseau's quest. On many points of interpretation I have found Judith N. Shklar's *Men and Citizens: A Study of Rousseau's Social Themes* (Cambridge, Mass., 1969) provocative, though I do not accept her perception of radical disjunction between the two. On the patterns of Rousseau's mind, William H. Blanchard, *Rousseau and the Spirit of Revolt: A Psychological Study* (Ann Arbor, Mich., 1967) is useful; Peter Gay's "Blueprint for a Biography" in Gay, ed., *The Party of Humanity* (New York, 1964) is persuasive; Jean Starobinski's *Jean-Jacques Rousseau: La transparence et l'obstacle* (Paris, 1958) is brilliant and indispensable.

genes' dog, or rather a dog descended from that dog's bastard son."[5] Some of Rousseau's contemporaries appreciated his revival of the austere spirit of Diogenes,[6] but whether they approved or disapproved, the image of Rousseau the uncompromising moralist struck them as just.

The title "moralist" in no way exhausts the thought of Rousseau, but it does point to his central patterns and habits of thought. Though he was aware of the practical, legislative concerns of his contemporary philosophes, economic and social issues inexorably shifted in his mind from problems of utility and happiness to problems of conscience and virtue. In the second of his famous series of letters to Malesherbes, he described that revelation on the way to Vincennes which first set him on his career as the moral judge of enlightened society: He had just glanced at the proposed topic for the *prix de morale* of the Dijon Academy (the future subject of his fateful *Discours sur les sciences et les arts*) when he was overcome by the frenzy of his thoughts. Resting beneath a tree he had tried to understand his revelation. "Oh Monsieur," he wrote to Malesherbes,

> if I had been able to record a quarter of what I saw and felt underneath that tree, with what clarity would I have pointed out the contradictions of the social system, with what force would I have exposed all the abuses in our institutions, with what simplicity would I have shown that man is naturally good and that it is by institutions alone that men become evil.[7]

Though sensitive to the abuses within his society, Rousseau's perception of abuse was bracketed by two other perceptions: his sense of paradox and contradiction—the instinct of the Sophist—and above all his sense of the overriding importance of the problems of good, evil, and justification—the quest of the Cynic. The philosophes were content to dwell in the middle ground—abuse and its cures. Rousseau preferred the more taxing realms outside.

5. In Rousseau, *Correspondance complète*, ed. R. A. Leigh, 16 vols. to date (Geneva, 1965–): Diderot to Sophie Volland, 26 May 1759 (820); d'Alembert to Voltaire, 9 April 1761 (1391); Voltaire to d'Alembert, 17 June 1762 (1887).

6. E.g., Pierre de la Roche, who admired the Diogenes in Rousseau and feared relaxation in Rousseau's moral temper after reading *La nouvelle Hélosie*: "I very much fear that in place of the name 'cynic' which worldly men have given you, those you call 'austere' will call you 'Temporizer,' and be sure to note that this name is infamous." Rousseau, *Correspondance complète* (1337).

7. 12 January 1762, Rousseau, *Correspondance complète* (1633); also in *Oeuvres complètes*, 1:1135–36.

Like all persons tortured by psychological problems left unresolved from childhood, Rousseau was condemned to think in patterns, to work out repeatedly the puzzles of guilt and innocence, moral opaqueness and transparency. When in 1759 Controller General Silhouette failed in his attempt, supported by the philosophes, to reform the finances of France, Rousseau addressed a letter to him:

> Deign to receive the homage of a solitary man who is unknown to you but who admires you for your talents, respects you for your administration, and who did you the honor of expecting it would not last long. Unable to save the state except at the expense of the capital which has destroyed it, you have braved the cries of the money men. Seeing you crush these wicked men, I envied your position; seeing you leave without having given in, I admire you. Be satisfied with yourself, Monsieur; [your tenure] leaves you with an honor which you will long enjoy without rival. The curses of the wicked are the glory of the just man.[8]

The problems of this administrator (who, it should be pointed out, used luxury taxes as Rousseau had recommended in the *Encyclopédie*) became transformed into the battles of the just man in the world of the wicked, as the dilemmas of the man of good will who faces inevitable defeat in a corrupt world and accepts that fate, unsullied and unbowed.[9]

Once recognized, the insistent moralization of economic and social issues can be seen at work in almost all that Rousseau wrote. In his private notes he outlined a set of economic goals very much in the manner of the philosophes, defining a just economic order as one in

8. To Etienne de Silhouette, 2 December 1759, Rousseau, *Correspondance complète* (899).

9. Cf. Rousseau's response (3 May 1759, *Correspondance complète* [806]) to a prospectus of a work on finances sent to him in 1759 by Charles Etienne Pesselier: "I understand nothing . . . of the matter which you have treated and, to tell the truth, I wish that no one needed to understand it. It seems most unfortunate to me that so many taxes are necessary to assure the condition of citizens and that they must be ruined for their own good. I believe I have seen countries where civil surety is no less solidly established and where one does not pay so much." Rousseau closed by expressing his confidence in Pesselier to handle such matters. Compare his reaction to that of Voltaire, who first complimented Pesselier on his work in the prospectus and in the *Encyclopédie* (30 October 1758, Voltaire, *Correspondence* [7211]), and then later requested a countersigned copy from d'Argental, adding, "I'll put it on the shelves of my little library destined for project-makers. I already have a goodly number." (18 June 1759, Voltaire, *Correspondence* [7642].)

which "everyone can, by his work, easily amass all that is necessary for his subsistence."[10] But when Rousseau tried to formulate his economic goals in *Du Contrat social*, he infused the issue with moral concerns. There he required a society with "no citizen so rich as to be able to buy another, none so poor as to be forced to sell himself." This economic order created duties for both estates: moderation of goods and credit by the rich, curbing of avarice and greed by the poor.[11] The simple observation of his notes, much in the legislative spirit of the philosophes, easily and inevitably changed into the more complex demand of the moralist.

This same impulse impelled Rousseau to praise the potential benefits of the corvée while the philosophes were attacking its oppressive workings in the institutions of France. Though Rousseau considered the corvée an evil in a corrupt society, he appreciated the possible virtue of citizens cooperating in the work of the state; hence he prescribed the corvée as a tax proper for the laborer in a just political order.[12] Similarly, while Voltaire and others were campaigning for elimination of servile status in France and elsewhere, Rousseau integrated the status of serfdom into a scheme for moral education for the Polish nation. Freedom would become a reward for service, a stage in the moral and civic education of the peasant granted by those already free. Rapid freeing of the serfs by decree posed, he thought, a threat to social order. "Do not free their bodies," he warned Polish leaders, "until you have freed their souls." He therefore envisioned a gradual liberation of men and villages, much in the manner of the high and late Middle Ages, but for reasons of virtue, not economics.[13]

Rousseau's moral vision effectively separated him from the mainstream of the Enlightenment.[14] Nor could he find a secure home within the moralist traditions of his day. He echoed enough of the common sentiments against the very wealthy and the evils of the

10. "Fragments politiques," *Oeuvres complètes*, 3:524.

11. *Oeuvres complètes*, 2:391–92.

12. *Du Contrat social, Oeuvres complètes*, 3:429; *Projet de constitution pour la Corse* (hereafter *Corse*), ibid., p. 932; *Considérations sur le gouvernement de Pologne et sur sa réformation projettée* (hereafter *Pologne*), ibid, p. 1009.

13. *Oeuvres complètes*, 3:974 (quotation) and pp. 1026–27.

14. For a good indication of the divorce of moralism from the utilitarian perspective of the Enlightenment, see Bentham's discussion "On Motives," chapter 10 of his *An Introduction to the Principles of Morals and Legislation* (1780).

passions to find support ranging from the academicians of Dijon[15] to the pastors of Geneva. That support, however, remained fragile, since he shared enough of the radical values of the Enlightenment to place him on the edge of moral acceptability. He saw the workings of economic and social forces as a *philosophe*, even if he eventually refused to adopt economic values as his legislative standard. He refused, as a *philosophe*, to recognize an innate sinfulness in men, even if he remained obsessed with issues of virtue and corruption. He tested, analyzed, and demystified traditions, even if he often chose to do so with the traditional tools of the moralist. The critical spirit was not lost on Rousseau, but though he shared in it, he chose to remain apart from the company of philosophes as well as the company of traditional moralists. His obsession with the clarities of virtue removed him from the gray ambience of reform and compromise that typified the Enlightenment. His favorite means of underscoring and defining this separation was an insistence on identifying himself with society's outcasts, the people.

At times Rousseau took pride in belonging to no class, the proper condition of a man speaking as society's conscience. "Being nothing and wanting nothing," he once wrote, "I troubled and importuned no one; I entered everywhere without holding on to anything, sometimes dining with Princes in the morning and supping with peasants in the evening."[16] Rousseau could not, however, always remain neutral among the classes, and in times of intellectual and psychological stress he chose to align himself with the outcast lower orders of society. Though professing to value independence above all else and frequently rejecting the favors of the wealthy, he also craved submission and dependence. His identification with the lowly suited this dual need. He sought a symbolic, voluntary poverty as both a club to beat back the favors and temptations of wealth and status and, psychologically, a guarantee of his dependence on wealthy women. In 1758 he complained to Madame d'Houdetot, that her letters had begun to show equivocation and ambiguities. "The sincerity of you *gens du monde*," he wrote,

is never to say what you think except with precautions, with

15. On the appeal of Rousseau's ideas to the academicians of Dijon, see Marcel Bouchard, *L'Académie de Dijon et le Premier Discours de Rousseau* (Paris, 1950).
16. "Ebauches des confessions," *Oeuvres complètes*, 1:1151.

reserves, politely, double-edged, half-said. My childish sincerity with myself, as you yourself call it, is to interpret all of that in my rustic tongue, and to respond directly to what was spoken to me cleverly.[17]

The pose of Rousseau the boyish rustic, the "worker," the man without means helped him move through the ambivalent demands of literary patronage and his own divided needs.[18]

From this unique perspective, quite apart from the elitist logic of the philosophe, Rousseau went about judging and unmasking the society, not merely indicating its foundation in human passions but pointing to its inner contradictions. He stripped this world of any claims to righteousness and legitimacy by holding up images of its corruption against images of moral perfection. Rousseau found his theme in the *Discours sur les sciences et les arts* of 1750 and never thereafter foresook his role as moral censor. Within each institution he discussed, from the arts to the laws, he saw the workings of self-interest gone wrong, the corruption of the will, and the oppression of the weak.

Like the philosophes, Rousseau sensed early in his career that the values of society had often strayed from real to artificial needs. The poorest man, he recognized in the first discourse, is often the most useful to society.[19] Here he was at one with Diderot, but, unlike Diderot, he was unwilling to make peace with the values of an unequal, apparently illogical economic order. Rather than call for a reform of legislative values in the manner of the Encyclopedists, Rousseau moved immediately toward a deeper perception and broader portrayal of a society corrupted at its heart—in its law. He realized and stated in the 1750s what other philosophes only gradually learned over the course of the following two decades: laws usually serve the rich and oppress the poor. The *Discours sur l'inégalité* of 1754 was, in effect, his declaration of independence from the growing

17. 5 January 1758, Rousseau, *Correspondance complète* (602).

18. E.g., his ambivalent reactions to the favors of Montmorency; see Rousseau, *Correspondance complète* (803 and 1116); *Confessions, Oeuvres complètes*, 1:543.

19. E.g., *Oeuvres complètes*, 3:26: "We have Physicists, Geometers, Chemists, Astronomers, Poets, Musicians, Painters; we no longer have citizens, or if any remain, they perish indigent and scorned, scattered over the countryside. Such is the state to which those who give us bread and nurse our children are reduced; such are the opinions we hold of them."

reformist spirit of the philosophes. Rousseau used a favorite tactic of the Enlightenment, the subversive genealogy,[20] to undermine the legitimacy of an institution which philosophes did not want to subvert. In the first discourse he sketched a self-satisfied, corrupt world; in its sequel he traced the origins of that corruption. The movement downward began, as he described it, with the first enclosure of private property. From that moment, the forms of inequality evolved inevitably through three stages: eras of proprietary rights, magistracy, and arbitrary power, successively dividing society into rich and poor, powerful and weak, master and slave.[21] Far from finding an order in which rank and distinction rested on merit, Rousseau discerned an order of exploitation, in which the powerful found joy only in the misery of the poor. And though he recognized that some forms of inequality might be authorized by natural law, he refused to give any sanction to the existing order. There can be no doubt of our judgment of the standing of civilized society before that standard, he concluded, "since it is clearly contrary to natural law, by any definition, that a child rule a grown man, an imbecile lead a wise man, and that a handful of men be glutted with excesses while the starving multitude lacks the necessities of life."[22] Luxury, the arts, feudal laws,[23] oppressive taxation,[24] and even the wickedness of servants[25] mirrored this illegitimacy.

Had Rousseau moved from this perception to advocacy of radical reform, he might have appeared more dangerous to his contemporaries than merely a new Diogenes. Instead, he virtually refused to propose legislation in the reformist manner of his onetime companions. In his entry on "Economie politique" in the *Encyclopédie*, he lent his voice to the idea of proportional taxation but even in that analysis he concentrated more on the difficulties of attaining fair taxation in a corrupt society and on the uses of luxury taxes to

20. On the technique of "subversive genealogy" and Rousseau's place in the tradition from Hesiod to Nietzsche, see Judith N. Shklar, "Subversive Genealogies," *Daedalus* 101, no. 1 (Winter 1972): 129–54.

21. *Oeuvres complètes*, 3:187.

22. Ibid., p. 194.

23. See Rousseau's attack on the droit de chasse in *Emile, Oeuvres complètes*, 4:690, and *Confessions, Oeuvres complètes*, 1:575–76.

24. "Discours sur l'économie politique," *Oeuvres complètes*, 3:273–78.

25. E.g., *La nouvelle Héloïse* (hereafter *NH*), *Oeuvres complètes*, 2:455, 491.

reform morals than on the details of a new tax system.[26] After that, his reforming voice fell silent. He rejected the claims of practicality in the preface to *Emile*:

> People are always asking me to propose something practical. They might just as well say, "Propose what we are doing already, or at least propose some good to mix with the existing evil." In certain respects such a plan is much more fanciful than mine, because in such a mixture the good spoils, the evil never improves.[27]

Rousseau likewise spurned the path of reform in social affairs. Advocacy of mere reform implied tacit admission that the evils of the day could be set right by the administrator. Such an admission implied in turn giving moral legitimacy, however slight, to the existing order, and that Rousseau was unwilling to do. Thus, he accepted property and its products as inevitable and regrettable results of human self-interest. Even the corruption of law he accepted fatalistically. "The universal spirit of the laws of all nations," he noted in *Emile*, "is always to favor the strong against the weak, the haves against the have-nots; this inconvenience is inevitable and without exception."[28] Nowhere did he see the possibility of a return to purity.[29] He accepted the arts as a consolation in a corrupt world, a necessary evil where men are already wicked.[30] The sanctity of property would be one of the first and most important lessons of his moral man, Emile, as he learned to make his way in the world.[31] But nowhere did he judge the arts and property intrinsically good or even bad but amendable. Rather than respond to the disease with accessible cures, he chose instead to hold up models of ideal health, near enough to the existing world to underscore the moral illegiti-

26. *Oeuvres complètes*, 3:273–78.

27. *Oeuvres complètes*, 3:242–43.

28. *Oeuvres complètes*, 4:524 note; see also the discussion, pp. 524–25.

29. E.g., his letter responding to Voltaire's ridicule, in which he explained that he had no pretensions of making humanity go back to walking on all fours: "There comes a time when the evil is such that the causes which brought it about are necessary to keep it from spreading: it's the bullet that must be left in the wound lest the wounded man die in trying to extract it." Rousseau to Voltaire, 7 September 1755, Rousseau, *Correspondance complète* (319).

30. See his various responses to criticisms in *Correspondance complète*, nos. 319, 418, 424, 1176.

31. *Oeuvres complètes*, 4:330.

macy of his times, far enough removed to lie beyond the powers of a legislator.

Just as Rousseau used his own poverty and common origin to fend off the rich, he used the image of the virtuous poor man to illuminate the corruption of the higher orders and dramatize his unwillingness to compromise with them. The honest peasant, uncorrupted by the example of rich masters and luxury in the cities, became his symbol of moral health. The image of peasant virtue was by no means new in the annals of moralism, but Rousseau insisted on it with a seriousness and intensity which differentiated his vision from the pastoral niceties of eighteenth-century art and literature. He projected onto his peasants all of those qualities which to his mind constituted true virtue. His rustic Valaisians recreated the order which he had considered ideal in his second discourse, the golden mean between the stupid primitive and the mendacious civilized man.[32] Rousseau fabricated an image of the poor man, blessed by simplicity and independence, in which he chose to see qualities which the philosophes had denied to the man of the people. The simple existence of the Valaisian peasant, pitied by the philosophe, became for Rousseau a source of happiness. "I dare claim," he wrote to Voltaire, "that in the upper Valais region there is perhaps not one mountain dweller unhappy with his virtually mechanical existence and who would not accept it in place of paradise itself."[33] This simplicity brought in its wake all those virtues Rousseau professed to admire—modesty, honesty, openness, hospitality.[34]

A framer of hypothetical histories and ideal models, Rousseau felt released from the bonds of fact and embroidered on the theme of peasant superiority. For him, the peasant diet came to symbolize health and simplicity.[35] The peasants' speech lacked the stuttering of that of urban children coddled in their youth and badly edu-

32. *Oeuvres complètes*, 3:171.

33. To Voltaire, 18 August 1756, Rousseau, *Correspondance complète* (424). The reaction of Formey to Rousseau's use of the adjective *automate* to describe his happy peasants was characteristic: "Rousseau destroys what he pretended to establish by the use of this word alone. A *vie automate* could never be happy. And men stupid enough to prefer the mountains of upper Valais to Paradise are not competent judges of happiness." (See editor's note "*t*" to no. 424.)

34. For Rousseau's admiration of the Valais, which he knew hardly at all, see *NH*, *Oeuvres complètes*, 2:76–78, and editor's note to p. 76 in ibid., pp. 1387–90.

35. *Emile, Oeuvres complètes*, 4:414–17.

cated in adolescence.[36] Even the labor of the men of the people, including those craftsmen who might ply their trade in the rural village, became invested with a moral value and purpose denied in the writings of Rousseau's contemporary philosophes. That labor which Diderot admired for its skill and complexity, the trades of the *artiste*, Rousseau deplored as physically and morally debilitating. He required his Emile to learn a simple trade, one which would give him a measure of independence from the workings of fortune and teach him the virtues of honest, useful labor. In his choice of a trade for Emile, the tutor did not ignore the mechanical nature of most labor. But he saw enough value in the simple arts—their independence, their utility, their lack of pretension—to make apprenticeship in a manual art part of the "apprenticeship of a man."[37]

Rousseau thus adopted the Enlightenment's apology for utility and the useful arts, but then pushed it beyond appreciation of the arts in general to esteem for the laborer himself. As we have indicated,[38] Helvétius distinguished two hierarchies, of utility and of rarity, to explain away society's esteem for the craft but not the craftsman. Rousseau similarly delineated two hierarchies, but designed them so that the simple artisan and the farmer would rank at the top of both. Obeying the standard of utility, Rousseau's Emile would shun the standards of the *haut monde* and honor the shoemaker or the mason "more than the Emperor, a Le Blanc, or all the jewellers of Europe." As his second standard, Emile would choose not the economic value of rarity but the moral value of independence, whereby the arts which deal in primary materials rank above the more advanced and skilled arts. The farmer, the metalworker, and the carpenter would then precede all others on this second scale.[39] Rousseau thus denied the philosophes and his Emile any escape from the implications of utility; the individual artisan and the worker would share in the dignity of his art.

Though Rousseau dealt with ideals, he did not always automatically associate virtue with the people. The corruption of society spread to the lower orders. Rousseau's moral world, therefore, did not lack a classical populace, an ignorant and violent lower class. He

36. Ibid., pp. 294–96.
37. Ibid., pp. 470–78.
38. See above, p. 37.
39. *Emile, Oeuvres complètes*, 4:458–60.

could on occasion speak of the people in terms worthy of an angry Voltaire. Servants especially earned his scorn as reflections of the duplicity and cruelty of their masters.[40] But Rousseau's populace was a created one, born from the oppression and corruption of those above. "It is certain," he wrote in *Discours sur l'économie politique*, "that peoples are in the long run what the government makes of them. Warriors, citizens, men if it wishes; populace or canaille when it so pleases. . . ."[41] In *Emile*, Rousseau similarly allowed that the peasant was usually "rustic, base, and clumsy," but only because his life had become automatic, routine, continually given over to burdensome work, habit, and obedience.[42] And when he spoke to Voltaire of the happiness of the simple peasant, he took care to differentiate between the free and prosperous peasants of the Valais and the peasants of France, "where it is maintained that they must die of misery to give you a living."[43] Poverty and simplicity in the real world did not bring virtue, but in Rousseau's moral world the ignorance of the poor still contrasted favorably with the errors of the rich.[44]

Rousseau could not remain content with images of the virtue of the simple, isolated man or family any more than society, in his vision of history, could remain in its ideal state between savagery and luxury. Though no man insisted more on the need for independence, none was more sensitive to the workings of hierarchy in civilization. With the notable exception of the theoretical model of *Du Contrat social*, Rousseau's pictures of social order revolve not around equality and independence but around deference and dependence. In the microcosm of the estates of Baron Wolmar of *La nouvelle Héloïse* and in the macrocosms of his ideal Corsica and Poland, Rousseau portrayed social life in hierarchies as being more rigid and static than did most of the philosophes in their writings. Accepting the order of rich and poor (and even that of lord and serf in Poland), he tried to explore its moral potential. He found solutions in those hierarchical

40. See, e.g., *NH, Oeuvres complètes*, 2:585, and *Emile, Oeuvres complètes*, 4:287, 326, 500.

41. *Oeuvres complètes*, 3:251.

42. *Oeuvres complètes*, 4:360.

43. To Voltaire, 18 August 1756, Rousseau, *Correspondance complète* (424).

44. Rousseau frequently distinguished between "ignorance" and "error"; see, e.g., *Emile, Oeuvres complètes*, 4:428, and letter to Voltaire, 7 September 1755, Rousseau, *Correspondance complète* (319).

orders which met three standards: that the people remain simple, uncorrupted, and content with their lot; that the masters see the world through the eyes of an Emile, aware of the duties of their station; and that all men recognize each other's moral dignity.

The first standard remained essential and allowed the ideal of the autonomous, virtuous peasant to pass over into the social order. Social mobility was a symptom of social corruption to Rousseau. In *La nouvelle Héloïse* he even attacked the idea of "talent" as disruptive of good social order. People have, he observed, "talent" only for rising in station and never for descending. Were a society possible where rank could exactly coincide with talent and virtue, it would be ideal. But in a society where the most corrupt professions bring the greatest fortunes, the peasant should learn the contentment and value of his station and the unhappiness of the condition of the rich. "Simple and good peoples," Rousseau wrote, "have no need of talents; they support themselves better by their simplicity alone than others do with all their industry." Within this framework even rudimentary education for the villager seemed dangerous to rural order.[45] Within an ideal order, change marks decay; stability is the outward glow of inner well-being.[46]

The role of the master in the ideal society is to encourage and maintain moral and economic contentment. No one leaves Clarens (the estate of Baron Wolmar) for any other condition.[47] Wolmar's exercise of authority far exceeds the philosophes' prescriptions for bienfaisance. Not only does he oversee economic order and insure prosperity; he also creates by his example a climate of virtue and satisfaction. The influence of the master, though often invisible, is omnipresent, much as it is in the "natural" education of Emile. The philosophes hoped that the enlightened pursuit of self-interest by the man of wealth might create a healthy economy in which wages might rest somewhere above the level of mere subsistence. In the autarchic economic order of Clarens, wages are manipulated to inspire emulation, industry, and security. Wolmar pays two wages—one the going rate and the other a *prix de bénéficence*, rewarding excellent service and

45. *Oeuvres complètes*, 2:537–38, 566–67.
46. See also "Economie politique," *Oeuvres complètes*, 3:264. In a fragment on Corsica (*Oeuvres complètes*, 3:941), he proposed a fine and three years' disfranchisement for moving from one district to another.
47. *Oeuvres complètes*, 3:445, 547–48.

often exceeding the profit gained by the worker's assiduousness. Overseers toil alongside the workers and earn a percentage of the total product. Every eight days Julie rewards the best worker with a substantial prize.[48] Beyond this economic supervision and encouragement, the master attends to the moral order of his household, mediating any quarrels and inspiring virtue in the actions of those below him.[49]

This exaggerated *bienfaisance* alone, however, does not bring full legitimacy to the ideal world of Clarens. That legitimacy comes only with the culmination of the agricultural year, the harvest and its festival. Though they do not lose their identity as masters, Julie and Wolmar work alongside their laborers, keeping workers' hours, eating at the workers' table, sharing the workers' joys and amusements.[50] The harvest becomes a purified saturnalia. "The sweet equality which reigns here," Rousseau wrote, "reestablishes the order of nature, forming a lesson for one side, a consolation for the other, and a tie of friendship for all."[51] The experience of the equality of the season of the harvest *fête* brings moral legitimacy to the hierarchical social order, allowing a time for mutual recognition of moral dignity.[52]

Late in life, Rousseau remembered in his *Rêveries* the experience of the fête. In corrupted France, he wrote, festivity has lost its joy. But in Geneva and Switzerland

> everyone exudes contentment and joy at the fêtes, misery does not show its ugly face or pomp its insolence; well-being, fraternity, concord cause hearts to open up, and often in the transports of innocent joy strangers greet one another, embrace, and enjoy together the day's pleasures.[53]

48. *Ibid.*, p. 443; in a rare appeal to economic self-interest he did predict that this economic order would produce greater revenues. See also *Emile, Oeuvres complètes,* 4:805.

49. *Oeuvres complètes,* 2:459–66.

50. *Ibid.*, pp. 607–09.

51. *Ibid.*, p. 608. Cf. the corrupt, luxuriant feast and Emile's guilty reflections on it, in *Emile, Oeuvres complètes,* 4:463.

52. Starobinski, *Rousseau,* pp. 120–29, discusses the egalitarian fête in some detail, but primarily with a view toward its illusory nature; for Rousseau, I think, its transitory nature in no way undermined its meaning and importance. Christie Vance discusses the meaning of the harvest fête in "The Extravagant Shepherd: A Study of the Pastoral Vision in Rousseau's *Nouvelle Héloïse,*" *VS* 105 (1973):133–44.

53. *Oeuvres complètes,* 1:1094–95.

Festivity possessed the magic of dignity and harmony.

Rousseau extended his vision of the potential of festivity far beyond the isolated region of Clarens. At a time when reformers—puritans and philosophes—were seeking to curtail popular amusements for being violent, wasteful, and vulgar, Rousseau characteristically tried to envision purified fêtes to bring social harmony. In 1758 he proposed an alternative to the Geneva theater in the form of public festivals, modeled after those of ancient Sparta, as a means of promoting feelings of concord and public fraternity among Genevans.[54] His plans for Poland included public festivals to replace the exclusive entertainment of the rich. Ranks would not disappear, but all would share the common joy.[55] This structure of the fête, a temporary egalitarian rite giving legitimacy to an unequal society, enters even into the structure of *Du Contrat social*. The original pact, whereby each individual recognizes the other as a moral equal and a part of the community, raises the spirit of the fête to the level of formal theory. The pact legitimizes the social order and places an egalitarian base beneath the necessarily separate and unequal structure of government. For the philosophes, government would mirror the economic hierarchy. For Rousseau, legitimacy could only come through an institution which, at least temporarily, denied that hierarchy and recognized the equal dignity of all men.

Rousseau moved away from his theoretical democratic ideal toward political models more consonant with human nature, just as the fête had to give way to the normal relations of seigneur and laborer. The Roman order described at length in the fourth part of *Du Contrat social* did not meet the egalitarian standards expounded in the first part. But the republic of Rome still reflected enough of that mutual recognition among classes and individuals to warrant praise and imitation. Similarly, the Genevan, Polish, and Corsican societies which Rousseau mentally constructed revealed the spirit but not the letter of the social contract and the harvest fête. Though unwilling to accept gradual reform and/or sponsor utilitarian legislation, Rousseau still nursed enough hope to think that if men were shown their capability for virtue, they might at least salvage that measure of innocence which remained free from the corruption of inequality.

54. *Lettre à M. d'Alembert*, in *Du Contrat social, . . . Lettre à M. d'Alembert, etc.* (Paris, 1962), pp. 224–34.
55. *Oeuvres complètes*, 3:962–63.

His schemes for legislation attempted to freeze that capacity and nurture its full possibilities. In the end, therefore, Rousseau offered the people both an uncompromising awareness of its oppression and an insistence on its dignity. Beyond these gifts—abstract, tenuous, yet unique within the Enlightenment period—he had little to offer his "idol." In the manner of the philosophes, he occasionally insisted on the need for equal laws which might encircle dependence with liberty, but he doubted whether any change would actually take place.[56] He often spoke of an ideal order in which rank would be determined by merit.[57] He supported taxation which would vary with the ability to pay.[58] These gestures to the legislative spirit of other philosophes, though they mark his affinity with their causes, were only tangential to his interests and goals. He questioned the fundamental assumption of the philosophes that the self-interest of those with power might be turned to the public good.[59] Recapturing the golden age could only be an act of love and that was impossible.[60] "I am the Botanist who describes the plant," Rousseau observed late in life. "It is up to the doctor to determine its use."[61] In this light, Rousseau considered the legislation of the philosophes more inadequate than unworthy. He could, however, feel their lack of love.

## THE PHILOSOPHES: THE LOGIC OF RESPONSIBILITY

As the self-appointed conscience of his society, Rousseau saw more clearly and immediately than any philosophe the abuses and contradictions of that society. In a sense he became paralyzed by what he saw, unable to move comfortably from his perception of fundamental abuse, paradox, and contradiction to a legislatable program of

56. For Rousseau's demands for equality before the laws, see *Oeuvres complètes*, 3:248, 258, 294, 310, 332, 367, 374, 391, 496, 891, 911; and letter to Damilaville, 1755 (?), Rousseau, *Correspondance complète* (267).

57. "Fragments politiques," *Oeuvres complètes*, 3:522; *NH, Oeuvres complètes*, 2:194.

58. *Oeuvres complètes*, 3:271–72, 1011.

59. Hendel makes this essential point in his *Rousseau*, 1:129–30.

60. See *Emile, Oeuvres complètes*, 4:859: "Men consider the golden age an illusion, and so it will always remain for those with corrupted hearts and inclinations. Men do not truly miss it, their regrets are always hollow. What must be done to recapture it? One thing alone, and that is impossible; that would be to love the golden age."

61. "Mon portrait," *Oeuvres complètes*, 1:1120. The fragment begins, "I am an observer, and not a moralist," meaning by "moralist" someone who recommends cures and a course of action. He was, of course, a true moralist, but in a deeper sense that he did not recognize here.

change. His was the logic of dignity in a world which denied the possibility of equal dignity for all men. He sought ways, even within highly deferential societies, to insure mutual recognition of a dignity equal in all persons as moral agents. The philosophes, on the other hand, grew only gradually into an awareness of corruption. They moved carefully, against their elitist bias, from a stark sense of the separation of classes to an appreciation of the people's role in society and a perception of society's ingratitude. Theirs was the logic of responsibility. They experienced much comfort within the economic hierarchy and perceived society in terms of the power which economic dominance gave to an elite over the rest of society, the people. They acted not as spokesmen for any eternal moral sense but rather as the conscience of this elite, and they perceived in the actions and attitudes of the elite both the responsibility for the people's well-being and the culpability for the people's misery. They attacked the problems of the people primarily by appealing to the best instincts of men with power. Condorcet once distinguished three types of opinion: enlightened, public, and popular. In his optimism he insisted that the first will always rule the second, and the second in turn rules the third.[62] The philosophes scorned the popular mind and found little to say to it; they fought their battles in the gray zone between enlightened and public opinion.

The philosophes were the agents of a certain kind of class consciousness, not of the "middle class" but of the elite class of those with superior economic power and hence greater access to education This "class" was hardly of one mind, including everyone from kings to mayors, clergy to atheists, reactionaries to humanitarians. For the most part, it included men who had never thought about the structure of their society or its underpinnings. The philosophes explored that structure and tried to lay bare the real lines of power, with its incumbent problems and responsibilities. They approached their task with a certain confidence, since they proposed nothing without precedent in the world of the elite. Some officials had seen the need for equitable taxation decades before the philosophes made fair taxation part of their program for the people. The Catholic and Protestant faiths had established public instruction long before reformers proposed making universal elementary instruction a public

62. *Oeuvres complètes*, 11:201.

responsibility. Some private citizens and monarchs had acted as vigorous economic leaders long before philosophes insisted on the need for such leadership. Public officials had attacked feudal prerogatives, many of which had disappeared by the time the philosophes incorporated civil equality into their program. The open market had proved its value in England and the Netherlands before it appeared as a cornerstone of some economic proposals of the Enlightenment.

The spokesmen for the Enlightenment adopted these measures and publicized them, making them appear not as random possibilities but as the necessary dictates of equity and utility. They sought to gather those rays of enlightened thought and action and magnify them through the glass of public opinion; hence, their heavy reliance on the state and its legislative powers to institute their programs. Christian stewardship emphasized the private workings of charity; enlightened responsibility, for all its debts to this sense of private stewardship, emphasized the public workings of the law. Only through a universal public institution could their programs achieve the consistency which the responsibilities of power and dominance seemed to warrant. Even laissez-faire presupposed an activist state intervening in traditional market patterns to provide more stability and prosperity. The philosophes did not dwell in the providential world of the nineteenth-century marketplace where pursuit of self-interest automatically generated the public interest. Rather, they argued that public opinion and public power would have to see proposed actions in light of the general good and act accordingly. To those with power and influence, they held out the reward of dignified well-being within the framework of public happiness.

Their program was not without its ambiguities and occasional cruelties, especially in the hands of followers not possessing their broader public sense. Utilitarian schemes to make the poor work replaced at times the random cruelty of hôpitaux and poor rates with harsh, calculated discipline. The notion that large tracts of land accessible to investment and larger returns should replace small tracts and common lands could and did provide justifications for enclosers and consolidators who disrupted village life without providing compensating rewards. The idea of the open market, generally a humane experiment in the minds of its proposers, became in the nineteenth century a dangerously fixed dogma. Like all thinkers, the philosophes were often victims of followers who seized upon specific doctrines without examining the context or the animus behind them.

The philosophes tried to speak for the interests of both the elite and the people. Proposing legislation from the perspective of the economic hierarchy of the eighteenth century, they offered the elite continued power and dominance, more fully insured by beneficent and wise treatment of the mass of men. They gave substance to the ideal of the public welfare as the necessary alternative to ideals of dynastic glory, aristocratic honor, and corporate status that had ruled public life since the Middle Ages. In sum, the philosophes insisted that the price of dominance must be responsibility.

The Enlightenment's program for public welfare may well seem modest by modern standards. Two centuries of industrialization and revolution have radically transformed ways of perceiving what society owes the people. But it is unfair to fault men for not seeing what they could not see. To the philosophes the people seemed, despite its numbers, relatively helpless, defined by its dependence on others.[63] The philosophes could not foresee the process over the subsequent century by which the gens des bras would become the "working class." Nor did the future resources of industrialization inform the philosophes' thinking about the people. The possibility of an egalitarian society which could exist substantially above the subsistence level did not seem the viable option it would after a century of technological revolution. Still, for all its limitations, paternalism, and haughtiness, the philosophes' approach to the people was not unworthy. They assumed that at all times power and responsibility would rest in the hands of relatively few. But they also insisted that this elite could best serve itself and its trust by giving to the people the most it could afford, short of abjuring its own power. Their program for the people thus included economic stability, assured subsistence, fiscal equity, efficient charity, minimal instruction, and evenhanded justice—a program adventurous enough in the face of the realities of eighteenth-century society. In other economic, technological, and social circumstances the same program might have dictated much more.

Perhaps there was something naive in the philosophes' approach to social problems. They knew neither the misery of the people nor the selfishness of the elite as well as they might have. Working mostly in

63. Asa Briggs, "The Language of Class in Early Nineteenth-Century England," pp. 62–63.

the domain of public opinion—rather than in the fields of Europe, the streets of Paris, or the councils of kings—certainly allowed for much misperception, arrogance, and wishful thinking. But then again, there will probably always be something naive in the vocation of the philosophe in a world of unenlightened people and irresponsible leaders.

# Bibliography

PART I: PRIMARY SOURCES

The following printed sources and collected works served as primary source material for this essay. Bracketed dates indicate initial year of publication.

Alembert, Jean le Rond d'. *Oeuvres complètes*. Vol. 4. Paris, 1822.

Augustine, bishop of Hippo. *The City of God*. Translated by M. Dods. New York, 1950.

[Barbeu-Dubourg, Jacques]. *Petit Code de la raison humaine, ou exposition succincte de ce que la raison dicte à tous les hommes, pour éclairer leur conduite & assurer leur bonheur*. N.p., 1782 [1774].

[Baudeau, Abbé Nicolas]. *Avis au peuple sur son premier besoin*. 3 vols. in 1. Amsterdam, 1768.

[————]. *Idées d'un citoyen sur les besoins, les droits, et les devoirs des vrais pauvres*. Amsterdam, 1765.

[————]. *Première introduction à la philosophie économique, ou Analyse des états policés* [1771]. Edited by A. Dubois. Paris, 1910.

[————]. *Principes de la science morale et politique sur le luxe et les loix somptuaires* [1767]. Edited by A. Dubois. Paris, 1912.

[Bayle, Pierre]. *Pensées diverses, écrites à un docteur de Sorbonne à l'occasion de la comète qui parut au mois de décembre 1680*. Third ed. Rotterdam, 1699 [1682].

Beccaria, Cesare. *An Essay on Crimes and Punishments*. Translated by E. D. Ingraham. Philadelphia, 1819.

Bentham, Jeremy. *A Fragment on Government and An Introduction to the Principles of Morals and Legislation*. Edited by Wilfrid Harrison. Oxford, 1967.

[Boncerf, Pierre François]. *Les inconvéniens des droits féodaux*. Paris, 1776.

Bossuet, Jacques Bénigne, bishop of Meaux. *Oeuvres oratoires de Bossuet*. Edited by Abbé J. Lébarq, et al. 7 vols. Paris, 1926–27.

Condorcet, Marie-Jean-Antoine-Nicolas Caritat, marquis de. *Oeuvres complètes*. Edited by M. F. Arago and A. C. O'Connor. 12 vols. Paris, 1847.

————, and Turgot, Anne-Robert-Jacques, baron de l'Aulne. *Correspondance inédite de Condorcet et de Turgot: 1770–1778*. Edited by C. Henry. Paris, 1883.

Coyer, Abbé Gabriel François. *Dissertations pour êtres lues: La première sur le vieux mot de patrie: La seconde, sur la nature du peuple.* The Hague, 1755.

[————]. *Plan d'éducation publique.* Paris, 1770.

*De l'éducation. Ouvrage utile aux Parens, aux Gouverneurs, &c. Et à tous ceux qui se chargent de l'Education.* Amsterdam, 1768.

Diderot, Denis. *Correspondance.* Edited by G. Roth and J. Varloot. 16 vols. Paris, 1955–70.

————. *Mémoires pour Catherine II.* Edited by P. Vernière. Paris, 1966.

————. *Oeuvres complètes.* Edited by J. Assézat and M. Tourneux. 20 vols. Paris, 1875–77.

————. *Oeuvres esthétiques.* Edited by P. Vernière. Paris, 1959.

————. *Oeuvres philosophiques.* Edited by P. Vernière. Paris, 1964.

————. *Oeuvres politiques.* Edited by P. Vernière. Paris, 1963.

————. *Oeuvres romanesques.* Edited by H. Bénac. Paris, 1951.

————, et al. *Encyclopédie, ou Dictionnaire raisonné des sciences, des arts et des métiers, par une société de gens de lettres.* 17 vols. Paris, 1751–65.

Dieckmann, Herbert, ed. *Le philosophe: Texts and Interpretation.* St. Louis, 1948.

Domat, Jean. *The Civil Law in its Natural Order. Together With the Public Law.* Translated by William Strahan. Second ed. London, 1737.

Duclos, Charles. *Considérations sur les moeurs de ce siècle. Oeuvres complètes.* Vol. 1. Paris, 1820.

Fleury, Abbé Claude. *Droit public de France.* Edited by J. B. Daragon. 2 vols. in 3. Paris, 1769.

Friedrich, Karl, grand-duke of Baden. *Brieflicher Verkehr mit Mirabeau und Dupont.* Vol. 2. Edited by K. Knies. Heidelberg, 1892.

Friedrich II, king of Prussia. *Oeuvres.* Vols. 24–25. Berlin, 1854.

Furetière, Antoine, ed. *Dictionnaire universel, contenant généralement tous les mots françois tant vieux que modernes.* Second ed. Hague and Rotterdam, 1694 [1690].

————, et al. *Dictionnaire universel françois et latin* [*Dictionnaire de Trevoux*]. 6 vols. Paris, 1743.

Galiani, Ferdinando. *Dialogue entre M. Marquis de Roquemaure et Mˢ. le Chevalier Zanobi.* Edited by Philip Koch. Vol. 21 of *Analectica Romana,* edited by F. Schalk. Frankfurt am Main, 1968.

*Le grand vocabulaire françois.* Vol. 21. Paris, 1772.

Graslin, J.-J. Louis. *Essai analytique sur la richesse et sur l'impôt.* [1767]. Edited by A. Dubois. Paris, 1911.

Helvétius, Claude Adrien. "Correspondance d'Helvétius avec sa femme." Edited by A. Guillois. In *Le carnet historique et littéraire* 6 (Nov.–Dec. 1900), pp. 424–46, 481–98.

————. *Notes de la main d'Helvétius.* Edited by A. Keim. Paris, 1907.

————. *Oeuvres complètes.* 5 vols. Paris, 1795.

————. "La tournée du fermier général Helvétius dans les Ardennes (1738)." Edited by R. Desné. In *Dix-huitième siècle,* 3 (1971), pp. 3–40.

[Holbach, Paul-Henri Thiry, baron d']. *Le Bon Sens, ou Idées naturelles opposées aux idées surnaturelles.* London [?], 1772.

[————]. *Le Christianisme dévoilé, ou Examen des principes et des effects de la religion chrétienne.* London [?], 1756 [1761].

[————]. *La Contagion sacrée, ou Histoire naturelle de la superstition.* London [?], 1772 [1768].

[————]. *Essai sur les Préjugés, ou, de l'Influence des opinions sur les moeurs & sur le bonheur des hommes.* London[?], 1770 [1769].

[————]. *Ethocratie, ou le Gouvernement fondé sur la morale.* Amsterdam, 1776.

[————]. *La Morale universelle, ou les Devoirs de l'homme fondés sur la nature.* 3 vols. Amsterdam, 1776.

[————]. *La Politique naturelle, ou Discours sur les vrais principes du gouvernement.* 2 vols. London[?], 1773.

[————]. "Problème important. La religion est-elle nécessaire à la morale & utile à la politique?" [Jacques André Naigeon, ed.]. *Recueil philosophique.* 2 vols. in 1. London[?], 1770, pp. 70–112.

[————]. *Système de la Nature, ou des Loix du monde physique & du monde moral.* 2 vols. London[?], 1770.

Hume, David. *Essays Moral, Political and Literary.* Oxford, 1963.

————. *David Hume: Writings on Economics.* Edited by E. Rotwein. Madison, Wisc., 1970.

Institut National d'Études Démographiques. *François Quesnay et la Physiocratie.* Vol. 2. Paris, 1958.

Johnson, Samuel. *Works.* Edited by W. Pickering. Vol. 6. London, 1825.

Kant, Immanuel. *Kant's Political Writings.* Edited by Hans Reiss. Cambridge, 1970.

Krauss, Werner, ed. *Est-il utile de tromper le peuple? Concours de la classe de philosophie speculative de l'Académie des Sciences et des Belles-Lettres de Berlin pour l'année 1780.* Berlin, 1966.

La Chalotais, Louis René de Caradeuc de. *Essai d'éducation nationale, ou Plan d'études pour la jeunesse.* N.p., 1763.

[La Rivière, Pierre François Joachim Mercier de]. *De l'instruction publique, ou considérations morales et politiques sur la nécessité, la nature et la source de cette instruction.* Stockholm, 1775.

[————]. *L'ordre naturel et essentiel des sociétés politiques.* 2 vols. London[?], 1767.

[Linguet, Simon-Nicolas-Henri]. *Théorie des loix civiles, ou principes fondamentaux de la société.* 2 vols. London[?], 1767.

Machiavelli, Niccolò. *The Prince and The Discourses.* Translated by L. Ricci and E. R. P. Vincent. New York, 1950.

Mandeville, Bernard. *The Fable of the Bees.* Edited by P. Harth. Baltimore, 1970.

[Mirabeau, Victor de Riquetti, marquis de]. *Théorie de l'impôt.* Paris, 1760.

Montesquieu, Charles de Secondat, baron de. *Oeuvres complètes.* Edited by A. Masson. 3 vols. Paris, 1950–55.

More, Saint Thomas. *Utopia.* Edited by E. Surtz, S. J. New Haven, 1964.

Morveau, Louis Bernard Guyton de. *Mémoire sur l'éducation publique, avec le prospectus d'un Collège.* N.p., 1764.

Necker, Jacques. *De l'importance des opinions religieuses* [1788]. *Oeuvres complètes.* Edited by Baron de Staël. Vol. 12. Paris, 1821.

———. *Sur la législation et le commerce des grains* [1775]. *Oeuvres complètes.* Edited by Baron de Staël. Vol. 1. Paris, 1820.

Pluche, Abbé Noël. *Le Spectacle de la Nature, ou Entretiens sur les particularités de l'histoire naturelle.* Vol. 6. Paris, 1770 [1746].

Plutarch. *Plutarch's Lives: The Translation called Dryden's.* Edited and revised by A. H. Clough. Vol. 1. Boston, 1878.

Ranconet, Aimar de. *Thresor de la langve françoise.* Revised and expanded by Jean Nicot. Paris, 1621. Reprint. Paris, 1960.

Richelet, Pierre, ed. *Nouveau dictionnaire françois.* Paris, 1712.

Richelieu, Armand-Jean du Plessis, cardinal duc de. *Testament politique.* Edited by L. André. Paris, 1947.

Robinet, M., ed. *Dictionnaire universel des sciences morale, économique, politique, et diplomatique.* Vol. 26. Paris, 1782.

Rousseau, Jean-Jacques. *Correspondance complète.* Edited by R. A. Leigh. 16 vols. to date. Geneva, 1965–.

———. *Correspondance générale.* Edited by T. Dufour. 20 vols. Paris, 1924–34.

———. *Du Contrat social, Discours, Lettre à M. d'Alembert, Considérations sur le Gouvernement de Pologne, Lettre à Mgr de Beaumont.* Paris, 1962.

———. *Oeuvres complètes.* Edited by B. Gagnebin, et al. 4 vols. to date. Paris, 1959–.

[Saint-Lambert, Jean François, marquis de]. *Les Saisons, poëme.* Amsterdam, 1769.

Tisserand, Roger, ed. *Les concurrents de J.-J. Rousseau à l'Académie de Dijon pour le prix de 1754.* Paris, 1936.

Turgot, Anne-Robert-Jacques, baron de l'Aulne. *Oeuvres de Turgot et documents le concernant.* Edited by G. Schelle. 5 vols. Paris, 1912–13.

Voltaire [François-Marie Arouet]. *Voltaire's Correspondence.* Edited by T. Besterman. 107 vols. Geneva, 1953–65.

————. *Dictionnaire philosophique.* Edited by J. Benda and R. Naves. Paris, 1967.

————. *Essai sur les moeurs et l'esprit des nations et sur les principaux faits de l'histoire depuis Charlemagne jusqu'à Louis XIII.* Edited by R. Pomeau. 2 vols. Paris, 1963.

————. *La Henriade.* Edited by O. R. Taylor. *VS,* nos. 38–40. Geneva, 1965.

————. *Notebooks.* Edited by T. Besterman. 2 vols. Vols. 81 and 82 of T. Besterman, et al., ed., *The Complete Works of Voltaire.* Geneva, 1968.

————. *Oeuvres complètes.* Edited by L. Moland. 52 vols. Paris, 1877–85.

Warburton, William. *The Alliance of Church and State.* London, 1736.

PART II: SECONDARY WORKS

The following secondary works served as significant background or stimuli to thought.

A. *Articles and dissertations*

Angers, Julien-Eymard d'. "Richesse et pauvreté dans l'oeuvre d'Yves de Paris." *XVII^e siècle* 90–91 (1971): 17–46.

Bahner, Werner. "Le mot et la notion de 'peuple' dans l'oeuvre de Rousseau." *VS* 55 (1967): 113–27.

Baker, Keith M. "Scientism, Elitism, and Liberalism: The Case of Condorcet." *VS* 55 (1967): 129–65.

Barennes, Jean. "Montesquieu et le braconnage à la Brède." *Revue historique de Bordeaux et du département de la Gironde* 5 (May–June 1912): 158–63.

Begin, Luc. "Le rôle du peuple dans la philosophie sociale de Voltaire." Master's thesis, McGill University, 1966.

Behrens, Betty. "Cultural History as Infrastructure, Part 2." *VS* 86 (1971): 14–24.

Bertière, A. "Montesquieu lecteur de Machiavel." *Actes du congrès Montesquieu,* pp. 143–58. Bordeaux, 1956.

Besthorn, Rudolph. "Zeitgenössische Zeugnisse für das Werk Holbachs." In *Neue Beiträge zur Literatur der Aufklärung,* edited by W. Krauss, pp. 85–94. Berlin, 1964.

————. "Zur Verfasserfrage des *Essai sur les préjugés.*" *Beitraege zur romanischen Philologie* 8, no. 1 (1969): 10–46.

Boisis, Philippe. "L'impôt de la corvée et la structure socio-professionnelle des campagnes à la veille de la révolution." *Annales historiques de la révolution française* 207 (Jan.–Mar. 1972): 82–91.

Bollème, Geneviève. "Littérature populaire et littérature de colportage au 18^e siècle." In *Livre et société dans la France du XVIII^e siècle,* pp. 61–92. Paris, 1965.

Boss, Ronald I. "The Development of Social Religion: A Contradiction of French Free Thought." *Journal of the History of Ideas* 34 (1973): 577–89.

———. "Rousseau's Civil Religion and the Meaning of Belief: An Answer to Bayle's Paradox." *VS* 84 (1971): 123–93.

Briggs, Asa. "The Language of Class in Early Nineteenth-Century England." In *Essays in Labour History*, edited by A. Briggs, pp. 43–73. London, 1960.

Burgelin, Pierre. "Le social et le politique chez Rousseau." In *Etudes sur le Contrat social de Jean-Jacques Rousseau: Actes des journées d'études*, pp. 165–76. Dijon, 1962.

Cavanaugh, Gerald J. "Turgot: The Rejection of Enlightened Despotism." *French Historical Studies* 6, no. 1 (1969): 31–58.

———. "Vauban, D'Argenson, Turgot: From Absolutism to Constitutionalism in Eighteenth-Century France." Ph.D. dissertation, Columbia University, 1967.

Cherpack, Clifton. "Warburton and Some Aspects of the Search for the Primitive in Eighteenth-Century France." *Philological Quarterly* 36 (1957): 221–32.

———. "Warburton and the *Encyclopédie*." *Comparative Literature* 17 (1955): 226–39.

Chisick, Harvey. "Attitudes Toward the Education of the *Peuple* in the French Enlightenment: 1762–1789." Ph.D. dissertation, Johns Hopkins University, 1974.

Church, William F. "The Decline of French Jurists as Political Theorists, 1660–1789." *French Historical Studies* 5, no. 1 (1967): 1–40.

Clarke, Jack A. "Turgot's Critique of Perpetual Endowments." *French Historical Studies* 3, no. 4 (1964): 495–506.

Coats, A. W. "Changing Attitudes to Labour in the Mid-Eighteenth Century." *Economic History Review*, 2d ser. 11 (Aug. 1958): 35–61.

———. "The Classical Economists and the Labourer." In *Land, Labour and Population in the Industrial Revolution*, edited by C. L. Jones and G. E. Mingay. New York, 1967.

———. "Economic Thought and Poor Law Policy in the Eighteenth Century." *Economic History Review*, 2d ser. 13, no. 1 (Aug. 1960): 39–51.

Dainville, François de. "Collèges et fréquentation scolaire au XVIII<sup>e</sup> siècle." *Population* 3 (July–Sept. 1957): 467–94.

Dieckmann, Herbert. "Diderot's Conception of Genius." *Journal of the History of Ideas* 2, no. 2 (April 1941): 151–82.

Duchet, Michèle. "Le primitivisme de Diderot." *Europe*, nos. 405–06 (Jan.–Feb. 1963): 126–32.

Dulac, Georges. "La question des blés." *Europe,* nos. 405–06 (Jan.–Feb. 1963): 103–09.

Eerde, John van. "The People in Eighteenth-Century Tragedy From *Oedipe* to *Guillaume Tell.*" *VS* 27 (1963): 1703–13.

Ehrenpreis, Irvin. "Poverty and Poetry: Representations of the Poor in Augustan Literature" and "Discussion." *Studies in Eighteenth-Century Culture. Proceedings of the American Society for Eighteenth-Century Studies* 1 (1971): 3–35.

Fletcher, F. T. H. "Montesquieu et la politique religieuse en Angleterre au xviiie siècle." In *Actes du congrès Montesquieu,* pp. 295–304. Bordeaux, 1956.

Forster, Robert. "Obstacles to Agricultural Growth in Eighteenth-Century France." *American Historical Review* 75 (1970): 1600–15.

Gagnegin, B. "Le rôle du législateur dans les conceptions politiques de Rousseau." In *Etudes sur le Contrat social de Jean-Jacques Rousseau: Actes des journées d'études,* pp. 277–90. Dijon, 1962.

Gembruch, Werner. "Reformförderungen in Frankreich um die Wende vom 17. zum 18. Jahrhundert." *Historische Zeitschrift,* no. 209 (Oct. 1969): 265–317.

Goldmann, Lucien. "La pensée des lumières." *Annales* 22, no. 4 (July–Aug. 1967): 752–79.

Grange, H. "Turgot et Necker devant le problème du salaire." *Annales historiques de la révolution française* 29 (1957): 19–33.

Green, F.C. "L'Abbé Coyer—A Society in Transition." In *The Eighteenth Century: Six Essays,* edited by F. C. Green. London, 1929.

Havens, G. R. "Diderot, Rousseau, and the *Discours sur l'inégalité.*" *Diderot Studies* 3 (1961): 219–62.

Healey, F. G. "The Enlightenment View of *Homo Faber.*" *VS* 25 (1963): 837–59.

Hill, Christopher. "Puritans and the Poor." *Past and Present* 2 (Nov. 1952): 32–50.

Hufton, Olwen. "Begging, Vagrancy, Vagabondage and the Law: An Aspect of the Problem of Poverty in Eighteenth-Century France." *European Studies Review* 2 (1972): 97–123.

———. "Toward an Understanding of the Poor of Eighteenth-century France." In *French Government and Society, 1500–1850,* edited by J. F. Bosher, pp. 145–65. London, 1973.

Hundert, E.J. "The Making of *Homo Faber*: John Locke Between Ideology and History." *Journal of the History of Ideas* 33, no. 1 (Jan.–Mar. 1972): 3–22.

Hutchinson, T. W. "Bentham as an Economist." *Economic Journal* 66, no. 262 (June 1956): 288–306.

Johnson, Richard. "Educational Policy and Social Control in Early Victorian England." *Past and Present* 49 (Nov. 1970): 96–116.

Jouvenel, Bertrand de. "Rousseau's Theory of the Forms of Government." In *Hobbes and Rousseau*, edited by M. Cranston and R. S. Peters, pp. 484–97. New York, 1972.

Julia, Dominique. "L'enseignement des pauvres dans le diocèse de Reims à la fin de l'Ancien Régime." *Annales historiques de la révolution française* 200 (April–June 1970): 233–86.

Klaits, Joseph. "Men of Letters and Political Reform in France at the End of the Reign of Louis XIV: The Founding of the Académie Politique." *Journal of Modern History* 43, no. 4 (Dec. 1971): 577–97.

Kortum, Hans. "Frugalité et luxe à travers la querelle des anciens et des modernes." *VS* 56 (1967): 765–75.

Ladd, Everett C. "Helvétius and Holbach: *La Moralisation de la Politique*." *Journal of the History of Ideas* 23, no. 2 (April–June 1962): 221–38.

Laget, M. "Petites écoles en Languedoc au xviiie siècle." *Annales* 26, no. 6 (Nov.–Dec. 1971): 1398–1418.

Levy, Darlene Gay. "Simon Linguet's Sociological System: An Exhortation to Patience and Invitation to Revolution." *VS* 70 (1970): 219–93.

Lipton, Charles. "The Social Thought of Diderot." *Science and Society* 8 (1944): 126–42.

Loupès, Philippe. "L'assistance paroissale aux pauvres malades dans le diocèse de Bordeaux au xviiie siècle." *Annales du Midi* 84 (1972): 37–61.

McManners, John. "The Social Contract and Rousseau's Revolt Against Society." In *Hobbes and Rousseau,* edited by M. Cranston and R. S. Peters, pp. 291–317. New York, 1972.

Meuvret, Jean. "Les idées économiques en France au xviie siècle." *XVIIe siècle* 70–71 (1966): 3–19.

Meyer, Paul H. "Politics and Morals in the Thought of Montesquieu." *VS* 56 (1967): 845–91.

Michaud, Gérard. "Le Paris de Diderot." *Europe,* nos. 405–06 (Jan.–Feb. 1963): 29–47.

Middendorf, John H. "Dr. Johnson and Mercantilism." *Journal of the History of Ideas* 21, no. 1 (Jan.–Mar. 1960): 66–83.

Mortier, Roland. "Diderot et la notion de 'peuple'." *Europe,* nos. 405–06 (Jan.–Feb. 1963): 78–88.

———. "The 'Philosophes' and Public Education." *Yale French Studies* 40 (1968): 62–76.

———. "Voltaire et le peuple." In *The Age of Enlightenment: Studies Presented to Theodore Besterman,* edited by W. H. Barber et al., pp. 137–51. London, 1967.

Mousnier, Roland. "D'Aguesseau et le tournant des ordres aux classes sociales." *Revue d'histoire économique et sociale* 49, no. 4 (1971): 449–64.

Naumann, Manfred. "Zur Publikationsgeschichte des *Christianisme dévoilé.*" *Neue Beiträge zur Literaturwissenschaft* 21 (1964): 155–83.

Niklaus, Robert. "La propagande philosophique au théâtre au siècle des lumières." *VS* 27 (1963): 1223–61.

Oake, Roger B. "Montesquieu's Analysis of Roman History." *Journal of the History of Ideas* 16 (1955): 44–59.

Parry, Geraint. "Enlightened Government and Its Critics in Eighteenth-Century Germany." *The Historical Journal* 6, no. 2 (1963): 178–92.

Perkins, M. L. "Voltaire on the Source of National Power." *VS* 20 (1962): 141–73.

Polin, Raymond. "Le sens de l'égalité et de l'inégalité chez J.-J. Rousseau." In *Etudes sur le Contrat social de Jean-Jacques Rousseau: Actes des journées d'études,* pp. 143–64. Dijon, 1962.

Poutet, Yves. "L'enseignement des pauvres dans la France du xvii$^e$ siècle." *XVII$^e$ siècle* 90–91 (1971): 87–110.

Proust, Jacques. "La fête chez Rousseau et chez Diderot." *Annales Jean-Jacques Rousseau* 37 (1968): 175–96.

Raymond, Agnes. "Le problème de la population chez les Encyclopédistes." *VS* 26 (1963): 1379–88.

Roche, Daniel. "Milieux académiques provinciaux et société des lumières." In *Livre et société dans la France du XVIII$^e$ siècle,* pp. 93–184. Paris, 1965.

Rogers, John West, Jr. "The Opposition to the Physiocrats: A Study of Economic Thought and Policy in the Ancien Régime, 1750–1789." Ph.D. dissertation, Johns Hopkins University, 1971.

Sée, H. "La doctrine politique de Turgot." *Annales historiques de la révolution française* 1 (1924): 413–16.

Shklar, Judith N. "Rousseau's Images of Authority." In *Hobbes and Rousseau,* edited by M. Cranston and R. S. Peters, pp. 333–65. New York, 1972.

———. "Subversive Genealogies." *Daedalus* 101, no. 1 (Winter 1972): 129–54.

Stelling-Michaud, Sven. "Lumières et politique." *VS* 27 (1963): 1519–43.

Strauss, Leo. "On the Intention of Rousseau." In *Hobbes and Rousseau,* edited by M. Cranston and R. S. Peters, pp. 254–90. New York, 1972.

Stricklen, Charles G. "The Philosophe's Political Mission: The Creation of an Idea, 1750–1789." *VS* 86 (1971): 137–228.

Tavenaux, René. "Les écoles de campagne en Lorraine au xviii$^e$ siècle, à-propos d'une étude récente." *Annales de l'Est* 2(1970): 159–71.

Thomas, Keith. "Work and Leisure in Pre-Industrial Society." *Past and Present* 29 (Dec. 1964): 50–66.

Vance, Christie McDonald. "The Extravagant Shepherd: A Study of the Pastoral Vision in Rousseau's *Nouvelle Héloïse.*" *VS* 105(1973): 1–184.

Vartanian, Aram. "From Deist to Atheist: Diderot's Philosophical Orientation, 1746–1749." *Diderot Studies* 1(1949): 46–63.

Vovelle, Michel. "L'Elite ou le mensonge des mots." *Annales* 29, no. 1 (1974): 49–72.

Vyverberg, Henry. "The Limits of Nonconformity in the Enlightenment: The Case of Simon-Nicolas-Henri Linguet." *French Historical Studies* 6, no. 4 (1970): 474–91.

Wade, Ira. "Poverty in the Enlightenment." In *Europäische Aufklärung,* edited by F. Schalk and H. Friedrich, pp. 311–25. Munich, 1967.

Weintraub, Karl J. "Toward the History of the Common Man: Voltaire and Condorcet." In *Ideas in History: Essays Presented to Louis R. Gottschalk,* edited by R. Herr, pp. 39–64. Durham, N.C., 1965.

Williams, William H. "Voltaire and the Utility of the Lower Clergy." *VS* 58(1967): 1869–91.

Wilson, Arthur M. "The Concept of *Moeurs* in Diderot's Social and Political Thought." In *The Age of Enlightenment: Studies Presented to Theodore Besterman,* edited by W. H. Barber et al., pp. 188–99. London, 1967.

————. "The Development and Scope of Diderot's Political Thought." *VS* 27(1963): 1871–1900.

————. "Why Did the Political Theory of the Encyclopedists Not Prevail?" *French Historical Studies* no. 3 (1960): 283–94.

Womack, William R. "Eighteenth-Century Themes in the *Histoire philosophique et politique des Deux Indes* of Guillaume Raynal." *VS* 96 (1972): 129–265.

## B. *Books*

Agulhon, Maurice. *La sociabilité méridionale.* 2 vols. Aix-en-Provence, 1966.

Airiau, Jean. *L'opposition aux Physiocrates à la fin de l'Ancien Régime: Aspects économiques et politiques d'un libéralisme éclectique.* Paris, 1965.

Andlau, B. d'. *Helvétius, seigneur de Voré.* Paris, 1939.

Ariès, Phillippe. *Centuries of Childhood: A Social History of Family Life.* Translated by R. Baldick. New York, 1962.

Armogathe, Jean-Robert, et al. *Images du peuple au XVIIIe siècle.* Paris, 1973.

Arneth, Alfred Ritter von. *Geschichte Maria Theresias,* vol. 9. Vienna, 1879.

Barckhausen, H. *Montesquieu, ses idées et ses oeuvres d'après les papiers de la Brède.* Paris, 1907.

Barnard, F. M. *Herder's Social and Political Thought*. Oxford, 1965.

Barnard, H. C. *Education and the French Revolution*. Cambridge, 1969.

Barrière, Pierre. *Un grand provincial: Charles-Louis de Secondat, baron de la Brède et de Montesquieu*. Paris, 1946.

Besterman, Theodore. *Voltaire*. London, 1969.

Bigot, Henri. *Les idées de Condorcet sur l'instruction publique*. Poitiers, 1912.

Blanchard, William H. *Rousseau and the Spirit of Revolt: A Psychological Study*. Ann Arbor, Mich., 1967.

Bloch, Camille. *L'assistance et l'état en France à la veille de la Révolution*. Paris, 1908.

Bloch, Marc. *French Rural History: An Essay on its Basic Characteristics*. Translated by J. Sondheimer. Berkeley, 1970.

Boas, George. *Vox Populi: Essays in the History of an Idea*. Baltimore, 1969.

Bollème, Geneviève. *Les almanachs populaires au XVIIe et au XVIIIe siècles*. Paris, 1969.

―――. *La Bibliothèque bleue: Littérature populaire en France du XVIIe au XIXe siècle*. Paris, 1971.

Bosher, J. F. *French Finances, 1770–1795: From Business to Bureaucracy*. Cambridge, 1970.

―――. *The Single-Duty Project*. London, 1964.

Bouchard, Marcel. *L'Académie de Dijon et le Premier Discours de Rousseau*. Paris, 1950.

Bourde, André J. *Agronomie et agronomes en France au XVIIIe siècle*. 3 vols. Paris, 1967.

―――. *The Influence of England on the French Agronomes: 1750–1789*. Cambridge, 1953.

Bruford, W. H. *Culture and Society in Classical Weimar, 1775–1806*. Cambridge, 1962.

Bryson, Gladys. *Man and Society: The Scottish Inquiry of the Eighteenth Century*. Princeton, 1945.

Carcassonne, E. *Montesquieu et le problème de la constitution française au xviiie siècle*. Paris, n.d.

Cassirer, Ernst. *The Philosophy of the Enlightenment*. Translated by F. C. A. Koelln and J. P. Pettegrove. Princeton, 1951.

―――. *Rousseau, Kant and Goethe*. Translated by J. Gutmann, P. O. Kristeller, and J. H. Randall, Jr. Princeton, 1945.

―――. *The Question of Jean-Jacques Rousseau*. Translated by P. Gay. Bloomington, 1963.

Caussy, Fernand. *Voltaire, seigneur de village*. Paris, 1912.

Ceitac, Jean. *Voltaire et l'affaire des Natifs: Un aspect de la carrière humanitaire du patriarch de Ferney*. Geneva, 1956.

Charbonnaud, R. *Les idées économiques de Voltaire.* Paris, 1907. Reprint 1971.

Chaussinand-Nogaret, Guy. *Les financiers de Languedoc au xviiie siècle.* Paris, 1970.

Cherel, Albert. *Fénelon au xviiie siècle en France.* Paris, 1917.

Clifford, James L., ed. *Man Versus Society in Eighteenth-Century Britain.* Cambridge, 1968.

Cobb. R. C. *The Police and the People: French Popular Protest, 1789–1820.* Oxford, 1970.

Coleman, D. C., ed. *Revisions in Mercantilism.* London, 1969.

Couturier, Marcel. *Recherches sur les structures sociales de Chateaudun, 1525–1789.* Paris, 1969.

Cragg, Gerald R. *The Church in the Age of Reason.* New York, 1961.

Cumming, Ian. *Helvétius: His Life and Place in the History of Educational Thought.* London, 1955.

Dakin, Douglas. *Turgot and the Ancien Régime in France.* Reprint edition. New York, 1965.

Dedieu, Joseph. *Montesquieu.* Paris, 1913.

Delvaille, Jules. *La Chalotais, éducateur.* Paris, 1911.

Derathé, Robert. *Jean-Jacques Rousseau et la science politique de son temps.* Paris, 1950.

Deyon, Pierre. *Amiens au xviie siècle.* Paris, 1967.

Dommanget, Maurice. *Le curé Meslier: Athée, communiste et révolutionnaire.* Paris, 1965.

Evans, A. W. *Warburton and the Warburtonians: A Study in Some Eighteenth-Century Controversies.* Oxford, 1932.

Eylaud, J. M. *Montesquieu chez ses notaires de la Brède.* Bordeaux, 1956.

Faure-Soulet, J. F. *Economie politique et progrès au "siècle des lumières."* Paris, 1964.

Flitner, Andreas. *Die Politische Erziehung in Deutschland: Geschichte und Probleme, 1750–1880.* Tübingen, 1957.

Ford, Franklin. *Robe and Sword; The Regrouping of the French Aristocracy after Louis XIV.* New York, 1953.

Forster, Robert. *The House of Saulx-Tavanes.* Baltimore, 1971.

Foucault, Michel. *Madness and Civilization: A History of Insanity in the Age of Reason.* Translated by R. Howard. New York, 1967.

Fréville, Henri. *L'intendance de Bretagne (1689–1790).* 3 vols. Rennes, 1953.

Furniss, Edgar S. *The Position of the Laborer in a System of Nationalism.* Boston, 1920.

Gagliardo, John. *From Pariah to Patriot; The Changing Image of the German Peasant, 1770–1840.* Lexington, Ky., 1969.

Garden, Maurice. *Lyon et les Lyonnais au xviii^e siècle.* Paris, n.d.

Gay, Peter. *The Enlightenment: An Interpretation.* Vol. 1. *The Rise of Modern Paganism.* New York, 1966. Vol. 2. *The Science of Freedom.* New York, 1969.

———. *The Party of Humanity: Essays in the French Enlightenment.* New York, 1964.

———. *Voltaire's Politics: The Poet as Realist.* Princeton, 1959.

Gontard, Maurice. *L'enseignement primaire en France de la Révolution à la Loi Guizot (1789–1833).* Paris, 1959.

Goubard, Marguerite. *Voltaire et l'impôt: Les idées fiscales de Voltaire.* Paris, 1931.

Goubert, Pierre. *Beauvais et le Beauvaisis de 1600 à 1730.* Paris, 1959.

Granger, Gilles-Gaston. *La mathématique sociale du Marquis de Condorcet.* Paris, 1956.

Grente, Cardinal Georges, ed. *Dictionnaire de lettres françaises: XVII^e siècle.* Paris, 1954. *XVIII^e siècle.* Paris, 1960.

Grimsley, Ronald. *Jean d'Alembert.* Oxford, 1963.

Groethuysen, B. *The Bourgeois: Catholicism Vs. Capitalism in Eighteenth-Century France.* Translated by M. Ilford. New York, 1966.

Gruder, Vivian R. *The Royal Provincial Intendants in Eighteenth-Century France.* Ithaca, N.Y., 1968.

Guglielmi, Jean-Louis. *Essai sur le développement de la théorie du salaire.* Nice, 1945.

Gutton, Jean-Pierre. *La société et les pauvres: L'example de la généralité de Lyon, 1534–1789.* Paris, 1970.

Haar, Johann. *Jean Meslier und die Beziehungen von Voltaire und Holbach zu ihm.* Hamburg, 1928.

Hauser, Henri. *La pensée et l'action économiques du Cardinal de Richelieu.* Paris, 1944.

Havens, G. R. *Voltaire's Marginalia on the Pages of Rousseau: A Comparative Study of Ideas.* Columbus, Ohio, 1933.

Heckscher, Eli F. *Mercantilism.* Translated by M. Shapiro. Vol. 2. London, 1955.

Hendel, Charles W. *Jean-Jacques Rousseau, Moralist.* 2 vols. New York, 1934.

Hertz, Frederick. *The Development of the German Public Mind: The Age of Enlightenment.* London, 1962.

Higonnet, Patrice L.-R. *Pont-de-Montvert: Social Structure and Politics in a French Village, 1700–1914.* Cambridge, Mass., 1971.

Hobsbawm, E. J. *Social Bandits and Primitive Rebels.* Glencoe, Ill., 1958.

Holborn, Hajo. *A History of Modern Germany, 1648–1840.* New York, 1964.

Hubert, René. *D'Holbach et ses amis.* Paris, 1928.

————. *Les sciences sociales dans l'Encyclopédie.* Paris, 1923.

Hufton, Olwen H. *Bayeux in the Late Eighteenth Century: A Social Study.* Oxford, 1967.

Huizinga, J. *Homo Ludens: A Study of the Play Element in Culture.* London, 1949.

Inglis, Brian. *Poverty and the Industrial Revolution.* London, 1971.

James, E. O. *Seasonal Feasts and Festivals.* New York, 1961.

Jones, E. L., and Mingay, G. E., eds. *Land, Labour and Population in the Industrial Revolution.* New York, 1967.

Jones, M. G. *The Charity School Movement in the Eighteenth Century.* Cambridge, 1937.

Kann, Robert A. *A Study in Austrian Intellectual History: From Late Baroque to Romanticism.* New York, 1960.

Kaplow, Jeffry. *The Names of Kings: The Parisian Laboring Poor in the Eighteenth Century.* New York, 1972.

Keim, A. *Helvétius, sa vie et son oeuvre.* Paris, 1907.

Kotta, Nuçi. *"L'homme aux quarante écus"; A Study of Voltairean Themes.* The Hague, 1966.

Kra, Pauline. *Religion in Montesquieu's Lettres persanes. VS* 72. Geneva, 1970.

Krauss, Werner, ed. *Studien zur deutschen und französischen Aufklärung.* Berlin, 1963.

Lakoff, Sanford A. *Equality in Political Philosophy.* Cambridge, 1964.

Levasseur, Emile. *Histoire des classes ouvrières en France.* Vol. 2. Paris, 1859.

Levi, Anthony, S. J. *French Moralists: The Theory of the Passions, 1585 to 1649.* Oxford, 1964.

Lichtenberger, André. *Le socialisme au xviiiᵉ siècle.* Paris, 1895.

Liebel, Helen P. *Enlightened Bureaucracy Versus Enlightened Despotism in Baden, 1750–1792. Transactions of the American Philosophical Society.* 55, part 5. Philadelphia, 1965.

Ljublinski, W. S. *Voltaire-Studien.* Berlin, 1961.

Lough, John. *Essays on the Encyclopédie of Diderot and D'Alembert.* London, 1968.

McCloy, Shelby. *Government Assistance in Eighteenth-Century France.* Durham, N.C., 1946.

————. *The Humanitarian Movement in Eighteenth-Century France.* Lexington, Ky., 1957.

Mack, Mary P. *Jeremy Bentham: An Odyssey of Ideas.* New York, 1963.

Mackrell, J. Q. C. *The Attack on "Feudalism" in Eighteenth-Century France.* London, 1973.

McManners, John. *French Ecclesiastical Society under the Ancien Régime: A Study of Angers in the Eighteenth Century.* Manchester, 1960.

Malcolmson, R. W. *Popular Recreations in English Society, 1700–1850.* Cambridge, 1973.

Manuel, Frank E. *The Eighteenth Century Confronts the Gods.* Reprint edition. New York, 1967.

———. *The Prophets of Paris.* Cambridge, Mass., 1962.

Marshall, Dorothy. *The English Poor in the Eighteenth Century.* London, 1926.

Mason, H. T. *Pierre Bayle and Voltaire.* Oxford, 1963.

Mason, Lester B. *The French Constitution and the Social Question in the Old Regime, 1700–1789.* Bonn, 1954.

Mauzi, Robert. *L'idée du bonheur dans la littérature et la pensée française au xviiie siècle.* Paris, 1960.

Meek, Ronald. *The Economics of Physiocracy.* Cambridge, Mass., 1963.

Merry, Henry J. *Montesquieu's System of Natural Government.* Purdue, 1970.

Montfort, H. Archambeault de. *Les idées de Condorcet sur le suffrage.* Paris, 1915.

Morehouse, Andrew R. *Voltaire and Jean Meslier.* New Haven, 1936.

Morizé, André. *L'apologie du luxe au xviiie siècle et "Le mondain" de Voltaire.* Paris, 1909.

Mortier, Roland. *Clartés et ombres du siècle des lumières.* Geneva, 1969.

Mousnier, Roland. *La Dîme de Vauban.* Paris, 1968.

———. *Etat et société sous François Ier et pendant le gouvernement personnel de Louis XIV.* 2 vols. Paris, n.d.

———. *Les hiérarchies sociales de 1450 à nos jours.* Paris, 1969.

Naville, Pierre. *D'Holbach et la pensée scientifique au xviiie siècle.* Paris, 1967.

Oestreicher, Jean. *La pensée politique et économique de Diderot.* Paris, 1936.

Palmer, Robert R. *The Age of Democratic Revolution.* Vol. 1. *The Challenge.* New York, 1959.

Pappas, John N. *Voltaire and D'Alembert.* Bloomington, 1962.

Perkins, Merle L. *The Moral and Political Philosophy of the Abbé de Saint-Pierre.* Geneva, 1959.

Pomeau, René. *La religion de Voltaire.* Second ed. Paris, 1969.

Proust, Jacques. *Diderot et l'Encyclopédie.* Paris, 1962.

———. *L'Encyclopédie.* Paris, 1965.

Ridgway, Ronald S. *La propagande philosophique dans les tragédies de Voltaire.* VS 15. Geneva, 1961.

Roberts, Hazel Van Dyke. *Boisguilbert: Economist of the Reign of Louis XIV.* New York, 1935.

Robin, Régine. *La France en 1789: Sémur-en-aixois.* Paris, 1970.

Rossi, Paolo. *Philosophy, Technology, and the Arts in the Early Modern Era.* Translated by S. Antonasio. New York, 1970.

Roustan, Marius. *Les philosophes et la société moderne au xviii<sup>e</sup> siècle.* Paris, 1906.

Rowe, Constance. *Voltaire and the State.* New York, 1955.

Sarrailh, Jean. *L'espagne éclairée de la seconde moitié du xviii<sup>e</sup> siècle.* Paris, 1964.

Shackleton, Robert. *Montesquieu: A Critical Biography.* Oxford, 1961.

Shafer, R. J. *The Economic Societies in the Spanish World (1763–1821).* Syracuse, 1958.

Sheppard, Thomas F. *Lourmarin in the Eighteenth Century: A Study of a French Village.* Baltimore, 1971.

Shklar, Judith N. *Men and Citizens: A Study of Rousseau's Social Themes.* Cambridge, Mass., 1969.

Small, Albion W. *The Cameralists.* Chicago, 1909.

Smith, D. W. *Helvétius: A Study in Persecution.* Oxford, 1965.

Spengler, Joseph J. *The French Predecessors of Malthus.* Durham, N. C., 1942.

Spink, John S. *Jean-Jacques Rousseau et Genève.* Paris, 1934.

———. *French Free Thought From Gassendi to Voltaire.* London, 1960.

Starobinski, Jean. *Jean-Jacques Rousseau: La transparence et l'obstacle; Suivi de Sept essais sur Rousseau.* Paris, 1971 [1958].

Stromberg, Roland N. *Religious Liberalism in Eighteenth-Century England.* Oxford, 1954.

Tilgher, Adriano. *Homo Faber: Work through the Ages.* Translated by D. C. Fisher. New York, 1958.

Tilly, Charles. *The Vendée.* Cambridge, Mass., 1964.

Topazio, Virgil W. *D'Holbach's Moral Philosophy: Its Background and Development.* Geneva, 1956.

Torrey, Norman L. *Voltaire and the English Deists.* New Haven, 1930.

Turberville, A. S., ed. *Johnson's England: An Account of the Life and Manners of his Age.* 2 vols. Oxford, 1933.

Vaughn, C. E. *Studies in the History of Political Philosophy Before and After Rousseau.* 2 vols. London, 1925.

Venturi, Franco. *Italy and the Enlightenment.* Translated by Susan Cors. New York, 1972.

———. *Utopia and Reform in the Enlightenment.* Cambridge, Mass., 1971.

Voitle, Robert. *Samuel Johnson the Moralist.* Cambridge, Mass. 1961.

Vyverberg, Henry. *Historical Pessimism in the French Enlightenment.* Cambridge, Mass., 1958.

Waldinger, Renée. *Voltaire and Reform in the Light of the French Revolution.* Geneva, 1959.

Webb, R. K. *The British Working Class Reader, 1790–1848.* London, 1955.

Weis, Eberhard. *Geschichtsschreibung und Staatsauffassung in der Französischen Enzyklopädie.* Wiesbaden, 1956.

Wermel, Michael. *The Evolution of the Classical Wage Theory.* New York, 1939.

Weulersse, Georges. *Les physiocrates.* Paris, 1931.

————. *La physiocratie à la fin du règne de Louis XV (1770–1774).* Paris, 1959.

————. *La physiocratie sous les ministères de Turgot et de Necker (1774–1781).* Paris, 1950.

Wilson, Arthur M. *Diderot.* New York, 1972.

Wolpe, Hans. *Raynal et sa machine de guerre: "L'Histoire des deux Indes" et ses perfectionnements.* Stanford, 1957.

Zink, Anne. *Azereix: la vie d'une communité rurale à la fin du xviiie siècle.* Paris, 1969.

# Index

Alembert, Jean Le Rond d', 12, 126 $n$; on democracy, 170; on education, 107–08; *Encyclopédie* articles of, 33, 94; on Rousseau, 173

America: Turgot on, 163

Argental, Count and Countess of, 95, 170

Atheism: Damilaville's defense of, 95; of Diderot, 84–89; *Encyclopédie's* treatment of, 71–73; of philosophes, 66–67, 76–77; Voltaire on, 77; Yvon on, 71, 73 $n$

Augustine, Saint, 68

Bacon, Francis, 33

Barbeu-Dubourg, Jacques, 88, 105

Barbeyrac, Jean, 173 $n$

Baudeau, Abbé Nicolas, 99, 102, 105 $n$; on luxury, 134–35; charity proposal of, 126–28

Bayle, Pierre, 87, 170; paradox of, 67, 70, 71, 74, 84

Beccaria, Marchese de Cesare Bonesana, 56–57, 62, 63

Beggars, 123–26, 146 $n$

Bentham, Jeremy: on democracy, 171; on economics, 133; on laws, 57, 62

Besthorn, Rudolph, 19 $n$

Betski, Ivan Ivanovich, 88 $n$

Boisguillebert, Pierre Le Pesant, 45, 46, 48

Bonnet, Charles, 24 $n$

Boss, Ronald I., 14 $n$, 67 $n$

Bossuet, Jacques, 1, 55

Boulanger, Nicholas, 46 $n$, 52; on religion, 66, 76; on republicanism, 167

Bourgelat, Claude, 51

Britain. *See* England

Buffon, Comte Georges Louis Leclerc de, 56

Butchers: Diderot on, 24–25

Caesar, Julius, 167

Camisard uprising, 51 $n$

Carolina (U.S.): Locke's constitution for, 62

Catherine II (empress, Russia): Diderot and, 15, 28, 62, 105, 110, 131, 140, 161, 164, 168–69

Catholicism. *See* Roman Catholic Church

Censorship, 44–45

Chamousset, C.H.P. de, 126

Charity, 127–28, 147, 172

Chisick, Harvey, 99 $n$

Choiseul (French family), 45

Christianity: duty to poor of, 1, 127; Montesquieu on, 74; Turgot on, 76

Cicero, 68, 82 $n$

Citizenship: property and, 165 $n$, 168–70

Clarke, Samuel, 87

Class: usage of, 13

Colbert, Jean Baptiste, 34, 112, 134

Condillac, Etienne Bonnot de, 108

Condorcet, Marquis de, 2; on beggars, 124; on education, 99–100, 102–03; 106–08; 111–12; on equality, 159, 164; on exploitation of countryside, 48; on free trade, 141; on holy days, 122; on justice, 25–26, 161 $n$; on luxury, 134–36; Mauzi on, 156 $n$; on opinion, 188; on religion, 81, 92–93; on rich and poor, 47, 54, 55, 127; on taxation, 139 $n$; on wages, 143–45

"Corporeal eye," 1–2, 4, 38

Corsica: Rousseau on, 183, 184 $n$, 186

Couturier, Marcel, 11 $n$

Cowper, William, 29

Coyer, Abbé, 7–8, 12 $n$, 17

Crafts. *See* Manual arts

D'Alembert, Jean Le Rond. *See* Alembert, Jean Le Rond d'

Damilaville, Etienne Noël, 46 *n*, 76, 85, 95–96

De Jaucourt, Chevalier Louis. *See* Jaucourt, Chevalier Louis de

Democracy: philosophes on, 166–71

Deux-Ponts, Duke of, 105 *n*

Diderot, Denis, 3; background of, 2, 14–15; on education, 100, 103, 105, 107–11; *Encyclopédie* editorship and writings of, 24–25, 34, 44, 53, 72, 85, 94, 123, 131, 146; on equality, 148–49, 154–55, 160–61, 163–65; on foundlings, 127; on guilds, 137; on Helvétius, 156–57; on hôpitaux, 126; as legislator to Russia, 15, 28, 62, 84, 86–89, 100, 103, 105, 110–11, 131–32, 137, 140, 161, 164, 168–69; on luxury, 134, 135; on manual arts, 33, 34, 182; Mauzi on, 156 *n*; on monarchy, 57–58; on Physiocracy, 53–54; on religion, 22–23, 66, 72, 76, 81, 84–89; Rousseau and, 173, 178; Tahitians portrayed by, 27–28; on taxation, 138 *n*, 140; on use of Latin, 69–70; on wages, 145

Diogenes, 173–74

Discipline: of beggars, 123–26; holy days and, 121–22

Discord (goddess), 18

Domat, Jean, 9–11

Double truth, 67, 69–70, 78, 80, 94, 108

Duchet, Michèle, 28 *n*

Duclos, Charles, 37 *n*, 38

Dumarsais, César Cheneau, 19 *n*, 109

Dupont de Nemours, Pierre Samuel, 99, 102, 168

Education: philosophes on, 94–116

Eerde, John van, 23 *n*

Egypt, ancient, 69

*Encyclopédie*: d'Alembert writing in, 33, 94; Boulanger writing in, 52, 167; Diderot's editorship of and writing in, 24–25, 34, 44, 53, 72, 85, 94, 123, 131, 146; Dumarsais writing in, 109; Formey writing in, 69; Holbach writing in, 168; Jaucourt writing in, 20, 21, 32, 52–53, 72, 73 *n*, 119, 124, 138, 159–60; Joubert writing in, 34; leadership discussed in, 131; Quesnay writing in, 52, 118–19; religion discussed in, 69–73, 76, 79, 84, 85; Rousseau writing in, 137–38, 175, 179; Saint-Lambert writing in, 22, 135; Scythians in, 150; taxation discussed in, 138–39; "Travail" article in 37–38; Voltaire writing in, 21; workers portrayed in, 36; Yvon writing in, 71, 73 *n*

England: justice in, 161; mercantilism in, 117

Equality: philosophes on, 148–71, 172; Rousseau on, 179, 183–85, 188

Fénelon, François de Salignac de La Mothe-, 45–46, 48, 87

Ferney (France): Voltaire in, 62, 95, 129

Festivals: Rousseau on, 185–86

Fleury, Claude, 9–11

Flitner, Andreas, 98 *n*

Forbonnais, François Véron-Duverger de, 140

Formey, Samuel, 69–72, 181 *n*

Foucault, Michel, 29 *n*–30 *n*

France: beggars in, 123; in leadership of Enlightenment, 43; philosophes in administration of, 45–48; religious education in, 112–13; Rousseau on finances of, 175–76

Francis I (king, France), 12

Frederick II (king, Prussia), 79 *n*, 100, 107–08, 113, 170

Free trade: of grain, 140–42; philosophes on, 189; Quesnay on, 118–19

Friedrich, Karl (grand duke, Baden), 99, 100, 102, 111, 132

Furetière, Antoine, 8–9

Furniss, Edgar S., 117 *n*

Galiani, Abbé, 53, 141

Gay, Peter, 76 *n*, 155 *n*

Gembruch, Werner, 46 *n*

Geneva: Rousseau on, 185, 186; Voltaire in, 169

Genovesi, Antonio, 141

Gibbon, Edward, 2, 64

God. *See* Religion

Godwin, William, 172
Goldsmith, Oliver, 57
Gordon riots, 165–66
Graffigny, Françoise de, 151, 163
Grain: trade in, 140–42; wages dependent upon, 143, 144
Grange, H., 143 *n*–44 *n*
Graslin, J.-J., 119 *n*, 138 *n*, 140
Great Britain. *See* England
Greece, ancient: in *Encyclopédie*, 150; Formey on, 69; Montesquieu on, 169
Grotius, Hugo, 173 *n*
Guilds, 136–37

Haller, Albrecht, 30
Healey, F. G., 34 *n*
Helvétius, Claude Adrien, 2, 81; on ancient Greece, 150; censorship problems of, 44; Diderot on, 86 *n*; on equality, 153, 164–65; on execution crowds, 24; on ignorance, 27, 107; on land ownership, 168; on luxury, 135; on manual arts, 37, 182; on pleasure, 61–62, 156–59; on religion, 89–92; on rich and poor, 54, 127; on virtue, 28; on wages, 145
Herder, Johann Gottfried von, 13, 63
Herodotus, 150
Hierarchy: philosophes on, 148–71, 172
Hobbes, Thomas, 87
Holbach, Baron Paul Henri Dietrich, 2, 44; atheism, 16, 21–22; on democracy, 166, 168; on education, 100, 102, 105, 106, 109–10, 114; on equality, 152, 153, 155, 158, 164; on execution crowds, 24; on ignorance, 27; on legislation, 62; on luxury, 135; on manual arts, 35–36; on poverty, 32 *n*, 54, 55, 119 *n*, 127, 130–31; on reason, 19–21; on religion, 66, 76, 81–84, 86, 87, 89, 92; on taxation, 139; on wages, 145; on wealth, 28
Holland: Diderot on, 149 *n*, 160–61, 163
Holy days, 121–22, 132
*Hôpitaux*, 123, 124, 126, 127
Houdetot, Comtesse d', 177–78
Huber, Michel, 129
Humanitarianism, 42–43
Hume, David, 2, 43; on oppression of poor, 55–56; on taxation, 139–40; on wages, 144

India: Voltaire on education in, 94–95
Individual rights, 65
Instruction: philosophes on, 94–116
Iselin, Isaac, 115–16
Islam: Helevétius on, 89

Jaucourt, Chevalier Louis de: writing in *Encyclopédie*, 20, 21, 32, 52–53, 72, 73 *n*, 119, 124, 138, 159–60
Jenyns, Soame, 172
Jesuits: expulsion of, 98, 112
Jesus Christ: poor as representing, 1
Johnson, Samuel, 13, 29, 134
Joubert, Claude, 34
Justice: Condorcet and Turgot on, 25–26; equality in, 160–62

Kortum, Hans, 134 *n*
Krauss, Werner, 19 *n*

Labor: philosophes on, 117–47
La Bruyère, Jean de, 9
La Chalotais, Louis René de Caradeuc de, 108, 113
Land: division of, 164–65. *See also* Property
La Rivière, Mercier de. *See* Rivière, Mercier de la
Laws. *See* Legislation
Leadership: philosophes on, 128–31
Legislation: philosophes and, 56–57, 61–64, 73–75, 89–92, 159–65, 188–90; Rousseau on, 178–81, 187
Linguet, Simon Nicolas, 39, 57, 173
Locke, John, 26, 108; Carolina constitution of, 62; individual rights emphasized by, 65; on religious freedom, 66 *n*
Lorraine, Duke of, 131
Louis XIV (king, France), 43, 45, 46 *n*, 48, 112, 137
Louis XVI (king, France), 62, 83
Lower class. *See* Poor
Loyseau, Charles, 9–11
Luxury: philosophes on, 134–36
Lycurgus, 163, 164

Machault d'Arnouville, Jean Baptiste, 46–47, 49, 139
Machiavelli, Niccolò, 68 *n*, 82
Madrid Society, 141
Malesherbes (French family), 45
Malesherbes, Chrétien Guillaume de Lamoignon de, 174
Mallet, Abbé, 73, 121, 122 *n*
Mandeville, Bernard, 117
Manual arts: philosophes on, 32–40; Rousseau on, 182
Maria Theresa (archduchess, Austria), 100, 113, 132
Marmontel, Jean-François, 47
Mauzi, Robert, 155 *n*, 156
Maximilian III Joseph (elector, Bavaria), 100
Mayenne, Duc Charles de Lorraine de, 18
Mercantilism, 117–19
Mirabeau, Marquis de: on education, 99, 101–02, 104, 111, 115; on taxation, 138
Miromesnil, Armand-Thomas de, 139 *n*
Misery, 146–47
Mohammedism: Montesquieu on, 74
Monarchy: administrative powers of, 47–48; Diderot on, 57–58; education and, 97, 98, 100, 101, 108; Montesquieu on, 159
Money: Helvétius on, 150
Montesquieu, Baron de La Brède, 2, 3, 27, 28, 43; on ancient Rome, 67–69, 74, 159 *n*, 167, 169; on democracy, 169; on education, 112; on equality, 154, 165; on legislation, 61, 159; Mauzi on, 156 *n*; on religion, 23, 67–69, 74–75
More, Hannah, 113
More, Thomas, 119 *n*
Moreau, François, 127 *n*
Morelly, 172
Möser, Justus, 30–31, 141
Moses, 63
Mousnier, Roland, 12 *n*
Müntzer, Thomas, 50

Necker, Jacques, 1, 141, 172; on wages, 143 *n*–44 *n*
Numa Pompilius (king, Rome), 62–63

Open market. *See* Free trade
Opinion: Condorcet on, 188

Palmieri, Giuseppe, 133
Pappas, John, 81 *n*
Pascal, Blaise, 156
*Pauvreté*: Diderot on, 146
Peasants: freeing of, 132
People: usage of, 7–17. See also *Peuple; Poor*
Pergen, Anton, 113–14
Pesselier, Charles Etienne, 175 *n*
*Peuple*: Jaucourt on, 20, 32; usage of, 7–13, 16. *See also* Poor
Philosophes: on education, 94–116; on equality, 148–71, 172; in French administration, 45–48; legislation and, 61–64, 73–75, 89–92, 159–65, 188–90; on poor, 2–4, 7–17; on religion, 66–93; on workers, 117–47
Physiocrats: Diderot and, 53–54; economics of, 118–19; education and, 98–100, 108; on free trade, 141; on leadership, 129–31; on luxury, 134–35; on taxation, 138–40; on wages, 142–45
Plato, 30
Pleasure: Helvétius on, 61–62, 156–59
Pluche, Abbé, 35 *n*, 126 *n*
Plutarch, 61–63, 71, 87, 114, 150
*Pöbel*: usage of, 13
Poland: Rousseau's plan for, 176, 183, 186
Polybius, 71
Pompadour (French family), 45
Pompey, 167
Pomponazzi, Pietro, 71
Poor: in Christian tradition, 1, 127; philosophes' view of, 2–4, 7–17, 117–47; workshops for, 124–26. See also *Peuple*
Pope, Alexander, 172
Poverty: usage of, 146; utility of, 117–19
Private rights, 65
Property: citizenship and, 165 *n*, 168–70; Rousseau on, 179, 180; Smith on, 152–53
Pufendorf, Samuel von, 153

Quesnay, François, 52; on free trade,

Quesnay, François (*con't.*) 118–19; on sharecropping, 130; on taxation, 16–17, 139; on wages, 142–43

Ranconet, Aimar de, 8
Reason: Holbach on, 19–21; religion and, 22–23
Reinhard, Johann, 36, 132
Religion: education and, 97–98, 100–02, 108, 112; philosophes on, 66–93; reason and, 22–23
Religious freedom, 66
Republicanism: philosophes on, 167–70
Richelieu, Duc Armand Jean du Plessis de, 40
Rights, private, 65
Rivière, Mercier de la, 62; on education, 99, 105, 109; on ignorance, 27; on justice, 161–62
Roche, Pierre de la, 174 *n*
Roman Catholic Church: duty to poor of, 127; education by, 97, 100–02, 112
Rome, ancient: Gibbon on, 64; Helvétius on, 91; Holbach on, 82; Jaucourt on, 138; Montesquieu on, 67–69, 74, 159 *n*, 167, 169; Plutarch on, 62–63; Rousseau on, 186; Voltaire on, 21
Rossi, Paolo, 34 *n*
Rothkrug, Lionel, 45 *n*
Roubaud, P. J. A., 123 *n*, 125 *n*
Rousseau, Jean-Jacques, 14, 108, 172–88; on ancient Greece, 150; on equality, 152; on execution crowds, 24; on insensitivity of people, 26; on laws, 57; political experiences of, 62; social contract doctrine of, 65–66, 72, 148 *n*; on taxation, 119 *n*, 137–38
Russia: Diderot in, 62, 84, 86–89, 100, 103, 105, 110–11, 131–32, 137, 140, 161, 164, 168-69

Saint-Lambert, Marquis Jean François de, 22, 57, 72 *n*, 135
Saint-Pierre, Abbé de, 80 *n*
Saint-Simon, Henri de, 48
Sander, Nicolaus, 103
Saxe-Gotha, Duke of, 104–05
Schlosser, Johann, 103–06

Scythians, 150, 163
Seneca, Marcus Annaeus, 71
Sentimentalists, 31
Serfdom: Rousseau on, 176
Sextus Empiricus, 71
Shaftesbury, Anthony Ashley Cooper, third earl of, 26
Silhouette, Etienne de, 175
Smith, Adam, 2, 43; on education, 114–15; on equality, 151 *n*, 152–53; on free trade, 141; on justice, 161 *n;* labor in political economy of, 16, 36; on leisure, 26; on taxation, 139; on wages, 120–21, 144–47
Sonnenfels, Joseph von, 63–64, 132–33
Spain: education in, 100
Sparta, 150, 163, 164
Starobinski, Jean, 185 *n*
Strabo, 71
Sturm und Drang, 31
Sweden: Rivière on, 99, 109
Symbols: in religion, 21–22

Tacitus, 150
Tahitians: Diderot's portrayal of, 27–28, 163
Talbert, Abbé, 153 *n*
Talent: Rousseau on, 184
Taxation, 49–53; Diderot's policies of, 132; reforms of, 137–40, 147; Rousseau on, 175, 179–80, 187
Temple, William, 117
Third estate: definitions of, 9–10
Turgot, Anne Robert Jacques, 11, 54; on democracy, 168; on education, 99, 102–05, 109, 110; on equality, 150–53, 163; on free trade, 141; on guilds, 136; on holy days, 121 *n*; on justice, 25, 26, 28–29, 161 *n*; political experiences of, 44, 46 *n*, 47, 48, 51, 62, 165–66; on poor, 127, 128; on religion, 75–76, 80, 83; on taxation, 139 *n*; on wages, 119, 125, 143–44; on workshops, 124–26

Vauban, Marquis de, 9, 45, 46; on misery of countryside, 48–49
Venturi, Franco, 48 *n*
Villers de Billy, Madame, 104
Volland, Sophie, 22, 86, 154

*Volk*: usage of, 13

Voltaire: on ancient Rome, 21; on beggars, 123–24, 125 *n*, 126; on cruelty of people, 24; on democracy, 169–70; on education, 39–40, 94–98, 113; on equality, 152–54, 162–63; on foundlings, 127; on free trade, 141; on holy days, 121 *n*, 122; on leadership, 128–29; on legislation, 61, 162; on luxury, 134; on manual arts, 34–35; Mauzi on, 156 *n*; on Pascal, 156; people portrayed in *La Henriade* by, 18–19; on Pesselier, 175 *n*; political experiences of, 44, 62; on poor, 2–3, 11, 29, 55; populace in plays by, 23; on religion, 16, 70, 76–87, 89, 92–93; Rousseau and, 66, 173–74, 180 *n*, 181, 183; Scythians portrayed by, 27; on serfs, 176; shoemaker's release won by, 1–2; on taxation, 49–52, 139, 140

Wages: Condorcet on, 143–45; Quesnay on, 142–43; Rousseau on, 184–85; Smith on, 120–21, 144–47; Turgot on, 119, 125, 143–44

Warburton, William, 69, 71

Ward, Bernard, 128

Wealth: corrupting influence of, 28–29

Weulersse, Georges, 142 *n*–43 *n*

Whiston, William, 74

Workers: philosophes on, 117–47; skilled, 32–40

Workshops, 124–26

Young, Arthur, 117

Yvon, Abbé, 71, 73 *n*